Reader Reviews

"Rooted in the rich wisdom of India yet warm and welcoming to any reader, *Satsang of One* feels less like a book and more like a conversation with a trusted friend who has walked the path before you. Honest, gentle, and refreshingly real, it is filled with reflections you will recognize and practical guidance you can actually use.

"A luminous blend of spiritual memoir, travelogue, and seeker's diary. We all sense it at some point: that quiet, persistent feeling that there must be something more. ZenHealer felt it too, and he followed it.

"From childhood through school, relationships, and the demands of a corporate career, he walked the same roads many of us walk. But all along the way, he was listening to something deeper, something calling him inward. And what he found there is both profound and deeply personal: true awakening isn't something you find in a crowd. It lives in the stillness within you.

"If you have ever longed to begin your own inner journey but didn't know where to start, or felt you lacked the courage, the resources, or the understanding, then this book was written for you. With patience and compassion, it shows that awakening isn't far away. It is right here. Right now. You only need to take the first step.

"One step. One surrender. One Satsang."

Sherry L. Granader
Ghostwriter
Sherrywritesforyou.com

"Satsang of One by ZenHealer is a luminous spiritual memoir, travelogue and diary of a seeker who bridged the corporate world and the inner quest. From childhood through education, relationships and a corporate career, he traces his path of discovery, realization and intuitive understanding of his highest nature, finally recognizing that true awakening is an inward, solitary realization, distinct from communal ritual or devotional song. Rooted in Indian wisdom yet universal in appeal, this candid book traces how discipline, surrender and steady practice led him to fall in love with who he truly is. Practical and inspiring, the book is full of candid reflections and actionable tips—part self-help guide, part spiritual testimony. Essential reading for anyone on the same path who lacks the courage, means or understanding to begin, it shows how discipline and steadfast determination can bring realization here and now. One step, one surrender, one satsang."

Dipak Haksar
Spiritual Aspirant
Retired Chief Executive ITC Hotels

"I have been fascinated, going through *Satsang of One*. It is a loosely woven but beautiful tapestry of down-to-earth experiences, spiritual and otherwise, as well as philosophical insights, creating a unique narrative that engages multiple sensitivities of the reader. It is laid bare to be imbibed at various levels. It is a travelogue covering much of the globe for travellers with a penchant for the unusual. It is a set of experiences for those who desire to immerse themselves in spirituality, as well as for those who are fascinated by the life journey of a rebel. It is an "open book" of a most amazing ongoing life, for anyone to dip into, whatever catches their fancy."

Jehangir
Philanthropist, Photographer, Jazz Player

"I discovered my Indian roots in the USA."

In our fake-news-hyped-up world, this is a book to read: an honest account of ZenHealer's spiritual journey through 130 countries, searching to answer the classic question, "Who am I?" Fearless in writing openly about the differences between spirituality and religion, male and female energies, and sexuality, his experiences of connection with the Shakti energies through the women in his life, and the differences between East and West sensibilities, he hints at the capacity for Middle-East culture to be a synapse between them

This is a celebration of life, the importance of living with values, and being grateful for all the gifts received, and includes ZenHealer's own step-by-step process for freeing himself from the beliefs that weighed on him. His journey continues as he quotes Robert Frost, with ". . . miles to go before I sleep."

"Be the witness and revel in the divine play all around."

Ayo Oum Shanti
Author, Founder of World Water Hub

I have edited many spiritual books, but none by a maverick like ZenHealer. In it, you get a candid take on life and spirituality, which reflects the spirit dwelling in this "rebel" who was unsatisfied with conventional answers to the questions that plagued him. Ultimately, his spiritual thirst was quenched by the eternal springs (his teachers) he drank from in the course of his journey, which takes you around the world in 388 pages.

Mehernosh Unwalla
Editor

SATSANG OF ONE

In Love with Myself

ZenHealer

For more information, contact: TanTienPraMonA@yahoo.com

ISBN: 979-8-234-06235-2 (paperback)
ISBN: 979-8-234-06236-9 (eBook)
Library of Congress Control Number: 2026910382

Cover Art by Ramona Manea
Cover Layout by Paula Ribiero
Book Interior and E-book formatting by Amit Dey
Editing by Mehernosh Unwalla

|| There Is No Past
There Is No Future
Only the Eternal Present ||

Table of Contents

Acknowledgements

This book is dedicated to Maa, the *Adi Shakti*, and to all the *Shaktis* of the world who may or may not have crossed my path. I am because of them.

I offer this book with reverence to all my gurus and teachers who have guided me along on this *Satsang* of One, starting with Osho, Ramesh Balsekar, Pandit Rajmani Tigunait, Maa Gyaan Suveera, Baba Harihar Ramji, and many others in spirit.

I thankfully acknowledge the support of my immediate and extended family, who have showered their unbounded love on me throughout my life.

This book would not have been possible without the relentless prodding and encouragement from my sister Urmila Roongta.

I am forever grateful to Anjali, my wife of thirty-three years, who endured my regular absences and proclivities, and who remains a Shakti in my life even today.

I offer my heartfelt thanks to Suma Varughese, the ex-editor of *Life Positive*, who encouraged me from the time I contributed to her magazine. She graciously agreed to give me her valuable feedback for this book.

I am grateful to Sherry Granader who started as my ghostwriter but quickly went on to guide me through the publishing world. She referred me to Michelle Hill who helped bring this book to life along with Paula Ribiero in Brazil and Amit Dey in India.

Through his painstaking editing, Mehernosh Unwalla has captured my intent while indulging my quirks and rebellious style of writing.

Lastly, I would like to express my undying gratitude to Ramona. Maa handed me over to Ramona for a good reason. For all our disagreements, she has been my Rock of Gibraltar while we paved the way together as PraMonA. Only she could have captured the essence of this book with the cover design that came as a vision to her when we first met.

ZenHealer

Introduction

Who is ZenHealer? The answer to this question takes the form of the investigation "Who am I?" The answer, as we know, is "I Am That." If I Am That, there is no need to individuate ZenHealer, as in reality, there is no such entity. It is as much an illusion as the entire manifestation. Hence, even though this book has been written by ZenHealer, the writer as well as the words are just a figment of imagination. My given name identifies my parents and my family. ZenHealer identifies me and my inner child.

However, as this is about the spiritual journey of an individual who lives his life in flesh and blood as a three-dimensional object (as Ramesh Balsekar would say), there are enough clues throughout the book to identify ZenHealer for those whose curiosity is miles ahead of their spirituality. Those close to me—family and friends—who pick up the book will, of course, know who I am, but just a handful will identify with the content, and claim to really know me. Those readers who do not know anything about me will allow their curiosity to get the better of them initially, but then, hopefully, they will gradually immerse themselves in the book as it unfolds, and connect with my experiences.

This journey is mine and mine alone. It is purely experiential and observational. From a young age, I have been a voracious reader of the esoteric, gravitating toward theosophy, philosophy, and spirituality. My eyes, my mind, and my heart devoured the writings of almost all the great ancient and modern masters, teachers, and sages, and most of the scriptures from different spiritual traditions. But none of these writings or discourses rang true unless I experienced their essence for myself and felt them vibrate within me. Until then, it was secondhand knowledge, someone else's word. One's own experience seals the learning, and then there is conviction and credibility in what I write and say. In turn, if you happen to read or hear that, it will not become yours unless you experience it. This is the stark difference between religion and spirituality. In all organized religions, you are constantly told about the existence of God, and you believe it. It is only on the spiritual path that you experience the *Brahma Leela* firsthand, as I did.

I was born a rebel, have lived my life as a rebel, and will breathe my last as a rebel. Spirituality is not for the faint-hearted. It takes you into unchartered dimensions; elevates you to the highest peaks; gives you a taste of the sublime; frees you from the shackles of mediocrity, cliches, herd mentality, and the mundane, pedantic world of illusory existence; and brings you closer to Divinity, your own Self. Logic and intelligence are impediments on this journey. One of my brothers-in-law has been struggling for years to seek answers, but to no avail, because he insists on using his mind. It is not for nothing that Osho and all the Zen masters have said, "You have to drop the mind first."

I have lived a very rich, fulfilling life on my own terms, and even if I had free will, I would not have wanted it any other way. There are many more Happenings, Wanderings, and Shaktis that have crisscrossed my journey. It is impossible to capture all of them in this book. Each moment of my life has been a divine moment full of joy and peace, even when I have been disturbed or unwell. How could it be otherwise? It has been a Satsang of One after all.

In the conventional sense, this is my memoir and, therefore, should include mention of both my immediate and extended family. However, it is first and foremost a spiritual journey of One, and only when someone in the family has had any impact on my journey have I mentioned that person. As you will see, *Maa* (my mother) is the anchor of this journey, along with *Babuji* (my father). However, there is not a single member of my family, besides Ramona, I can call my spiritual friend or companion on this journey.

There was a reason I was not gifted with a child, as shown in my horoscope. I could not have been on this journey of One otherwise.

The East and the West are diametrically opposite in almost every aspect of life, and my spiritual journey has straddled the two. When I set out on this mission to describe my journey, deciding on the audience became a challenge. Would this book appeal to a universal audience? Then it dawned on me that I was not writing for an audience but for myself, and that the book should speak for itself, regardless of who was reading it.

This book is universal but deeply rooted in India, the cradle of civilization and eternal wisdom. It is for serious seekers or at least for those who are earnestly treading the spiritual path. In this age of artificiality, I have delved deep into my body, mind, and spirit to write this book about my life journey. It is meant to awaken seekers to the fact that spirituality is not just buried in scriptures and arcane teachings but is alive and vibrating. We just need to open our eyes and experience it as we live each moment.

I have intentionally refrained from organizing the book in chronological order. Life may appear to move in a linear manner, but since there is no beginning and no end, it makes more sense to let my understanding of life take precedence over chronology. The book starts with the Source, follows the *Trinity* of *Brahma*, *Vishnu*, and Mahesh (*Shiva*), and moves on to *Tantra* and Zen, all interspersed with anecdotes and experiences. I have mentioned certain dates throughout for convenience sake and to jog my memory about certain events. But they have no relevance to how things have unfolded in my life. In Tantra, there is no *kaal* (time). For those who need proof, quantum physics has already shown that atoms move in a random manner and that their path cannot be predicted. Such is life—a series of random happenings, albeit all connected in a mysterious and metaphysical manner.

My body and spirit originated in India, but I have lived and wandered more than half my life in the West. My ethos is Indian; my sensibilities are Western. I think, converse, and write in English, and even though my journey has taken me to all corners of the world, my roots remain in India. Hence, I refer to many concepts and phrases in Hindi and Sanskrit, gathered and absorbed throughout my journey. Although I have not explained them in detail, since this is not meant to be a treatise or textbook, they are briefly explained in the glossary at the end. All the first instances of the words therein appear in italics in the text. Those italicized words that are explained in the text itself are not included in the glossary. Some words are also italicized as they are the names of book, films, plays, etc., and they may not appear in the glossary. The words are not important. Either you are already familiar with the concepts they represent, or their meanings will surface when you resonate with them at a subtle level.

There had always been a subconscious desire to share my journey with others by way of a book, beyond just the workshops and satsangs I have conducted so far. The push came from my sister Uma *Jiji*, herself a prolific writer. Without her encouragement and prodding, I doubt if this book would have come to light.

Ramona, my Shakti and *ardhangini*, whose presence in my life made Shiva Shakti alive and provided me with the impetus to keep moving forward, deserves special mention.

I have been blessed to have been gifted this life by Shiva and Maa to experience this blissful journey, my own Satsang of One.

I am Shiva. I am *Krishna*. I am *Hanuman*.

I am all there is.

Satchidananda.

ZenHealer

|| In the Beginning was the Word
And the Word was "Aum" ||

1.
|| The Source ||
|| MAA ||

October 24, 2004

I woke up with a start.

I was engulfed in bright white light. There was a strange glow all around. Never had I experienced anything like this before. I could feel something wet underneath me. My pajamas seemed totally soaked. It was 3:45 AM on my cell phone. Suddenly, a smile crossed my face, and I went back to sleep.

Sunila Jiji, my youngest sister, knocked on the door and simply said, "We have to go." I was in Pune, India, at her home, having come there from Mumbai the night before. I switched on the light. It was 4:15 AM. When I went to the bathroom to change, I noticed that my white pajamas had blots of red on the back side, and my underpants were soaked in red. I felt the area below my navel near the groin. The lump was no longer there. It was gone. I scanned the *hara*; it was glowing purple! The *Muladhara Chakra* was on fire.

Maa finally passed on, in *Brahma Muhurta* on *Kartik Ekadashi*. She had chosen the most opportune time . . . or was it chosen for her? My *sankalpa* was for that Sunday, October 24. But I had lost all track of *tithis* and had no idea that my sankalpa coincided with Kartik Ekadashi. I had definitely not asked for Brahma Muhurta.

We reached her bedside at Bhatia Hospital in less than two hours. It was as if I had developed wings to be with her. I was on the cell phone almost the entire drive from Pune to Mumbai, gathering my *Reiki* circle together and performing the closing circle. We completed it before sunrise.

When I got to Maa's bedside, she was as calm as a lake. I touched her forehead; it was still warm. Her skin felt as soft and supple as a newborn baby's. There was not a single wrinkle on her face. In fact, she was glowing. The *Sahasrara Chakra* had already closed.

I touched her feet and put my forehead to them. She blessed me. In that moment, I experienced the Divine.

The Good Doctor

I first met Dr. Suhas Shah in August 1999.

I was in London when I received a call from my nephew in Mumbai, asking me to come immediately, as Maa was in a coma in the ICU. I rushed to Bhatia Hospital the next morning after flying in late at night. Dr. Shah, under whose care Maa had been admitted to the ICU, had already informed the family that the inevitable could happen any day. When I first met him that morning, I took an instant dislike to him, as I do with most doctors. I was not allowed to enter the ICU. Later, I was allowed to "visit" Maa for five minutes. I desperately wanted to reach out to her as she was calling me. I pleaded with the doctors, the nurses, and the officials to allow me to be with her for an hour or so. I told them about Reiki, explaining that I would just place my hands on her body without talking to her or disturbing her in any way. All to no avail. Finally, that evening, after much convincing and pleading, Dr. Shah agreed to allow me near her. Tears arose, and I thanked him profusely.

The next two days were a blur. Once I gained admission to her bedside, the nurses became more friendly and inquisitive as they saw me placing my hands all over Maa. Most of the time, I was in a daze, and my eyes were shut. The only thing I still remember is a surge of fire in the form of a ball—a strange sensation in the *Anahata Chakra*. In the three years since my Reiki initiation, I had never experienced this sensation. On the second day, I remember watching Maa opening her eyes and locking them with mine. My *Ajna Chakra* was on fire.

Two days later, Maa came back home. It was a homecoming for me too.

After a few days, when I met Dr. Shah to settle his fees, he was a changed person. Or, perhaps, I was a changed person. I took an instant liking to him. In the middle of his busy consulting hours in the hospital, we spent almost thirty minutes talking about Maa's condition and recovery, and what he perceived as a "miracle." I told him there were no miracles, only Happenings (this was well before I came across Ramesh and his teachings!). I thanked him for his help and support. Even though I doubt that his textbook-conditioned mind allowed him to acknowledge something such as Reiki or grasp the phenomenon of healing beyond that induced by drugs, I was genuinely touched by his warmth and sincerity, so rare in the medical profession. We both became converts to a degree. And more importantly, a connection had been established.

Spiritual Immersion

The next five years were an intense period of spiritual and personal awakening and awareness for me. It was a serene whirl of yog, meditation, healing, scriptures, satsangs, naturopathy, Ayurveda, martial arts, shamanism, crystals, aroma, sound, *chakras*, auras, astrology, *Nadi Shastra* . . . all coming together and building up on the foundation laid by Sheryl Benson, my Reiki teacher, who initiated me about eight years earlier in Boston. My curiosity and intense travel bug took me to Dharamsala, Rishikesh, Bodh Gaya, Ganeshpuri, Pondicherry, Kerala, Pune, Osho, the Kumbh Mela, the Himalayan Institute, Kripalu Center, and Sivananda Ashram in India, and shaman healers and various monasteries in Southeast Asia and the USA. It was a journey I wished would never end. My sabbaticals from the corporate world were getting longer. Maa thought I had taken *sanyasa* and started preaching to me the importance of *Grihastha Ashram* before *Sanyasa Ashram*! I asked her how it mattered, so long as I was in some ashram. She had her intellectual and spiritual limitations, typical of most Indian women conditioned by and trapped in the ignorance of what passes for Hindu religion in India.

Each sojourn brought me in and out of Mumbai. It brought me to Maa, who lived alone ever since my father passed away eighteen years earlier, and whom all her three sons had abandoned for greener pastures abroad. When I left the shores of India to go to the USA, my father asked me whether I would ever return. I said yes, absolutely, but I just did not know when. I could not fulfill this promise during his lifetime, and the time to redeem had still not arrived. But I knew it would.

Living Maa's Life

Maa was the matriarch of a family she had raised amid adverse circumstances. A family of eight children, thirteen grandchildren, twelve great-grandchildren, and their varied spouses. After coming to the bustle of Karachi from the sleepy town of Akola after her marriage, she eventually got uprooted from Karachi to move to Calcutta, and then to Bombay, after the brutal and inhuman Partition orchestrated and perpetrated by the arrogant and ignorant British.

As my interaction with Maa increased, a certain quietude started creeping into our relationship. Words became redundant. Expectations, emotions, responsibilities, and duties started fading. As the youngest of her eight children and being almost an afterthought for my parents (there was a six-year gap between me and my sibling immediately elder to me), I always felt very close to her. She supported and protected me in my angst concerning my father. We always had a certain understanding and bond typical between the youngest child and their doting Indian mother. Yet it felt different now. Something had changed in these five years.

Maa and I had transcended certain barriers inherent between any two individuals. I had started living her life. Her pains and discomforts had become mine. She did not need to express or ask; I just knew it. She had already become enshrined within me. There was no need for that thread of white light for healing. As her heart kept shrinking, I started breathing for her. As her kidneys started failing, my incontinence increased. As her digestion became weaker, my appetite for her favorite items increased. After all these years, I finally learned to say no to her. There were no pangs of guilt. She understood. She knew it wasn't me saying no—it was she herself. It did not matter anymore.

In Mumbai with Maa

My interest in astrology had reached a crescendo by 2001. I had my readings done under three different schools: Indian Vedic astrology (*Jyotish*), Western astrology, and Nadi Shastra. I was amazed at the confluence of the three readings. Besides touching upon myriad aspects of my life, each reading mentioned 2004, and one of them mentioned October 2004. That is when my Reiki intuition took over.

I was back in the USA, feeling like I was at a dead end. My corporate career seemed as if it had faded into the distant past, and neither were my dreams of a healing center in India materializing. Maa was becoming weaker and lonelier, but I was away from her and could not be with her for various reasons. My sojourns became less frequent.

And then I got a call. I landed a six-week consulting assignment in Mumbai. It seemed the stars had lined up for me. But then, out of the blue, something called 9/11 happened. Despite this Happening, I resolved that nothing was going to come in my way. I landed in Mumbai on September 24, 2001. I surprised Maa by reaching home the morning she was having a *havan* performed on my father's *shraddha*.

I was elated to meet her. It seemed her joy was subdued, but not really, as she knew I had come home, even though I was staying in a plush hotel in the distant suburbs close to my place of work.

The six-week assignment became a two-year project. I spent most of this period in the hotel and barely visited her once or twice a week. Each time I visited her, she cooked her favorite items, without asking me. She knew I would eat, and she would relish it. Her appetite had diminished considerably. But how did it matter? As long as *I* was eating. We hardly spoke of anything consequential. She knew I would take care of everything as I could intuit what she wanted.

Shiva's Child

On one of these visits to Maa, I was sitting next to her on the sofa, and she was patting my head in her familiar way, which I loved so much. Spontaneously, I asked her, "Maa, you had seven children already, including two sons. Why did you have one more?"

With a soft smile, she replied, "You were a gift from Shiva. I asked for you."

I was taken aback.

She went on: "You are the only one who will be there when I need you for myself and your three siblings."

"What do you mean, Maa?"

"You have to take care of Nirmala (my eldest sister), Krishna (my eldest brother), and Sunila (my youngest sister). They have no one except you. I needed you for that. Promise me you will be there for them. I asked Shiva for this, and He granted me this boon."

I was already very close to my three siblings whom Maa mentioned. Nirmala Jiji had no children. *Bhaisahab* (Krishna) had a broken marriage and a dysfunctional family that disavowed him. Sunila Jiji, too, had no children until she adopted Ankur many years after her marriage. But it took some time for Maa's revelation to sink in. I was steadily proceeding on my spiritual path, and this was the first of many events and Happenings that would, in time, reinforce my journey. I hugged Maa, and there were tears in our eyes.

Moving to Pune

My assignment was over in October 2003, and I decided to move back to India from the USA. I bought an apartment in Pune as I could not imagine living in Mumbai, let alone with Maa. She knew, she understood. Never once did she ask that I move in with her. She was so overjoyed at my moving to India, and that was enough for her. How could she ask for anything? I felt her unexpressed desire and cried. I was helpless as all I could do was watch and be a witness. (I had discovered Osho but not Ramesh yet.) I started getting the apartment ready and furnished to move in by the middle of next year. I was running against time. The October 2004 astrological reading had stayed with me. I quietly told myself, *Whatever has to happen during this period will go away only after it has come; not a day before, not a day after.*

Meeting Ramesh

I finally met Ramesh in January 2004 at his apartment in Mumbai for his morning discourse (after having heard about him from a Brazilian friend four years earlier while on a trip to Bodh Gaya). It was the year after I started reading his books. He turned out to be everything except what I had imagined him to be. I had tears in my eyes that first day when I touched his feet. I knew my search was over.

The Beginning of the End

As I was practicing my morning *asanas*, I felt a twitch in my chest on the left side. I ignored it, but it persisted. While it was not painful, I could feel it now and then. As I gave myself Reiki, I felt the lump gradually moving toward the Anahata Chakra. During visualization, I saw something dark brown, almost black and dirty. It was quite small—small enough not to cause any concern. It had almost become a plaything. I sought it out each night before I fell asleep. Over the next few weeks, I felt it increasing in size and shifting downward.

It was time for me to go back to the USA and pack up, and come back for good. I was in the car after one of Ramesh's discourses, on my way to visit Maa, when Lalloo (her servant of many years) called on the cell. Maa had fallen on the balcony and was in pain. Nirmala Jiji called soon after, asking me to get to Maa as soon as possible. We were in the month of July 2004, and it was pouring cats and dogs outside. It was one of those days in the Bombay monsoon, when everything is flooded, and you cannot get anywhere.

I was able to reach Maa only later that evening. She had fallen on the plants in the balcony, and her chest seemed to have taken the brunt of the pressure. She complained of pain in the chest, but was otherwise quiet. Her maid, Archana, was applying hot-water bottles. The next day, the X-ray did not show any broken bones. Dr. Parikh, the family doctor, suggested a chest brace, which unfortunately gave her no comfort.

Maa kept complaining of pain in her chest. Everyone thought it was muscular because of the fall and would heal itself gradually. During the Reiki I gave her that evening, I saw that her chest was ablaze. The Anahata Chakra was all dark and ominous. During visualization, I saw a lump, the size of a golf ball, on the left side. As earlier, it was dark brown, almost black and dirty. I let her sleep. I went back to bed and sought it out. It had moved further down, just above my navel. There was no pain, just a soft sensation. I felt divine.

At Home with Her Loved Ones

It was August 2004, and my apartment in Pune was still not ready. I was getting anxious. Maa had now lost almost all appetite; I was eating like a pig. Her kidneys had almost failed; my incontinence had become more intense. She was gasping for breath every so often; my *pranayama* became more powerful.

Maa could no longer stand erect, let alone walk with her walker. She was totally bedridden. Dr. Shah was back in charge. I spoke with him for the first time since August 1999. His advice was simple: "Hospitalize her." It would be extremely difficult, if not impossible, to care for her at home. But being a doctor, he was not sensitive enough to the nuances and the dynamic forces that were in play. He did not understand Maa; he did not understand me.

Maa was resolute. She would not go to the hospital. She wanted to be at home, under the care of Archana, Sarita, and Lalloo, who had all so lovingly cared for her all these years. She still wanted to know what was cooking in the kitchen, who was at the door, and whether Lalloo was shortchanging her while buying groceries.

I drafted her obit. I also had the handwritten piece of paper where, many years ago, Maa had scribbled her wishes to be carried out upon her passing away. I was leaving on the 15th for the USA. I got together with my four sisters the day before and discussed the entire plan in the event of anything happening in my absence. We all agreed that under no circumstances would we hospitalize Maa. We discussed and agreed on the funeral and post-funeral plans. I summarized everything and put it in an email to Bhaisahab, Pramila Jiji, and Dilip Bhaiya, my siblings in the USA. I could not have been less emotional.

I bid Maa farewell on the 15th, telling her I would be back soon. She patted me and blessed me. As I went to sleep on the flight, I felt the lump. It was in the hara, in the *Manipura Chakra*.

On September 1, 2004, I called Maa from Boston. She could barely speak or hear. I informed her that my flight reservation was for November 1. She could not hear me and kept asking, "You are coming on the 25th, aren't you?" I finally said yes, which seemed to make her happy. I called the airline and changed my reservation for September 24.

Mridula Jiji called from Bombay. She said Maa was in a lot of agony and discomfort but was not "letting go," waiting for me. She suggested I come back at the earliest and help relieve Maa of her misery. I said I would think about it, as it was September 5 then. I checked my hara. The lump had not moved much, and there was still no pain.

I was traveling in the USA on September 22, 2004, when I got a message on my voicemail to call Bombay immediately. I spoke with Pramila Jiji, my sister from California, who had already reached Bombay. She informed me that the doctor had found a lump in Maa's chest and wanted to test it for malignancy. They had finally figured out what was causing her the pain all along! She also informed me that Dr. Shah was adamant that Maa be hospitalized immediately, but Maa refused to listen to anyone until I returned. I reminded her that we had all decided not to hospitalize her under any circumstances. I asked for Maa, but she was in no position to speak on the phone.

I scanned my hara. The lump had moved to the *Swadhisthana Chakra*. I asked my sister not to bother putting Maa through the biopsy test. It was not relevant.

ICU and Advaita

I reached Bombay early morning on September 25, 2004. I finally saw Maa, a little later, after her morning rituals. She hugged me and started sobbing. I told her I had come back home. I finally redeemed my promise made to my father twenty-two years ago. I asked her whether she would like to go to the hospital, but she just kept looking at me and sobbing. All day long, there was a lot of pressure from my sisters, doctors, and others to take her to the hospital. I refused.

At 7:30 PM, Maa moved her bowels and then called me urgently. "I cannot breathe," she gasped. I scanned her Anahata Chakra. It was very dark. I panicked. I called Dr. Shah, the ambulance, and Bhatia Hospital, all in a space of five minutes. She was admitted to the ICU within half an hour. Ramesh's teachings were truly alive! That night, I recalled the conversation with her on September 1, when she was happy that I was coming on the 25th. After that, I slept like a log. I had never been happier.

Maa stayed in the ICU for a week. All her eight children were with her, including both my brothers from the USA. The medical diagnosis was clear: The kidneys had failed, and the heart was barely pumping. She refused all intakes. It was a matter of any day now, according to Dr. Shah. But I knew she was not ready yet. I scanned her Sahasrara; it was closed. I scanned myself; the lump had barely moved. Access to her in the ICU was very restricted, so we decided to take her out to a private room. The next few days became a routine. All of us slept in the room with her in rotation.

My sister Urmila Jiji had started sensing something. She asked me a few times about the date, but I kept quiet. Mridula Jiji insisted that I was "holding Maa back" and should "let her go." How could I? I was only a witness, not the doer.

I attended Ramesh's satsangs almost every morning and shared my daily experience with him and everyone present. His teaching was coming alive for me each day. *Advaita* was no longer just a concept; it had become real for me. What better teaching could I ask for? Osho says I could only be a witness. Balsekar says I am not the doer. It was all ringing true, each day, each moment.

Leela of Light

It was October 10, 2004—Maa's birthday. She was barely able to open her eyes. I asked her if she would like to come to Pune to my new home. She nodded and said, "Yes, take me there." Her eyes were moist. I scanned her. My hands froze on the back of her head. There was an unmistakable glow and heat. My heart jumped a beat. The Sahasara Chakra was open!

I felt a tightness in my groin. I scanned myself. The lump had moved all the way down. It seemed to have shrunk a bit, but it was ominously dark as always.

The next few days, I was with Maa as much as possible. She had become *Brahmaleen*—one with the Creator. I wanted to be as close to this *Leela* as possible; absorb and bask in as much of the divinity as possible. There was no thought, no emotion, no sensation. Her aura got brighter each day. The colors had started to fade. She was encircled in white light that became more intense with each passing day. Maa, Reiki, me . . . the distinctions had faded. There was no healer or healing; just pure, white light.

Dr. Shah continued his twice-a-day visits, amazed at her resilience. We no longer talked about Reiki or miracles or healing. It was not relevant, and he would not understand. All that mattered now was his warmth and caring attitude, as if his own mother were lying there. Ironically, he said, "We can only watch." I smiled. I wished Ramesh were there to hear it!

Letting Go

Everyone had left. It was 8:35 PM, and I was alone with Maa. She was in a deep sleep. It had been almost a month (October 20, 2004) since she was admitted to the hospital. I sat beside her and, as always, placed my right hand on her head and left hand on her Anahata. The Sahasrara was still open. I closed my eyes. I saw a red glow and felt a twitch in my right hand. When I opened my eyes, Maa was looking at me with eyes wide open, like a baby who had just woken up from a long, peaceful sleep. I quickly grabbed my cell phone and started shooting her video. She rolled her eyes and moved her head from side to side. I immediately called my sisters to tell them what was happening. They wanted to come over, asking how long this would continue. I hung up the phone and placed my hand on Maa's forehead. She looked into my eyes and nodded. A tear slipped from my right eye, and I nodded back. She closed her eyes. I needed to let go. She was ready.

I stayed awake all night in meditation. The sankalpa came into being at about five in the morning. All of the Reiki energy had accumulated. It was accompanied by a vision of a long highway leading away from a bright light into forests yonder. When I came out of my meditation, Maa was in a deep sleep.

I came back the next day to Maa's room in time (12:30 PM) for Dr. Shah's morning visit, and also to inform him that I was leaving tomorrow for Pune for a couple of days. He examined Maa and asked me not to leave town. I reluctantly agreed and closed my eyes. How could I explain my sankalpa to him? How could I tell him that Maa would not leave unless I left first? I kept quiet.

Two days later, at 7 AM, I scanned Maa for the last time. The Sahasrara Chakra was still open. I touched and kissed her forehead, touched her feet, and left immediately for Pune. Dr. Shah did not need to know.

That night at Sunila Jiji's place, I went to the bathroom before going to bed at 10 PM. As I was emptying my bladder, there was a sharp, excruciating pain in the groin. I almost screamed. After that, I went to sleep like a toddler.

The next day (October 24, 2004) was Maa's funeral. My pajamas were bleeding red during the entire ceremony, and I was emptying my bladder profusely.

The healing was complete. I had come full circle.

"Family" Doctor

A week later, when I went to settle Dr. Shah's fees in his consulting room, we spent almost an hour together. He had become part of the family. I wanted to give him a Reiki hug. I hesitated, thinking he would not understand. We talked mainly about Maa, from the time we first met him in August 1999 to the present. We touched upon my journey and my healing practice briefly, but there was no mention of Reiki, miracles, and the like this time. Later, he simply said, "After a point, even the doctor can only watch." I said to myself, *Dr. Shah, I would want you to be my doctor until that point.*

I went home to Maa.

All Is Maa

I had started visiting Rishikesh, India, regularly since 2000, when I attended the first International Yog Festival organized by Parmarth Ashram. During one of my visits (two years after Maa left us), I met Maa Gyaan Suveera, who has a beautiful ashram by the Ganga, away from the hustle-bustle of the main drag. We connected immediately, and it felt like I was in the presence of Maa and Shakti combined into one. Her story of how she ended up in that divine location was as inspiring as her presence. She became my Guru Maa.

After visiting Guru Maa one day, I proceeded to the *Vashishta Gufa* down the road. I sat in silence inside for a couple of hours, and when I started to emerge from the gufa, I saw a woman in a white saree with white light surrounding her. She approached me and said, "You have come, Pradeep!"

I had never seen or met her before. How did she know my name?

"I have been waiting for you. Now, I can go in peace."

I came closer to her and asked, "Maa, what do you mean? How do you know me?"

"You are my son. I was pregnant with you twenty years after you were born to your mother, but Shiva decided to manifest you earlier. I had a miscarriage in my fourth month. You are actually twenty years younger."

The date of her miscarriage was exactly twenty years after the date of my birth!

I stood there transfixed, not knowing what to say or do. Maa's revelation about my birth resonated loud and clear. Was this really happening? Yes, it was, and I was just a witness to yet another Leela. Osho and Ramesh were again ringing true. Spirituality was yet again coming alive right here.

I touched her feet, and she blessed me with a smile and a glow. I had experienced Shakti Herself.

I was in a daze, and not knowing what else to do, I went along my way without turning back.

Two days later, I returned to the Gufa and crossed paths with a *sadhu*. He looked at me and said, "Pradeepji, you have come for the last rites of your mother?" Yet again, I was in shock. How did he know my name?

"Lalitadevi had said you would come for her last rites. She passed away this morning. Please come with me."

He led me to a nearby hut, where I saw Lalitadevi, my spiritual mother, lying in all white, the way I had seen her two days earlier. I had tears in my eyes.

The sadhu helped me perform the last rites by the Ganga. There were just the two of us, and my two Maas. As I saw the flames go up by the cool waters of yet another Maa, the Ganga, I was wondering, *Who was the Source? Where did I come from? Shantadevi or Lalitadevi? Or was it the Mother Goddess Herself—Shakti?* My Ajna Chakra lit up, and Shiva appeared in his most benevolent form and blessed me. I had become a convert. Rather, I had become Shiva.

The first sound uttered by a newborn is "mmm," the beginning sound in "Maa" and the last sound in "*Aum.*" This sound represents the deep sleep state after "a" (the waking state) and "u" (the dreaming state). When they merge in Aum, it is the *Turiya* state—Satchidananda.

It was sheer bliss. Nothing mattered. A continuation of a journey with higher peaks to reach. The first taste of bliss was sweet, but it was just a taste.

|| Aum Namah Shivaya ||

|| Shiva and Shakti
The Cosmic Dance ||

2.
|| Bindu ||
|| Shakti ||

Shiva is incomplete without Shakti.

Maa Shakti is the divine Goddess who gives birth and nourishes all human beings. She is the consort of Shiva, the divine male form, who is Her protector. The two energies join together to manifest the unmanifest.

It is really as simple as that.

If Nature were allowed to follow its natural course, there would be no conflict between Shiva and Shakti, and the divine *Raas Leela* symbolized by *Radha* and Krishna would go on uninterrupted. But Nature has also bestowed upon man greater physical strength than that of a woman, and instead of using this to protect his beloved, he has, time and again, used it to attack her, as symbolized by the humiliation of Draupadi by Duryodhana and his brothers. This has continued for generations, and the results are evident in this *Kaliyuga*.

Laws are being enacted to protect women. They are up in arms, and sympathy for them is abundant. But the cycle of anger and angst, and remorse and pain, will continue unabated. Nothing will change with the degeneration of the rich, ancient Indian culture in this Kaliyuga. It requires a paradigm shift in awareness and consciousness.

No worldly laws can control the unbridled energy flowing within each human being. No government, police, or courts can take any action against this highly potent energy lying coiled at the bottom of the spine in each one of us. This energy in the Muladhara and Manipura chakras can either take the form of the divine *Kundalini* energy rising up the spine and connecting all the chakras with the Sahasrara Chakra and, thereby, with the Supreme Consciousness, or it can take an aggressive, violent form and attack the female energy. Of course, the third possibility is that it stays dormant for the most part, as with celibates and renunciates, but that requires a very high order of awareness and consciousness, which is absent even in many high-profile so-called godmen. It has also remained dormant within the typical Indian Shakti who has repressed and locked her sexuality, and thrown away the keys in the ocean of ignorance and darkness. All of this has further empowered the male energy to act the way it does in the modern world. The land of *Kama Sutra* and Khajuraho has become the hunting ground of the Duryodhanas and their ilk.

Decline of Tantra

The sexual energy in the bottom two chakras has two—and only two—specific purposes according to the Laws of Nature. The first and obvious purpose is procreation, to keep the manifestation going. The second purpose, which is highly sacred and esoteric, and steeped in mystique, is to bring the male and female energies into a spiritual union such that they become one with the Universe. This is the essence of Tantra.

So long as Tantra was alive and mainstream—as depicted in the temples of Khajuraho, Konark, and Kamakhya, and of the *Sixty-four Yoginis*, mentioned in many scriptures and reflected in various art forms—man worshipped woman and treated her as a goddess. When Tantra mysteriously disappeared into the background and became a taboo subject, male domination over the female commenced its journey and has continued till today.

Tantra celebrates the free spirits of Shiva and Shakti, and while recognizing them as individuals, also emphasizes the importance of their coming together as a form of cosmic union, which is highly symbolic, esoteric, and potent. All my workshops start and end with a Cosmic Dance. Unfortunately, not many Shivas show up at these workshops, so it remains unbalanced. So be it. The understanding of this cosmic union depends on the presupposition that the human being has evolved to a much higher plane of consciousness to understand and appreciate this union. When this higher level of consciousness is absent, the only purpose left for sexual energy is procreation and unbridled lust. And if procreation is not desired by a couple or if procreation cannot be the purpose of all copulation, then we are left with a problem. Lust.

The mention of lust as a human weakness in all religions, in some form or another, recognizes that it can be the cause for mankind's downfall, as evident in today's headlines. It brings us down to the level of beasts. When lust takes over, the intelligence that separates mankind from the animal world disappears. The chakras close up, and there is no higher flow of energy. There is just raw sexual energy waiting to unleash itself on the first victim. Even within the lowest of the three *gunas—tamas—*lust is at the bottom of the pile.

Avenues for Sexual Energy

Lust is the result of many factors, the most important being repressed sexual energy. Sexual energy needs an outlet; it cannot remain inert. It needs to manifest itself in some form or another. Other than the spiritual rising of the Kundalini and procreation, most societies have provided various avenues for this purpose. These have not been the result of some organized effort by society; rather, they have evolved naturally. They include a healthy interplay of man–woman relationships outside of marriage, and access to the arts, literature, and various media that depict sexuality in a healthy and aesthetically pleasing manner.

Meaningful sex education in schools plays a very important role in removing any taboos toward human sexuality. When boys and girls are brought up together, intermingling with each other freely, it helps create a healthy understanding and respect for the opposite gender. When they are segregated at each step, an element of curiosity and wonder starts taking over, and since the male energy is physically stronger, it starts making untoward advances. In India, men and women are segregated in almost all walks of life: weddings, parties, satsangs, funerals, temples, airports, and so on. There is no healthy touching, patting, and hugging, let alone kissing. My workshops start and end with hugs. It is really funny and sad to see Indian women give side hugs (that barely last a moment) instead of full, frontal hugs (which can last an eternity!).

Taboo

Something that is the very basis of life and a cause for celebration, joy, and happiness has been termed "dirty" and firmly relegated to a place behind closed doors. In the name of modesty, coyness, and shame, the human body has been hidden behind the *purdah*. Parents do not discuss it at home, teachers shy away from it, and the media only uses it for titillation. Whatever exposure it gets is mainly from the internet. There is an entire stratum of society, mainly the lower middle class in the semi-urban and semi-rural areas, that has access to the internet. But those comprising this stratum, consisting primarily of males in the fifteen-to-twenty-five-year age group, are disenfranchised, disillusioned, displaced, and only partly educated. Until they get married, they have no avenues for releasing their raging hormones. Frustration in an illiterate mind is fertile ground for giving rise to sexually violent thoughts. The result is inevitable.

Sexual violence has very little to do with bold attire or its portrayal on TV and movies. Many societies around the world, including those that are even less developed and more promiscuous than Indian society, have a far healthier attitude and approach toward this very basic human activity called sex. Yet the incidence of sexual violence is nowhere near what we see in India.

It is all in the mind. The mindset needs to change.

Societal Changes: Pros and Cons

Despite the deeply entrenched intolerance for human sexuality outside the conjugal world, there are significant changes taking place in India. This is coming about primarily as a result of both genders of the younger generation studying and working side by side, with an increasing number of women joining the workforce. There are more opportunities for interaction and interplay, and the dynamics are changing fast and for the better. This is both good and bad. To the extent that there is better tolerance and understanding of each other, this is a very healthy development. However, biologically and spiritually, a woman's role is that of a nurturing mother full of unconditional love and compassion. The extent to which that is sacrificed at the altar of equality of the sexes only contributes to cosmic imbalance. The feminists who strive for equality in all walks of life are as misplaced in their zeal as the masochistic men who only believe in physical domination and abuse of women. The balance between Shiva and Shakti, according to the Laws of Nature, which is the basis for manifestation itself, needs to be restored.

India is the land of the Kama Sutra and Tantra. Indian scriptures and mythology are replete with stories and anecdotes portraying free, noncommittal love and physical relationships between the two sexes. In fact, many of the stories revolve around the very same gods and goddesses that are so revered in India. But unlike the sex of today, it was spiritual and uplifting, and a play of the senses. Royalty as well as common folk equally indulged unabashedly in this most basic of human instincts.

Tantra is the masterful treatise on this subject; something that was looked upon by the entire world with awe and inspiration. There was no Sodom or Gomorrah, but there was no repression either. It was clean and sacred.

There was a long prelude to the sexual act itself, which took on numerous forms. Many yog asanas meant to strengthen the sexual organs and open up the energy channels in the lower chakras were practiced. *Kakasana* is one example. Food and nutrition, music, and dance forms were, in many ways, geared toward arousal of sexual energy.

Today, religious fundamentalism, political activism, and rampant ignorance and intolerance, along with a *tamasic* lifestyle, have played havoc. On the one hand, the so-called guardians of religion have woven a tight noose of intolerance around human sexuality, and on the other, the typical nutritional levels in India are so abysmally low that there is no possibility for any *sattvic* nourishment for the chakras to open up. Instead, they become more tightly clamped, abetted by the tight clothing fad prevalent today. Consequently, one cannot breathe freely, resulting in frustration and violent behavior.

Furthermore, most Indians today have access to all forms of titillation through movies, TV, the internet, and other media. However, their real life has not kept pace with what is depicted therein. The social mores are still Victorian or worse. Religion, parents, politicians, and teachers are all responsible for this total disconnect between Shiva and Shakti. During my travels, in no other country (except for the repressed and oppressive Muslim countries) have I seen such sexual repression and such intolerance for public display of affection, as is the case in India.

Unless this sacred connection between Shiva and Shakti is reestablished in India through a collective, conscious paradigm shift in society's outlook, Maa Shakti will continue to be abused and raped. No laws or other forms of action have the power to stop it. The evidence is right before our eyes.

The Essence of Shakti

From Maa onwards, to Ramona, my spiritual journey has been dotted with Shakti manifesting every step of the way, guiding me along, merging with my energy, and giving me a glimpse of Bindu—the beginning and end of all manifestation. Everything emerges from and merges into

Bindu. In modern terminology, it is "The Theory of Everything." Each of my experiences with the Divine Goddess brought me closer to Bindu, which sits on top of *Sri Yantra*, navigating the web of nine *yonis*. *Sri Sukta, Sri Vidya, Saundarya Lahiri,* and *Lalita Sahasranama* started to come alive in the presence of and merger with each Shakti.

Shakti is the pure, unbridled, unconditional, formless, feminine energy without attributes, that can only be experienced by Shiva, the pure, unbridled, unconditional, formless male energy without attributes. From the time mankind became aware of these unmistakable forces pervading the entire Universe, it started to visualize and depict them in its own image through symbols, sculptures, drawings, and writings. Shakti took the form of the human female body in its full splendor as extolled by *Adi Shankaracharya* in *Saundarya Lahari*. In *Sri Sukta*, She is even compared with a golden deer, a vision that appeared to me, as described later in this book in chapter seven, "Happenings."

Since Shakti has been described in the scriptures to have 108 forms, and chanted in the form of *Namavali,* each of these forms is denoted by a certain physical attribute: for instance, Saraswati is depicted with the *veena* in her hand, symbolizing the arts and learning, and Kali and Durga have multiple limbs and weapons of destruction to fight evil. Unfortunately, these pictorial depictions have taken on a religious tone with idols being worshipped by the ignorant masses led by the power-hungry and unscrupulous priests and other self-appointed caretakers of religion.

Shakti is that eternal, primordial energy that cannot be felt or experienced in any temple. It is all-pervasive and, at the same time, resides right inside you as Kundalini, coiled up like a serpent in the Muladhara Chakra. One of the many forms of spiritual awakenings is the uncoiling of Kundalini to rise through the chakras to merge with Shiva in the Ajna. Migle from Lithuania, one of the many Shaktis to have crossed my spiritual path, has some of the most frequent and spontaneous bursts of Kundalini I have ever seen. She is a *yogini* after all, and believes herself to have been a temple priestess in Kashi in a previous life. She spends most of her time in Kashi and Kamakhya these days.

Kamakhya is one of the fifty-one *Shakti Peeths* spread across this sacred land of Bharat. Many have disappeared or are in a very dilapidated state, devoid of any divine feminine energy. But some of the ones I have visited, including Kamakhya, are so potent as to cause a spontaneous burst of Kundalini awakening for the true *Devi sadhak*. Some texts mention sixty-four Shakti Peeths, known as Yogini Peeths, since they depict sixty-four forms of the Devi, typically in a circular setting. One of the most powerful of these is the one next to the Khajuraho temple, itself a potent *Tantric* site. Pandit Rajmani Tigunait of the Himalayan Institute has consecrated a beautiful Sri Vidya Peeth nearby, where he conducts regular Tantra retreats. That entire region is fertile with divine feminine energy. Many of these Peeths have been visited by me with the Shaktis in my life: Linda (USA), Neelima (India), and Laura (Lithuania), who appeared at the appropriate time to complete my Shiva Shakti connection and lead me deeper into this world of divine feminine energy. I have visited many others on my own, during my own Satsang of One.

The Shakti that I am talking about here, and which I have experienced on my journey, is part of the broad Tantra philosophy that precedes all other scriptures, and it is as vast as the Universe itself. It was largely an oral tradition passed down through the generations until the past thousand years, when it started to be transcribed. I will discuss more of this in a later chapter on Tantra. Suffice to say here that it is impossible to understand the Shiva Shakti connection without a knowledge of Tantra, and this has been my experience. This Shakti is largely unknown to the masses, even though, once upon a time, She ruled over Bharat conspicuously and still does, but inconspicuously.

The Feminine Presence in My Life

Maa is my Adi Shakti. Right from the time I emerged from her womb, I was surrounded mainly by the feminine form, and there was an unconscious force pulling me toward it—a quiet yet very potent pull, like the force of gravity beyond my control. I remember this well before I became aware of my *Shaivya* or heard the story of my birth from Maa or experienced the strong surge of sexuality from puberty onwards. The female form with its buxom curves is Divinity itself, sensuality oozing from each pore and fold of the skin. This physical form of the celestial Goddess has been eulogized by Kalidasa in his play, *Shakuntala*, and by Adi Sankaracharya in *Saundarya Lahari*. Shankaracharya, an avowed *Brahmachari*, had to shed his monkhood to experience this celestial form of the Mother Goddess in all Her glory and then compose a paean on her immense beauty. The composition itself is as mesmerizing as the form he describes therein. How can one not surrender to this sublimely breathtaking Divinity, which is the source of all Creation!

Indian scriptures are replete with tales of the most steadfast sages and mighty warriors falling prey to the charms of one such as Shakuntala, Radha, Draupadi. The Indian female form has descended straight from the heavens—full, rounded hips; perfect globes for breasts; long, black tresses; doe eyes; deep-set navel; slender fingers; and dusky complexion, oozing nurturing motherly instincts. When I was a toddler, I remember holding Maa's exposed midriff while going to sleep. It was *nirvana*.

I was surrounded by my aunts, *bhabhis*, and cousins, who doted on me. When Sneh Bhabhi came into the family, I was five years of age and under her care until she moved out. Even after that, the attraction was strong. The bhabhi–*devar* relationship in Indian folklore is very unique and replete with sensuality and sexual undertones. I had two brothers and numerous male cousins on both sides of my parents, and I was the youngest among them all. I ended up being doted upon by all the bhabhis, and the Shakti energy bubbled strongly around me.

Some of my male friends and I would play hide-and-seek with some of the girls in our apartment building. There was the inevitable crush on my schoolteachers and the principal. One of the first Shakti experiences I had was with Anita, sitting next to me for the SSC exams. We glanced at each other, but I was too shy and introverted to reach out. She became my classmate in college, yet in our four years together, we never exchanged a word. The irony was that she came from a family known to my parents and was also related to one of my aunts. Shaktis had started manifesting, but Shiva had not bloomed as yet.

In school, we were allowed to connect with pen pals from other countries. My destiny was starting to come alive. I connected with Pirkko from Finland and Vanitha from South Africa. I was barely in my teens, and the first blush of sexuality had started to arise. Pirkko and I stayed connected for the next ten years until I left for the USA, and then lost contact. We reconnected eighteen years later when I moved to London, and I tracked her down. The first thing she said upon seeing my LinkedIn profile picture was, "You should change your baby picture." She faded away after a while. Vanitha went on to propose to me, saying her parents wanted her to marry someone she did not like. When I wrote to her that I was getting married, she too gradually disappeared.

True to Indian tradition, there was a lot of pressure on me to find an arranged match before I left for the USA. The rebel in me took over, and I decided to find my own match on my own terms. In 1981, I met Anjali at work and quickly proposed to her, introduced her to my family, and took off for the USA via a short stint in Bahrain to earn my passageway and initial seed money. A couple of years later, Anjali followed. After many years, I learned that her father, a very simple and quiet man, was against this marriage because our horoscopes did not match. Destiny was playing out every step of the way, as we shall see later.

Anjali's mother was an equally simple and quiet person, unlike her three daughters. In 1994, when I was living in Bombay for my Morgan Stanley assignment, she was struck with cancer, and I was with her till the end. Anjali was in New York. After a couple of years, her father was struck with cancer, and I was with him too toward the end. Anjali was in Boston at the time. The two of us remained married for thirty-three years, with long intermittent periods of separation. Nonetheless, the Shakti connection was unique, and we are still connected. An aspect of Shiva is to protect his Shakti, no matter what.

It was the day after Diwali, 2002. I went to visit Nirmala Jiji and *Jijaji*. I rang the bell. As soon as the door opened, I saw a woman in a saree sitting directly in front of me, smiling away. It was Neelu (Neelima). It had been almost twenty years since we last met at my wedding. Our eyes met, and there was a current of instant reconnection, stronger than in all our meetings, years ago, when she was a teenager and we used to hang around with Nirmala Jiji and Jijaji (her maternal grandparents) or on our own. We had both moved on and gotten married. She had a daughter, her marriage was coming apart, and she was in Bombay with her mother. It was as if time had stood still. We picked up from where we had left off, and it quickly moved to the next level of Shiva Shakti connection. We traversed the length and breadth of India and Nepal. But Shakti is always fleeting and cannot be contained in a man–woman relationship. Her eternal nature is that of a cosmic dance with Shiva. Our Leela may have ended at the human level, but we still connect in Pondicherry (where she resides) when I am there.

The Lithuania Leela

In 2012, I was in Vilnius, Lithuania, one of the three relatively unknown and tiny Baltic countries that I was exploring, the other two being Estonia and Latvia. I was sitting in Vegafe, a cute little yog studio with an attached café. That is when I saw her. Our eyes locked, and we both smiled simultaneously. I was sitting on a cushion on the floor, sipping herbal tea, and she came and sat next to me. She introduced herself as Laura, a professional photographer and full-time accountant. We spent the rest of the warm summer day together while she showed me around her city. Eventually, we ended up lying on a blanket by the river that evening. Like all the other Shaktis who weave in and out of my life, she too darted out of the blue, led me by the hand, and we traversed the world. She, too, like Neelu, had a broken marriage and was the single parent of a teenage daughter. I start to see a certain pattern. Laura introduced me to Mindaugas and his wife, who run summer camps for teenagers, sponsored by UNICEF.

Mindaugas invited me to one of these camps, and Laura and I spent a whole day there. Everyone was running around, playing, and frolicking naked in the river. They were all as free as the birds soaring high above, with nothing to worry about. I ended up conducting a meditation session for everyone, as well as some individual mentoring sessions. This was my foray into the world of workshops, mentoring, and teaching in Europe.

Two days later, I was sitting in Raw 42, a raw vegan café, having a quiet supper before the full moon meditation that had been organized by Mindaugas in the nearby Tea House. All of a sudden, yet another Shakti appeared outside, stopped at the window, looked at me, smiled, and moved on. I finished my supper and made my way to the meditation workshop. As I entered the room, I saw her again, and she smiled at me once more. At the end of the session, during the question round, Juliya (the smiling stranger) said, "I have not menstruated in six years," and tears welled up in her eyes. I suggested that she should meditate regularly around full moon days and bring the powerful light into her Muladhara. (I had already talked about the connection between the lunar cycle and the female menstrual cycle.) Four months later, she called me up, crying, "Pradeep, I just had my menstruation after six years." We became the best of friends (Migle included), and in September 2024, I attended her wedding to her long-awaited Shiva. Six months later, along came little Ganesh.

The Juliya–Migle–Pradeep Happening can be better understood by what follows.

Sisters—in Life and Death

Two sisters, Lalitha and Sarangini, lived in a royal family somewhere near Benares, North India, in the middle of the nineteenth century. They were very close to each other. Their grandmother had brought them up as their mother had abandoned them in their childhood. They did not miss their mother because their grandmother loved them more than any mother could.

Lalitha was married to Shiva, who loved her dearly. She was his Shakti. Soon, Lalitha became pregnant. Shiva loved Sarangini too, but was fiercely loyal and committed to Lalitha.

Sarangini was young, beautiful, and longing for a man. She came under the charms of Yam, the head of the armed forces, who had his eyes on her. Having violence in his blood, he raped her brutally. Sarangini got pregnant, and Yam disappeared on the war front. Sarangini, who was left alone, cried inconsolably in the arms of her sister.

Lalitha vowed revenge for what was perpetrated on her sister and sought Shiva's help. Shiva remained the observer, asking her to be patient. But Lalitha was seething with anger and could not bear to see her sister in a sorrowful condition. Unbeknownst to anyone, she headed to the war front to confront Yam. Passing through a huge forest, she decided to rest since she was pregnant. While she was sleeping, she was bitten by a snake and died instantly.

Sarangini could not bear the loss of her sister and went mad. Her grandmother, though equally helpless, showered her with love, but it did nothing to console Sarangini. The grandmother requested Shiva to marry Sarangini. Shiva refused; he could not bear the thought of life without his beloved Lalitha. He took sanyasa and headed to the forest, never to return. Sarangini lost all hope and killed herself and her unborn child to become one with her beloved sister. The grandmother also died soon after.

Migle's Sister and Her Shiva

In 2010, when Migle visited the Santosh Puri Ashram near Haridwar, North India, Baba Santoshpuri had taken *samadhi,* and Narvada Puri Mataji was in charge of the ashram.

As soon as Migle arrived, Mataji asked her, "How is your sister?" Migle was surprised to hear that as she did not have a sister. Mataji took her in her arms, gave her a tight hug, and said, "Look after your sister."

After a month in the ashram, while Migle was leaving, Mataji told her, "Find your Shiva. He is waiting for you." Migle smiled. She already knew about this because a clairvoyant had told her the same when she was nineteen and had even described what he looked like: tall, dark, slim, long hair, and much older than her but young at heart. She was even told that her sister would help her find him. But she had no sister! And now, for the second time, someone (Mataji) had mentioned her sister.

Over the next two years, Migle traveled frequently to Benares from her home in Vilnius, in search of her Shiva. She wasn't quite sure who he was, but she knew she would recognize him as soon as she saw him.

One evening, she was on a boat in the Ganga, moving toward the *ghats.* Everyone was getting ready for the evening *aarti.* As she approached the ghats, she spotted him. Fair-skinned and well-built, with long hair, wearing a dhoti and holding the aarti. She recognized Yam instantly.

After the aarti was over, Migle followed Yam. When she got close to him, she seduced him with her radiant smile and mynah eyes. He was taken aback at what was happening. Being a Brahmin from Nepal, he was not supposed to be with any women, let alone foreign women. But he was also a man. Eventually, he could not resist her charms and fell for her. They became inseparable. She now had a reason to come to Benares frequently.

When Migle asked Yam to marry her, he refused, saying it was impossible; his family would never allow it. Also, he was much younger than her.

Thinking she just wanted to have fun, as most foreign women do, he was shocked that she was getting serious. He started avoiding her, but she did not relent and kept up the pressure. Desperate, he started verbally abusing and insulting her, hoping she would leave him alone.

Yam had no idea of their past-life relationship. He did not know Migle carried *shrapit dosha*, and that, now, he too was cursed by it.

Sisters in Arms

Migle was attending a yog camp in Lithuania in 2012, where she shared a room with another woman, also from Vilnius. This woman, Juliya, entered the room, and as soon as they saw each other, they fell into each other's arms. For the next seven days, they became almost inseparable, pouring out their hearts to each other and sharing their lives. It turned out that they both lived in Vilnius, not far from each other, and attended the same ashram there. It seemed as if they were long-lost sisters, Migle the older, and Juliya the younger.

Juliya Appears

Pradeep, a spiritual teacher from India, was visiting Vilnius for the first time in 2012 to conduct some workshops. It was full moon meditation day. He was sitting by the window in Raw 42, a raw food café, having a bite before the evening meditation. Juliya passed by on her way to the same meditation. She spotted Pradeep, stopped in her stride, and a smile crossed her face, after which she resumed her walk. Pradeep entered the meditation space soon after and spotted Juliya sitting in a corner with a huge smile on her face. Pradeep felt as if he had met her before, but could not remember when or where. After the session, they exchanged phone numbers, and Juliya requested him for an individual healing session. She was having menstrual problems and desperately wanted to become a mother.

The next few days, while Pradeep was still in Vilnius, they met every day, and a rapport instantly developed between them. Pradeep was interested in wooing her, but Juliya resisted. Her ego prevented her from reciprocating.

Pradeep returned to India. Four months later, Juliya called to share the wonderful news about her menstruating after six years. After that, there was no more contact between Pradeep and Juliya.

Shiva and Shakti Meet

One morning, in 2015, Pradeep was surprised to see an email in his inbox from Juliya. He opened it and read, "I was in the forest today, my favorite place for my spiritual practice, where I had a vision about you and the purple light from your Ajna Chakra." Thereafter, the connection was resumed, as if it had never broken during the last three years. They started sharing their dreams about each other, and Pradeep started flirting with her. She was a bit more receptive and open this time, but not fully.

One day, Juliya wrote to Pradeep, "I want you to meet my friend Migle; she is my elder sister." Pradeep agreed, and Juliya continued, "She will be coming to India soon, and the two of you can meet. Will you be there?" Pradeep had made plans to leave for his annual European trip and informed Juliya about it.

Meanwhile, Juliya told Migle about Pradeep and suggested that she should write to him and meet him when she was in India. Migle was not too interested but said, "OK, send me his picture; I just want to see his eyes." When she saw the picture, a smile crossed her face. He was her Shiva, the one that the clairvoyant had told her about!

Migle wrote to Pradeep, and when he received her email, he wrote back, "I have been waiting for you. Finally!" Migle made plans to visit Pradeep in Pune on her next trip to India. She was headed to India to do *tapasya* in Varanasi, as suggested by her Guruji. She also wanted to break off her relationship with Yam, who refused to meet her. He was in Nepal to help his family recover from the havoc wreaked by an earthquake.

Migle arrived at Pune station in Brahma Muhurta at 4 AM, dressed in pure white. Pradeep was waiting, also dressed completely in white. He was tall, dark, and slim, and had long hair—just like the clairvoyant had mentioned. They saw each other, smiled, and then fell into each other's arms. For the next ten days, they were inseparable.

Coming Full Circle

Migle went back to Vilnius after having had a wonderful time with Pradeep. He arrived there soon after. Juliya was already there, and the three of them bonded beautifully together. One day, as they were deep in Tantra meditation, holding each other's hands, Pradeep said, "Migle, you are Lalitha. Juliya, you are Sarangini." They both knew what he was talking about.

Two days earlier, Juliya had had a vision about an elderly woman wanting to meet her in India, whom she did not recognize. When she mentioned it to Migle, the latter showed her the picture of Mataji at Santosh Puri Ashram. "That is her," said Juliya, jumping for joy. Pradeep added, "She is your grandmother."

Back to the Present

Migle was now in Paris for her higher studies. I helped her set herself up there. Juliya quit her theater job and was on her way to Santosh Puri Ashram. Yam was afflicted with shapit dosha.

The awakened Shakti that she was, Migle was unable to see through the mask of this person whom she claimed to be her soulmate from her past life. Meanwhile, my Anahata had opened up wide and wanted to rescue this Shakti from the abyss she was in. However, something told me she did not want to be rescued. And if Shakti does not want to be rescued, Shiva is helpless and (in my case) heartbroken.

Our journey meandered from Pune to Vilnius to Paris to Benares. Migle was still in the throes of denial, awaiting her Shiva, as she was a confused and lost Shakti. First it was Yam, and then, Pradeep. Now she has taken off to Kamakhya, in search of her Shiva. But whenever Juliya, Migle, and I get together in Vilnius, where it all started, the intimacy between us is very much alive.

The Advent of the Shaktis

From September 2001 to December 2003, the ITC Maratha (a brand new, swanky hotel) was my home, under the aegis of the General Manager of the hotel, Dipak Haksar. Among other Happenings during this period, he introduced me to the Muktananda Ashram in Ganeshpuri, not far from the hotel. It was a potent period of my journey on many fronts, all anchored by the presence of Shakti in various forms. This was also the period of repaying my eternal debt to Maa. It was the last hurrah of sorts from *Lakshmi Narayan*. It was when my Reiki initiation by Sheryl Benson blossomed and took me higher on my spiritual journey. Also, my understanding of Advaita and nondoership went deeper. Many more Shaktis fleeted in and out of my life: Asmita, Vrinda, Ferzyn, Meher, Nikhat, Ruksana (Uganda), Gabriela (Mexico), and Silvuska (Slovakia). Unknowingly, each one contributed to my spiritual upliftment.

Vrinda stood steadfast by me as I was coming to terms with Maa's last days. She was the rare Indian woman I met on my journey who was not stuck up about her sexuality. As a Brahmin's daughter, she herself played the role of a priestess while performing the last rites of her father. There could hardly be anything more symbolic than this for a true Shakti.

Silvuska was an exchange student doing an internship at the hotel. She was young, naive, and inexperienced. I took her under my wing, and it is a connection that has continued to this day.

My world of Shaktis was interwoven with my wanderings and workshops. The Cosmic Dance would happen wherever we connected: Francesca

(Italy), Anina (Romania), Marina (Croatia), Gabriela (Serbia), Lucy (Ukraine), Jadranka (Bosnia), Karen (USA), Nela (Serbia), Maria (Romania/France), Flurina (Switzerland), Louise (Canada), Ivana (Serbia), Dorota (Krakow, Poland), Poonam (New Delhi), Olga (Moscow, Russia), Tanja (Denmark), Iluana (Romania), Aiga (Latvia), Lotta (Norway), Egle (Lithuania), Dorota (Warsaw, Poland), Olga (Saint Petersburg, Russia), Martina (Luxembourg), Linda (USA), Urta (Lithuania), Sandra (El Salvador), Christine (Sweden), Jadranka (Croatia), Haleh (Iran/Canada), Margo (Netherlands), Elizabeth (Italy) and Rosie (Hong Kong). The appearance of these Shaktis in my life was anything but random. Each of them crisscrossed my path for a reason, through a Happening that was divine intervention. They empowered my journey forward and passed me on to the next Shakti. Each was an individual in a three-dimensional form and fed me the nectar of joy and ecstasy.

If I were to pick a time when my journey truly started, it was sometime in 1996 when I moved to Boston. There was a *Shiatsu* school where I would go regularly for a Shiatsu massage. During one of the sessions, I started feeling strange sensations, never experienced before. The whole experience felt divine. At the end, I asked Sheryl, the therapist, what was going on. She replied, "I was giving you Reiki." I had never heard of Reiki. The next thing I knew, I was getting initiated into Reiki Level 1 within a month, Reiki Level 2 in three months, Reiki Level 3 in six months, and Reiki Master in less than a year. Sheryl told me she had never initiated anyone who progressed to Reiki Master so rapidly. Who were we to question the Universe's plan! My chakras were ablaze, and I was ready to go. Sheryl Benson was that unassuming Shakti, a corporate lawyer turned Reiki Master, who set me going on this journey that has taken me higher and higher.

While in Boston, I connected with Bonnie, a Shakti deeply anchored in Mother Earth, belonging to one of the Native American tribes in North America that were brutalized, destroyed, and deprived of their own lands and culture by the "white" people. After colonizing and destroying various cultures in the East, these vultures and barbarians had come West, to the New World. Bonnie was one of the most grounded Shaktis I ever met. Intuitive as she was, she was a Western astrologer and a *Tarot* reader as well. I would get my readings done regularly by her, and even though she followed a different line of astrology than Vedic Jyotish, the readings would be very similar. She was a wounded soul that cried out for healing, and we would do a barter, even after I moved to India.

When I moved to Pune in 2004, I started to write my experiences and thoughts in the form of articles, which were published in *Life Positive*, a monthly magazine focused on spirituality. A few sections in this book are based on those articles. At the time, Suma Varughese was the editor. Sadly, as a sign of the times, the magazine folded up in 2024, and Suma has moved on to other things. We became good acquaintances, and she encouraged me to write. She is a humble, simple person who (just like me) also needed to take care of her mother. I am grateful to her for the platform she gave me to write and be published, and her guidance for this book.

And then, there was Maria from California. She appeared like a bolt of lightning while I was in India and disappeared just as suddenly. It was a whirlwind dance lasting four weeks before she made me see reality and brought me down to earth. Only a Shakti could have done that most brutally, hurting Shiva where it would hurt the most. She abandoned me by the wayside once she discovered and exposed my Achilles' heel, which had been hidden all these years. It was not relevant to any of the other Shaktis but only to her. There cannot be Shiva with that Achilles' heel. It was one of the hardest lessons of my spiritual journey, and it took me a while to accept it and come to grips with it. But I am forever grateful to Maria for what she taught me.

I first heard Shruti Nada's divine voice in her album *Shivoham*, at Rhythm House, the place in Bombay to visit for all genres of music. (If they did not have it, they would get it.) It was my escape haunt, along with Samovar Café at the Jehangir Art Gallery across the street. Both of these iconic places have long disappeared. But I wake up to Shruti's *nada* every morning—her Aum rendition—a voice from the heavens gently waking me up. I ordered and gathered all her albums. There were not many, but it was Saraswati herself singing to Shiva.

Every note of Shruti's singing touched my chakras, and I felt the vibrations run through my body time and again. Was she a real person? Could the Devi's voice really resonate like that? I was happy to just listen to her at first, for a few years, but my yearning for her singing grew stronger, and I needed to seek her out. She was related to my sister by marriage. My sister reached out to Shruti's aunt, who lived in Benares and ran the Gyan Pravaha, a cultural and spiritual institution. I would pass by the Gyan Pravaha regularly while visiting Babaji (my Guruji) and the Aghor Ashram, and my curiosity had already been piqued. Acharya Vidyasagar Upadhaya, an astrologer I had met, told me a bit about this place, and Babaji knew of it too. As with many Happenings in my journey of One, it was a culmination of many streams coming together to form the *sangam*. I managed to contact Shruti and, finally, met her in New Delhi one wintry afternoon at a fair organized for women artisans from all over India. She supported a similar effort in Rajasthan, where she ran the family *haveli* as a boutique hotel and a gathering place for certain events. I feel a strong urge to go there, but for now, I am happy to wake up to her celestial voice each morning and immerse myself in her meditative rendering of *Shivoham* and *Saundarya Lahiri.*

I was in Fremont, CA, with my sister when I got the news that Harmeet was no more. I had learned to control my emotions since Maa passed away, but this time, I cried profusely. She was in Zurich on a work assignment, and I was scheduled to meet her there in two weeks. But it was not to be. She was the sweetest Shakti (of Punjabi origin, living in Singapore) that I had ever met, totally in tune with her feminine energy and sexuality. After Vrinda, she was another Indian Shakti I met who was refreshingly honest and different.

Harmeet was a divorcee with two grown-up children. Her entire family, including her children, as well as the *gurdwara,* had ostracized her for divorcing her abusive husband. She was as ardent a Sikh as one could find, but she was not willing to follow her faith blindly. She stood up as Shakti in her own right and lived life to the fullest on her own terms. No wonder we bonded so deeply.

I had met Harmeet in Singapore, and she had introduced me to some of the shops selling genuine Chinese medicine and herbs, as well as helped me start my collection of Chinese tea kettles. She knew all the secluded dining spots for authentic vegetarian Thai cuisine. She was as fond of the Thai red chili pepper as I was. When I underwent surgery in Pune, she came to spend a few days with me to help me recover. During this time, she cooked me some of the most delectable Punjabi dishes. Some Shaktis just show a glimpse of their magnitude and benevolence, and disappear into the yonder. Harmeet was one of them.

I was lying on the futon in Kalina's studio in Sofia, Bulgaria, while she was twisting and turning my body, especially my back, into all kinds of shapes—a contortionist's dream, so to speak. I was referred to her for Yumeiho therapy, a combination of Shiatsu, Thai massage, craniosacral therapy, and a couple of other modalities. However, it was not what she was doing to my body that was engaging me; it was her recitation of various *mantras*, Aum chanting, vocalizing of excerpts from Indian scriptures, and finally, her talking about her profound experience in Rishikesh, which engrossed my attention.

Before meeting Kalina, I had already met Antoneta, a reclusive and mysterious Tantrika. I was pleasantly surprised to see her already deeply immersed in the Shiva Shakti connection. Once again, I connected instantly, but it was to be a very enlightening and fleeting connection.

Here was yet another of those synchronicities and congruencies that came my way as I traversed Eastern Europe. While India is writ large all over Western Europe and North America, it is not so here. It is far more subtle, but also far deeper. Yog here is not just asanas; it is Patanjali's yogic way of life. India is not just a destination or vacation spot; it is a lifelong journey. And Kalina, a single mother of four, was a living example of what India is capable of doing to some individuals. One does not have to live in India to feel the Indian ethos. I discovered my Indian roots while living in the USA. One trip of six months was enough for Kalina to discover her connection with India. The vibrations reach far and deep. I have seen it, experienced it, and felt it in all corners of the world where I tread. It is in these moments that the adage "India is the cradle of civilization" rings true, with Shakti as the centerpiece.

Chandrika was introduced to me by Regina, who was our neighbor in New York. Chandrika was of Indian origin and had moved to the UK from

Burundi. I first met her in London when I was based there for a couple of years, enjoying some of her wonderful homemade meals. She then moved to Pune, the same time as I did, and the connection continued. In July 2003, we traveled to Kailash Mansarovar together, and she cared for me as I struggled with altitude sickness. I truly believe that was the purpose of her appearing in my life and then disappearing.

Lotte from Norway was given the name Poonam by her guru at the Sivananda Ashram, where she was initiated. She was one of the wounded Shaktis I have met, who needed healing but were lost. She showed me parts of Norway I would not have seen on my own. We ended up organizing a Tantra workshop in Oslo.

Elizabeth in Rome introduced me to a hospital that felt like heaven. We visited her friend who was admitted there. Shoes had to be removed at the main entrance, like in an Indian temple or ashram. Except for the soft, healing music playing throughout, there was pin drop silence. Doctors and nurses smiled when you passed them. The room itself (a regular, standard room alike for every patient) was done in soft, pastel hues and soft, warm lighting. The entire experience of visiting this hospital was sublime and calming. Like many other Shaktis who crossed my path, she disappeared soon thereafter, having shown me something I would not have known otherwise.

Louise was among the first Shaktis to appear in my life in the West. She was from Montreal but I first met her in New York. The connection was based upon a common interest in Ayurveda. Like most other Shaktis, she too was wounded and lost. Her dream of bringing Ayurveda within practical reach to the West, got lost along the way. But we stayed in touch.

Haleh from Toronto was to be my key to Iran, the country I was most in love with without having visited. However, she was a typical immigrant from the East who was more focused on blending into the Western lifestyle rather than maintaining her rich traditional connection.

I cannot end this section on Shaktis without being grateful for the support of those in my family.

Ayo Shanti was Bhaisahab's consort in the later part of his life, who cared for him as he neared the end, struck with cancer, and also protected him from his dysfunctional family. A grounded Shakti full of compassion and humility, she was the perfect balm for him to recover from his lifelong struggles. She held his hand until the end. Maa felt relieved knowing that Ayo was with her son. Ayo continues to communicate with him and seek his guidance as he watches over her. In spite of her own physical challenges since his passing on, she is running a campaign to clean up Maa Ganga and other polluted waterways of the world..

Maa had entrusted me with the responsibility for three of my siblings, Nirmala Jiji, Bhaisahab, and Sunila Jiji. In each instance, a Shakti appeared to help me fulfill my responsibility: Manju for Nirmala Jiji, Ayo for Bhaisahab, and Nupur for Sunila Jiji.

Manju was part of Nirmala Jiji's in-laws' family but had no reason to take on the responsibility the way she did. I have rarely seen the kind of unconditional support she rendered my sister in her last years, taking on full responsibility for her household, health, and finances. I was in the

USA for the most part, but Manju and I created a bond that has stood steadfast till today.

Nupur is Sunila Jiji's daughter-in-law. From tragedy arises hope. Nupur lost her husband (my nephew Ankur) and her father-in-law (Hari Jijaji) within a span of a year, while raising a two-year-old Shakti, Aanya. Sunila Jiji has been struggling with health issues since she was young. Her quiet and introverted nature does not allow her to reach out for help, and she suffers in silence. Sunila Jiji, Nupur, and Aanya are the three Devis who are now each other's support, full of love. Such are the ways of the Universe.

Gayatri *Mamiji* (my sister's aunt-in-law) lived next door to Nirmala Jiji and is now ninety-five. I became close to her in my sister's last days. She was a pillar of support, and along with Manju, watched over my sister as no family member would. She had a hip surgery due to a fall; despite this, she goes about doing her chores independently. She belongs to a generation that had different values and inner strengths, and sets an example for the younger generation glued to their devices.

Pushpa Bhabhi (my cousin's wife) is a Shakti who symbolizes tremendous resilience and strength to not just survive but thrive under the most adversarial circumstances. Having lost her husband over fifteen years ago, she has been living alone and has endured multiple falls and health issues. Each time, she got back on her feet with her resilience and fortitude. She was very close to my parents, and that is how we became close, in turn. Of course, we have that loving devar–bhabhi relationship where she dotes on me. She is yet another Shakti that belongs to a fast-disappearing generation.

And then, there are those we do not think about and take for granted. But they are Shaktis all the same. Archana was Maa's maid, and Sheila was Nirmala Jiji's, during their last years. These simple, folksy women from the villages of India, away from their own families, appeared just in time. Both literally arrived unannounced, straight from the street. Yet they were women of strength who provided the care that no family member could provide besides Manju.

A Few Good Men

In the world of Shaktis that I found myself in since my birth, there were a few men of strength and stature who stood up like pillars of support in my journey, and I connected with them as easily as I did with the Shaktis. Besides the realized teachers (Osho, Ramesh Balsekar, Pandit Tigunait, and Baba Harihar Ramji) who were my gurus, these men were the exception. I have not found it easy or natural to connect with the male energy. I had no tolerance for male chauvinism of any kind, and I had a fill of that during my corporate and personal life.

Within my family, Sushil Jijaji and Hari Jijaji, my oldest and youngest brothers-in-law, were bulwarks who made my journey, as well as that of my parents, that much easier. They both treated me like their own son. Then, there were two of my *Masajis*, Brijmohan Masaji in Nagpur and Srikrishna Masaji in Calcutta, who doted on me and inspired me since childhood. Brijmohan Masaji was that rare, down-to-earth, rustic, uneducated person who showered abundant love upon me. I was, perhaps, the son he never had. Srikrishna Masaji was the only person in the family with whom I could engage in a philosophical and intellectual discussion, right from my teen years when Bertrand Russell, G. B. Shaw, Annie Besant, and others had started to influence me. His command of English was chaste and perfect, better than that of a perfect Englishman.

Then there was Radheyshyamji in Pune, my niece's husband, but much older than me. He, too, was very close to my parents and a very practical, simple person. He only wore white trousers and a white shirt, no matter what the occasion or the weather. Along with his daughter Meera, he started a management institute in Pune and inducted me into the Academic Council to offer an alternative view on higher education. Unfortunately, I could not add much value due to certain entrenched views of other members. He was a foodie like me, and we hit it off.

Dr. GG Parikh passed away recently at the age of 101 in Bombay. When he turned a hundred, Ramona and I were with him for the celebrations at the iconic Bombay University. GG, as everyone fondly called him, was the family doctor. He lived and had a clinic next door to where my parents lived. When they were on their own, after all the children had left home, he was on call for their medical needs. GG became very close to my parents, especially my father, due to his connection with Gandhiji. He was among the last of the freedom fighters who worked alongside Gandhiji during India's freedom movement. He set up an upliftment center for Adivasis (tribals) in a rural area in memory of Yusuf Meherally, another freedom fighter. I supported the center financially for many years in memory of my parents and my sister. GG kept in touch, no matter where I was in the world. He was a giant of a human being in heart and spirit, and a true inspiration for me.

Though allopathy doctors have been anathema to me, two of them crossed paths in my journey for very specific reasons. I have talked about Dr. Suhas Shah in the context of Maa. I still consult with him when necessary. He introduced me to Dr. Jitendra Pandya when my eldest sister came down with Covid. I was in the USA and desperate to get medical help for her. During the dark days of the raging epidemic, when most doctors were hesitant or even reluctant to take on any patients, Dr. Pandya stepped in unhesitatingly. He was instrumental in getting my sister admitted to Bhatia Hospital. I felt at ease and immediately rushed down to be with her. She eventually recovered from COVID and came home. However, she developed a UTI, and her catheter needed to be changed regularly. It was Diwali night, the time for Lakshmi *Puja*. Dipika, the nurse at home, was having trouble changing the catheter. I called Dr. Pandya, and he immediately rushed to help with it. He has now become my personal physician, and I trust him fully.

Happenings have a way of happening at the most appropriate time.

I cannot but mention three more men whom I met at the most appropriate time on my journey and with whom I bonded quite easily. You will read about two of them, Dipak Haksar and JJ, later in the book. The third, Rajan, appeared out of nowhere when I was at my nadir and needed a levelheaded male presence. He was a thorough gentleman and one of those rare male energies that I could bond with.

The Eternal Connection

The man–woman relationship in the human dimension is just a microcosm of the cosmic Shiva Shakti connection. It plays out through a multitude of roles, and in the existential living dimension, most people remain oblivious of this. It is only when the chakras start to open up and vibrate, and awareness starts to seep into the human dimension, that this sacred connection begins to become apparent. My life has been one constant journey of the Shakti experience in all its myriad glory.

I have finally come home to my Shakti, Ramona, and I rest in her lap until my last breath.

|| Learning Never Ends
There is Always a Seeking ||

3.
|| Learning ||
|| Saraswati ||

Saraswati is the Goddess of learning and the consort of Brahma, the Creator. Brahma, as the Creator, needed Her by his side to infuse His Creation and mankind with Her knowledge. Like Brahma, She is rarely worshipped as a deity. You will not find Her as an idol in altars or temples. Unlike most of the other 108 forms of Shakti, She is the living Goddess from whom all knowledge emanates. In school, it was a tradition to sing a prayer in Her praise every morning. Also, we were taught to respect publications and written material by taking care not to step on them.

My learning started at home and in my immediate environment through observation, and has continued to do so to date. I consider myself a student of life. A large portion of my learning that has defined who I am has come from adopting the *sakshi bhava,* the sense of being merely an unbiased witness or an observer. It allows one to have a detached, objective view of happenings. The conscience absorbs whatever is in consonance with its own vibrations and thus sanskaras, or impressions, are formed. Over time, they become part of our genetic makeup and continue through generations. Sanskaras can be both positive and negative, depending on what is being observed and resonating with our own frequency. Like everything in Creation that is based on opposites, sanskaras are another example of this polarity.

The Only "Englishman" in the Family

My formal education started in the first standard at Magpherns English Medium School, located at Crawford Market, Bombay, a fifteen-minute drive from home. School education in India is very scattered and non-uniform, unlike the one to twelve–grade elementary, middle, and high school system in the USA. Grades are referred to as standards, and during my time, one had to pass through eleven standards to finish high school. I studied in Magpherns for standards one and two, and have some vague memories of the premises, the classroom, the teachers, the lunch break, and commuting to and fro, either in the school bus or our car.

As is evident from the school's name, it was an English medium school, and this is yet another unique feature of school education in India. Unlike almost all other countries where school education is imparted in a common national language, in India, that is not the case. While Hindi is the primary official language, it is neither the mother tongue of the vast majority of Indians nor is it widely prevalent in all parts of the country. So, three broad language streams exist for school education in India: first, Hindi medium; second, the regional language; and third, English. While English started mainly as an urban and metropolitan language, it has quickly made inroads into the semi-urban areas of India.

However, English is considered the language of the elite, and if one has an English medium education in India, that is considered a stepping stone to higher education, better job prospects, living and working abroad, and even better matrimonial matches—all prized accomplishments. Like everything in India where the class system exists in all walks of life, even the English medium education has two categories: convent and non-convent. Convent education refers to schools run and managed by English-era Church convents, and this is valued higher than non-convent education. Like many paradoxes and hypocrisies that exist in Indian society, political Hindu zealots, who try to appeal to their vote banks (mainly illiterate) with their nationalistic fervor, have no qualms about sending their own children to convent schools!

My school education was in the non-convent English medium, and I have to thank my father for this, as well as a stroke of higher intervention.

All my seven siblings went to Hindi medium schools, which teach English at a very basic level. So, English language proficiency was very rudimentary there. Since Hindi was our mother tongue and what we spoke at home, our ethos and thinking were Hindi-oriented. Newspapers, magazines, periodicals, radio and TV programs, letter writing, and all forms of communication were in Hindi. Except mine.

In those days, it was common practice to have tutors at home to supplement the school education. Ironically, this practice was not for the weaker students but, in fact, for those who already excelled in their studies. The prevalent thinking was that the child needs to continue to excel and not fall prey to distractions like friends and playing cricket! While this was an optional practice in school, it continued into college in the form of tutorials after regular lectures. In the present era, abundant in a multitude of distractions, these quaint practices have all but disappeared. In their place, coaching classes focused on specific higher studies, entrance examinations, or professional qualifications have mushroomed. This is yet another multimillion-dollar business in India. The sad part is that in the USA, where it is needed far more than in India, such supplementary teaching is not available. The results are clear for all to see.

My father, along with a group of other like-minded individuals who lived at Marine Drive (an elite part of Bombay), had decided to set up a school in the neighborhood. Marine Drive was the art deco district of the 1950s and an exclusive residential area on the seafront. But it lacked a school. So, Hindi Vidya Bhavan came into being. Those who had sponsored the school were all dhoti-clad upper-middle-class businessmen from Rajasthan, for whom English was as alien as eating meat.

As the name suggests, the school was to be a Hindi medium school exclusively for boys. This is yet another feature of the urban school system in India, where they have gender-specific schools, in addition to a few coed schools. But because of some divine intervention at the last moment, the sponsors had a change of heart, and it was decided that the school would impart education in the English medium. Well, what was to be done with the registered school name? Someone came up with a brainwave and "(English Medium)" was appended to the name. So, the official and full name became Hindi Vidya Bhavan (English Medium), and it quickly became the butt of jokes in town. Eventually, the parenthesis was dropped, and the school was referred to simply as HVB. Currently, it is officially called HVB Global Academy.

Once the name was sorted out, the next challenge was to find a new principal with an English medium education, to replace Mr. Sharma, who had been chosen earlier but did not fit the bill. Mrs. Daruwala was recruited from a reputed girls' school nearby, and I was fortunate to have had nine years of schooling under one of the most disciplined and strict individuals I would ever meet in my life. It was also the beginning of my Parsi connection. The icing on the cake was that she was the English teacher for my class in the eleventh standard, and I quickly became one of her favorite students.

By that time, English had deeply influenced my psyche, and I was already discovering the joys of English literature, that is, mainly of the England variety. Starting with Enid Blyton, I moved on to Agatha Christie, P.G. Wodehouse, James Thurber, Thomas Hardy, Jane Austen, and Aldous Huxley, not to mention a good sprinkling of English poetry by the greats— Shelley, Wordsworth, Byron, and Milton. Later, I slowly graduated to the world of Bertrand Russell and G. B. Shaw, getting my first insight into philosophy.

So Sanskrit It Is

Yet another episode of divine intervention took place.

The Universe was conspiring to lay the foundation for furthering my progress on the spiritual path. This foundation was the study of Sanskrit.

Since Sanskrit is the mother of all languages and the source of all the wisdom that exists in the world, it is of fundamental importance to anyone who intends to embark on the spiritual journey. Therefore, you need to have some basic understanding of how it has evolved and its relevance in Indian scriptures and spirituality. It may appear that it is a very difficult coded language with a grammar that is equally difficult, but in fact, Sanskrit is all about pronunciation and vibration. It is all about how the sounds of the language resonate with your own vibration and with that of the Universe. Remember, the Universe came into being with the primal sound, Aum, which is the *beej mantra*, the primal seed from which the entire Creation manifested. That is the sound of Brahma Himself. It is also the beginning of Sanskrit.

When I was in high school, we had to learn four languages, believe it or not! At least in those days. I went to an English medium school, so English was compulsory. We also had to learn Hindi because that was India's official language. For the third language, a regional language, the options were Marathi and Gujarati. I chose Marathi because the script was the same as that of Hindi and also because everyone on Maa's side of the family spoke Marathi fluently. The fourth language we had to choose, a "foreign" language, had French, German, and Sanskrit as options. Yes, Sanskrit was called a "foreign" language in India. I wanted to study French because, even in high school, I knew that I would be traveling all over the world and that French would be of tremendous use from a practical point of view.

But Babuji had other ideas. He insisted that I should choose to learn Sanskrit. I did not understand why he would want me to learn this dead, archaic language that was of no practical value and which no one was using. But I was not strong enough to stand up to him, and, sure enough, I gave in to his wishes.

Babuji's Prophecy Gets Vindicated

Fast forward twenty-eight years. I was in Boston in 1996, where there is a place called the Philosophy School. It held gatherings of highly educated and intellectual people from the field of medicine and research: doctors, engineers, and all the high-flying people from Harvard, MIT, and the other universities in Boston. They would gather twice or thrice a week to talk about Indian spirituality.

When I learned about it, I decided to participate in the gatherings and attended them twice a week. The gathering comprised Americans exclusively; I was the only Indian. At the time, we were discussing the *Bhagavad Gita.* Someone would first read an excerpt (chosen for that particular evening) from the Gita in Sanskrit, and then another person would translate it into English, after which we would discuss its meaning and relevance. As I sat listening to the pronunciation during the reading, it took me back to my high school days of learning Sanskrit. I found that their pronunciation was not ringing true, so I started correcting it as well as the translation and interpretation of some of the phrases. The principal soon took notice of this and, to my amazement, asked me to conduct a Sunday morning Sanskrit school! The first thought that came to mind was that of Babuji, and I had tears in my eyes. The foundation stone on which my spiritual journey was to proceed was not only laid but was getting firmly entrenched.

The Mother Language

For those of you who have heard Sanskrit, Hindi, or any of the other *Devanagari* languages from India being spoken by Indians in comparison to non-Indians, you know how different it sounds. During my travels around the world, I started noticing that there were many words in different languages—Lithuanian, Russian, Romanian, Serbian, and especially the Slavic languages—which were very similar to Sanskrit. And it really intrigued me into finding out how that could have happened. I started researching and talking to the locals, including some academicians. For example, I met a Sanskrit scholar teaching at Vilnius University. And then there was someone in Berlin who was researching the significance and impact of Sanskrit on the European languages. After a while, it was very clear to me that it does not take a rocket scientist to realize that Sanskrit is the mother of all languages.

Almost all the languages in the world can be traced back to Sanskrit. As languages spread around the world and people migrated to different lands, they carried the knowledge of Sanskrit with them. Of course, it evolved in different ways, in different parts of the world, as different dialects or languages. But there is no doubt that their origin is Sanskrit, and therefore, a lot of their words sound very similar to it. Furthermore, I particularly noticed that in some of the Slavic countries, especially in Romania and Serbia, the people and practices (their names, art forms, music, dance, culture, etc.) uncannily resemble those from India. In the Orthodox churches, for example, I discovered that some of their practices, as well as the *mudras* and icons, had their origin in Indian scriptures and philosophy, primarily written in Sanskrit.

I met some Orthodox priests in Belgrade and attended different ceremonies that had so much in common with Indian culture, which, over the years, had migrated to the West in different ways.

Language of the Gods

The most important part of Sanskrit, from my spiritual experience, is the chanting of mantras.

Mantras are the connection with the Universe, with the higher Self Itself. If you believe that there is a supreme Self, or a supreme Consciousness, then the language or the way to connect with that higher Self is through mantras. Chanting mantras is chanting the language of the gods. There are hundreds and thousands of mantras of all kinds for different purposes, but ultimately, they all have one common purpose, and that is to connect to the higher Self.

A mantra has to be chanted and pronounced correctly, and that accuracy, in my experience around the world, is something that is unique to the Indian ethos. I have met hundreds and thousands of Westerners, particularly in

Europe and the USA, and found that they have taken to Indian culture, Indian philosophy, Indian teaching methods, and Indian scriptures. However, their pronunciation of Sanskrit mantras does not ring true; it just does not create the necessary vibrations. This is something that has baffled me. I have never really understood why their enunciation leaves much to be desired, despite their sincerity and deep commitment to the Indian way of life. I can reasonably assume that this lack on their part has something to do with their local conditioning. Because I found that if the same Westerners spend enough time in India, they are able to imbibe that ability to pronounce mantras, just the way that Indians do. It is a matter of cultural acclimatization, which can only happen by living in this sacred land.

The way the alphabet, syllables, consonants, and vowels are put together, and how the sound emanates from inside the person's body and mind, is very different in India than it is abroad. And that is a very important aspect of understanding the sound aspect of Sanskrit. The more you chant and practice pronouncing these mantras daily, the better your ability to produce a resonant sound that comes from deep inside you and which connects to the higher Self.

I cannot emphasize enough what Sanskrit has done for me in my spiritual journey. And I am grateful and glad that my father insisted that I should learn it.

It was yet another Happening on my path of spirituality.

High Grades and Raging Hormones

Academic excellence was instilled in all eight of us siblings. Combined with Babuji's progressive views, his emphasis on higher education, and his strict discipline, it fostered a nourishing environment for all of us. I was a good student and had a healthy competition with Sanjeev Joshi, my classmate in school. We always ranked among the top two. I was a favorite student of most of my teachers except one—Mr. Crasto. We had a mutual dislike for each other, and his bias against me was reflected in the grades I received from him, which were completely inconsistent with the grades from other teachers. Even at that tender age, the rebel in me had no choice but to complain. And I did. To a designated official whom one could approach for any grievance. Suffice to say, Mr. Crasto did not return next year. My first act of rebellion was successful at the tender age of twelve! It was the first of many to punctuate my life. Shiva was starting to take shape.

Being in an all-boys school and primarily in an all-female teacher group, the first flush of my teenage years was starting to blossom. The hormones were starting to rage, but there were no girls to aim them at. Crushes were inevitable. I had two: Miss Zarin Patel, a short, buxom, prim and proper, perfectly attired Parsi woman, and Mrs. Daruwala, the principal. Wet dreams were the order of the day.

Other shenanigans were going on as well, both seen and imagined. A boys-will-be-boys attitude prevailed. I had a huge crush on a girl whom I passed every day on my way to school. Her face is still fresh in my memory. My first surge of sexual energy was unmistakable. But what could I do? I was living in a society where most men were virgins on their wedding night, and I would end up being one too. Shiva had something else in mind for me. I had to be patient.

From HVB Global Academy, the elite Sydenham College was just a hop, skip, and jump away. It was ironic that we no longer resided in Sadhana, the building which was bang opposite the college. That was where I lived during my school days. The admission process for getting into a college was simple and informal in those days, and consisted of filling out a form, attaching your SSC mark sheet, and waiting for your name to appear on the list of qualified entrants. Of course, I made it. I had the unbroken Darooka siblings' tradition of academic excellence to honor and also to fulfill Babuji's wish for all his eight children to complete their university education, which I did.

Smitten but Shy

After completing eleven years of school brilliantly, the four years of college turned out to be an anticlimax, characterized by my introverted nature and inability to be comfortable in coed social situations. Unlike school, college was more about social and extracurricular activities. If one did not participate in them actively, one quickly became a nerd, obviously not something I was keen on. I made efforts to join the Coop Stores, mainly because I had a crush on Sadhana, one of my classmates who also worked there. But I could not muster the courage to reach out to her. We barely spoke. Two of the girls sitting next to me in the SSC Board exams, Anita (a family friend's daughter) and Naina, too ended up in my class, and we barely made eye contact. Alka, another classmate from school, was also there, but again, I was too shy to approach her.

Shiva was not yet ready for his cosmic dance with Shakti.

The four long years of college education turned out to be a major waste of time; rather, an obstacle to be crossed before I could embark on my true passion for accountancy, and my eventual move to the USA. Post graduation, I underwent an enriching journey of three years of internship and two of the toughest professional exams in India to qualify as a chartered accountant, for the coveted CA title. These are all-India exams, and to top it all, I was a rank holder in both exams. My internship entailed working for the first two years with Shah & Co. and the last year with Richardson Hindustan, the predecessor to Procter & Gamble in India.

Here too, I developed two huge crushes, on Sandra and Vaishali, but I was still an introvert. Hormones were raging, but Shiva had to wait his turn. As Happenings happen, I connected with Sandra some twenty-two years later during my consulting assignment in Bombay, and this time, we connected instantly. Shiva had blossomed by then.

Male Bonding

During the CA internship, I met two individuals who became my closest friends: Pramod and Rajesh. Another character, Sunil, appeared out of the blue (a typical hot-blooded Delhiite). We were the inseparable CA quartet, and for the first and only time in my life, I experienced male bonding. Pramod was from Jaipur and lived in a hostel, Sunil lived in a paying guest accommodation (an arrangement unique to Bombay where single men or women rented a room in an apartment with no cooking facilities), and Rajesh was of the pedigreed kind whose father and brother already had a flourishing CA practice waiting for him to join it.

But first—fun. And did we have fun, including all of us (almost) losing our bursting virginities! It was a riot. Yankee Doodle on Marine Drive and Balwas at Marine Lines became our regular haunts. I had my first taste of beer and took an instant dislike to it. I have never touched it since then.

Chartered Munim

The date, July 21, 1979. It is imprinted in my memory forever. It was 4:30 PM. I got a call from my dear school and college friend Sampat, who was also a CA student. He asked me, "Have you seen the results?" I knew they were to be announced that day (though no one in the family knew that), and I was waiting with a thumping heart to go to the CA Institute office in Colaba to check. When I rushed there, a small crowd was already poring over the list on the board. I snaked my way through to the front with trepidation and ran my finger and eyes down the list, stopping at Darooka Pradip Kunjbeharilal. There it was, in black and white. I made it! The final hurdle had been crossed.

I rarely emote or swell up when I am alone; it is difficult to describe these emotions. I would feel the same a few more times later in life, but this was the first time. An achievement all my own! I was confident but still wanted validation. I needed to be hugged and held, and to share it with someone. But who? I was still in a situation where I was estranged from

Maa and Babuji. And four of my closest family members were traveling in the USA. Then I realized I was right next door to Uma Jiji, who lived at Badhwar Park. I excitedly walked to her apartment, with a bounce in my steps. As soon as she opened the door, I blurted out, "I have passed."

At first, it did not register; she was not expecting me or the news. Then a huge smile crossed her face as the news sank in. Smita (her daughter), who was to follow in my footsteps a few years later, was ten at that time. She was home, and I am sure the Universe conspired to pass on the baton to her right there. She was too young to realize what was happening. Uma Jiji immediately called Maa and Babuji, and gave them the news. Babuji wanted to throw a party for all my friends, and Maa organized it at home a few days later. We did not have international calling at that time, so I went to the post office across the street and shot off a telegram (for the first time in my life) to Sushil Jijaji. His *munim* had come into being!

"Munim" means a traditional accountant in Hindi, and every family business has one. A CA was a munim, as far as Sushil Jijaji was concerned. Right after having sat for the final exams in May earlier, I had gotten my first real job at SB Billimoria & Co. (a top CA firm in Bombay), paying me a princely sum of ₹1,200 per month. During the CA internship, I went from ₹60 to ₹100 to ₹650 per month. When I started my internship in May 1976 at Shah & Co., the first stipend of ₹60 seemed like a lottery. Apart from the occasional commission I would earn from Vishnu Jijaji selling magazine subscriptions, this was my first real earning. I finally had pocket money. Babuji never gave any of his children any pocket money. It was an alien concept. If I really wanted to indulge in something, I would have to cajole Maa into letting me have my way.

Real Education

My formal education was over, and Babuji was happy. Much later in life, I would realize that almost ninety percent of this education was of no practical use. I came to understand the difference between education and learning for life. As I traveled around in India and all over the world, this difference became starker.

No example illustrated this more clearly than the episode I watched in a village outside Pune. I was visiting the site of my future not-to-be healing and spiritual center. I was with my architect, contractor, and the local village head. The contractor was complaining of intense pain from stones in his bladder and the doctors' inability to do anything about his ailment. The village head coolly walked to a nearby shrub, plucked some leaves, crushed them in his palm, and asked the contractor to chew on them. He did so, and we all went home. We met again after a week, and the village head asked him about the pain. The contactor fell at his feet and, with gratitude, revealed that he had passed the stones in the urine the very next day, and that the pain had disappeared.

In years to come, similar lessons coming from unexpected sources would dot my life journey.

There is a snobbish craze with certain educated elites, especially the MBA kind, to attend postgraduate executive programs in elite colleges and universities to brush up their case study knowledge and, more importantly, to refresh and enhance their resume to make themselves more marketable. I ask them, "Do you really want more knowledge or just another jewel in your crown of degrees?" If you are looking for real knowledge on how the real world works, beyond case studies, spend the same six months traveling in remote, rural places, or become a volunteer of some kind.

I did an informal search and study of failed companies that had gone into Chapter 11 bankruptcy in the USA, and found that seventy-five percent of them were headed by an Ivy League CEO. Go figure. These CEOs just added their own company to the rich roster of case studies that are the backbone of the much-vaunted MBA programs all over the world, shallow to the core and inert from irrelevance in the real world. Another informal study I did suggested that not a single case study has ever replicated itself! MBAs find new ways to self-immolate.

Observation (sakshi bhava) and discernment (*vivek*) have been the two pillars of my education. The first foundations of these pillars were cast by Babuji. His passion for books, reading, and travel rubbed off on me in a way I would appreciate much later on in life. His penchant for staying abreast with world news through newspapers, radio, and TV inculcated the same in all of us, to the extent that each of us would rush to be the first to grab the daily newspaper. We stayed abreast of all world happenings and could discuss almost any topic under the sun. He would grill my two brothers, who were engineers, on various technical issues.

I still remember when Babuji visited us in the USA and stayed with me. When he saw the piston-style flush in the bathroom instead of the more common cistern tank, he asked my brother to explain how it works. He had barely completed his high school with no college education, but he was more organized and savvy in worldly matters than those with a chain of letters after their name.

The same was true of an uncle of mine, Brijmohan Masaji, who doted on me and was even less "educated" than my father. He could fix almost any item in the house and never believed in trashing anything. Memories of him would surface each time I saw people in the USA dumping their appliances and other articles by the curbside.

Babuji had subscribed to *National Geographic,* and it came to the doorstep each month with a new map inserted inside. We would pore over it and devour the contents to learn something new about this wonderful world that Babuji was exposing us to. Very soon, the monthly magazine started adorning the bookshelf in neatly bound annual binders. Everyone's heart broke when the time came to trash them one day. I learned more from this monthly "virtual traveling" than I did from any textbook in school or college. As a tribute to Babuji, I started a fresh collection of *National Geographic* when I reached the USA and kept it going for quite a few years.

Once again, I had to trash it. A few years later, the Universe would be teaching me a very important lesson of impermanence, and my life started building on that.

Babuji's passion for travel was pretty evident. Although finances were tight, he would take us on a summer vacation each year, eight children in tow. To this day (where we take the internet for granted for making all travel arrangements), it makes me wonder how he managed to accomplish so much all by himself. He was super organized and had an eye for detail that rubbed off on just two or three of his children, including me. He could spot a furniture piece or a wall hanging misplaced even by an inch and would not be satisfied until it was set right.

Babuji was my first teacher, and I acknowledged this only after he passed away. Due to the huge generation gap, we had a father–son relationship characterized by estrangement between us, but inwardly, I knew that he loved me very much. During the growing teenage years, as is typical, his stern, disciplined nature did not allow us to bond. Maa was the healing balm and mediator. When I, the last of the children and the youngest son, decided to migrate to the USA in 1982, I had not sought his permission or help in any way. I did not have the resources to buy myself a one-way ticket, so, while waiting for my coveted green card, I decided to take up a job in Bahrain to earn enough for my ticket to the USA. I was there for exactly three months, the first country I ever visited in what was to be a long chain of over 130 countries to date.

Secular Orientation

Most Indians are conditioned by their socioreligious environment, giving them an insular view of the world. They may have tolerance for people from other backgrounds but not much insight about them. I too was born and brought up in a Hindu family environment, but being a rebel, I never accepted being boxed into being a Hindu. My school, college, and work environment provided me with the opportunity to interact with people from other communities, many of them falling within the broad umbrella of "Hindu." However, two communities held a particular fascination for me: the Parsis and the Muslims.

My parents and older siblings lived in Karachi before the brutal and inhuman breakup of India, instigated by the British. They had to leave all their belongings behind and flee to Bombay. This left a deep scar on their psyche, for which they blamed the Muslims and not the British. I found this very ironic and sad. I did not have any close Muslim friends or acquaintances until much later, when I was introduced to the rich *Sufi* tradition during my "Wanderings (chapter ten)."

However, I grew up with Parsis from all walks of life, including some of my friends.

Parsi Connection

Mumbai is the city of the Parsis, a unique presence in the fabric of India. I was surrounded by Parsis in school and college: principal, teachers, colleagues, and friends. All my bosses in Bahrain as well as in Richardson Hindustan and S. B. Billimoria were also Parsis. Sarosh Kotwal has been my trusted Vedic astrologer for years. After all those years of camaraderie with them, I now frequent Chai Pani, a restaurant in Asheville, owned by Meherwan Irani, a Mumbai Parsi.

My corporate life afforded me the opportunity to interact with Ratan Tata, a gentleman who could not be more affable and humble despite being a name that needs no introduction. The highlight for me was the black and yellow cab ride we shared from Bombay airport upon returning from a board meeting in Goa, having sat next to him on the flight. He picked up his own bags; there was no chauffeured limousine waiting for him. He hailed a cab, and off we went.

Anjali went to Bengallee Girls' High School, lived on Princess Street (a Parsi hotspot, dotted with *atash behrams*, homeopathy pharmacies owned by Parsis, and even a Parsi bonesetter), and had numerous Parsi friends. Many of our Parsi friends migrated to Australia, and we would visit them.

They are an eccentric, funny, intelligent, close-knit but fast-dwindling community. South Bombay would not be South Bombay without them. They have been at the forefront of the freedom struggle and are the titans of society, business, and industry. The Parsi Dairy Farm and the Irani cafés are icons in Mumbai, and my regular haunts when I am there.

Later, in Pune, I met JJ (Sir Cowasji Jehangir), who was my neighbor. My apartment building was built by him on the ancestral land adjoining his two-hundred–year-old Victorian bungalow. He was also the chairman of the Jehangir Hospital set up by his grandfather, which would be the refuge for my family and me, in case of any medical need. Very soon, I came to know many of the doctors and staff at the hospital, including Dr. Divate, one of the most compassionate and skilled doctors I have met.

JJ and I hit it off through our common interests in travel and jazz. I gave him a hard time when Samovar, my favorite café at the Jehangir Art Gallery in Bombay (established by his family), was shut down. I have yet to meet a more humble and genteel individual who does not wear his legacy and pedigree on his sleeve.

One of my disappointments was that, as a non-Parsi, I could not visit any *agiary* in Bombay. The closest I got was when I visited the iconic Tara Baug for my friend Persis's wedding and enjoyed the vegetarian version of *lagan nu bhonu*. Years later, during my travels, the Universe would grant me the opportunity to visit the Ateshgah (House of Fire) in Azerbaijan.

My Parsi connection remains strong. How else can I explain meeting Mehernosh Unwalla, the editor of this book? There are no coincidences.

Saraswati Personified

Besides my schoolteachers and principal, there was just one other Shakti who appeared in my life that personified Saraswati: Madhuriji Nevatia from Bombay. She was a family friend and close to Uma Jiji. I first met her in New York when she was visiting her daughter, who lived close to where Anjali and I lived. My spiritual budding was still premature, but there is no doubt in my mind that this meeting was for Saraswati to appear and bless me Herself.

Madhuriji was a repository of Vedic knowledge, especially the Upanishads and the Bhagavad Gita. In one of the later meetings, I remember having an interesting discussion with her on Krishna, Radha, the *gopis*, and Raas Leela, one of my favorite subjects. She was adept in Hindi, Sanskrit, and English, which made the conversation very easy for me.

My last meeting with Madhuriji was in March 2025, during which she gave me valuable insights and tips for this book. It was my ardent wish that she would read this book and give me her blessings. But she passed away in January 2026. Saraswati will live on in this book and my heart.

Learning for Life

Right from my early years, I learned mainly by observation, to always respect any book or text, never step on it, and if we did, to bring it to our forehead as a gesture of making amends internally. Like every little ritual that I observed at home, it was never explained why. Later on in my journey, I realized that all books are looked upon as Maa Saraswati, the Goddess of learning, and the first goddess I encountered in my life.

But I had a long way to go. Education had ended, but learning was in full swing and would continue lifelong. For this, there are no degrees awarded or letters appended to your name. Just bliss.

|| Aum Narayana Aum ||

|| I Am the Witness
I Am That
I Am Not the Doer ||

4.
|| Sustenance ||
|| Vishnu ||

We cannot live on love and air alone.
We need the Mother to feed us.

We cannot live on learning alone.
We need to put knowledge to use.

We cannot live on chanting alone.
We need spirituality to feed the fire in the Manipura.

In the Trinity, Vishnu is the Lord of Sustenance. He is a *Bhogi* as well, and needs to be fed. Krishna, His *avatar,* is the epitome of that—one who enjoyed life to the fullest, who is appeased with *chhappan bhog* and indulges in Raas Leela. Gods too have their quirks, and Indian gods are no exception. The multiplicity of gods and goddesses in Indian culture accentuates their quirks and whims, all described in exquisite detail in Indian scriptures. Their egos precede them, and their bellies announce their arrival. But Vishnu, along with His consort Mahalakshmi (or Lakshmi), can be very generous. In fact, it is She who is the Shakti and has the power to bestow abundance and favors on those who appease Her. No wonder Lakshmi is the most worshipped goddess in India!

However, this Sri Lakshmi is different from the one that I discovered and fell in love with through *Sri Sukta, Sri Laksmi Tantra, Saundarya Lahiri,* and numerous other spiritual texts, extolling her beauty and virtues. Vishnu was relegated to the background, yet they were one as Lakshmi Narayan, Sita Ram, or Radha Krishna. There can be no sustenance without their blessings. And I received sustenance in abundance.

Ironically, my first sustenance check came from Vishnu Jijaji in the form of commissions earned from selling magazine subscriptions. But nothing comes unattached; he exacted a price for it, albeit unknowingly.

Dream Comes True

From the commission checks from Vishnu Jijaji, the CA internship stipend, the first salary from SB Billimoria, and the three months' worth of earnings in Bahrain at Jawad Habib & Co, I had managed to save enough to buy a ticket to the USA, with about $ 1,000 in my pocket to sustain me until I found my footing. I was anxious but confident. After all, I would be staying with Sita in New York, Nirmala Jiji's best friend forever, who had informally adopted me as her brother for reasons that became clear to me only after staying with her. And then there was Dilip Bhaiya in Philadelphia with Anmol, my favorite nephew, all of three years old. Pramila Jiji was in California, and it was she who sponsored my coveted green card. I had nothing to worry about.

But soon, reality began to sink in. Despite my shuttling between New York and Philadelphia, sending out hundreds of resumes, and knocking on numerous doors, there was no sign of an opening. I was too naive then to understand racism, but that was the bitter reality in a highly racist country, even in 1982, which has become far worse in the past couple of years. The same firm that had rejected me when I approached them directly, called me for an interview when an influential person intervened. It was Price Waterhouse, the most elite of the Big Eight accounting firms at the time. Needless to say, I landed the job in August 1982 at a salary of $18,500 per year! This was the second moment in my life when I felt on top of the world, the first being that of jubilation on seeing my name on the CA exams passing list. As before, I needed to share it with someone, but it was too expensive to call India. So I rushed to a public phone right after the interview and called Dilip Bhaiya and Lalita Bhabhi with the news. Needless to say, they were overjoyed.

I needed to set up home. By this time, Sita and I had fallen out. She wanted me to return some money she had loaned me (without my asking), but I could not comply with her demand until I received my first couple of paychecks. For the first and only time in my life ever, I borrowed $1,000 from Pramila Jiji and promised to return it as soon as I could. She insisted there was no need to return it. Sadly, in the process, I broke Babuji's rule in life to never ever borrow from anyone. But Babuji would understand. He was coming to visit me soon with Maa. I returned the amount to Pramila Jiji, having saved enough in about six months.

Lakshmi Matters

Money is a great leveler and teacher. This, too, I learned and inculcated while watching Babuji handle strained household finances in a very disciplined manner. I worked hard at making every penny go a long way. Slowly but surely, I built up some savings. However, when Babuji was visiting me in New York, I had to endure the pain of watching him take the stairs while traveling by subway and walking long blocks with the help of a walking stick. He had broken his hip in a fall a few years ago and was limping, managing to walk with a stick, albeit painfully. It broke my heart. But I could not afford taxis or rent a car, and he was eager to visit all the spots he had seen in *National Geographic* and other publications. He did not complain even once.

We would come back to my one-bedroom apartment after a long day, and he would crash on the bed. His excitement at his first trip abroad, visiting his three children in the USA, and enjoying all the sights he had looked forward to experiencing in person could not be taken away from him.

I felt the first flush of redemption of sorts. Lessons were coming in fast and furious.

Bias and the Rat Race

I was with Price Waterhouse for ten years, and looking back at my entire professional career of twenty-five years, it was the most satisfying period. Price Waterhouse was not just the elite of the Big Eight but a tight-knit professional firm. I blossomed despite certain built-in racial prejudices that popped up time and again with blatant insensitivity.

It was the practice to have a closing dinner for the entire audit team hosted by the partner-in-charge. At one such dinner, Ken and his subordinate, Frank, chose a steak restaurant for the occasion, not once but two years in a row, and devoured dead cows in my presence. They had not even asked for my opinion or choice, knowing I was vegetarian and assuming that "salad" was always available for me.

On another occasion, we went to a French restaurant. My wife Anjali was invited too, and we could not recognize anything on the menu. Seeing an item called "Sweetbreads," we innocently assumed that it would be "sweet" bread and we would manage with just that, even if it was only dessert. The partner-in-charge stopped us from ordering it, knowing we were vegetarians, and saved us from eating the innards of a dead cow! At least he was a bit more sensitive than the first guy.

Stuffy characters such as these abound everywhere, so gradually, I started choosing my company and controlling my life. The first seeds of Satsang were being sown. There were enough people on the other side to facilitate that, and I quit Price Waterhouse with a heavy heart but with the belief that the whole world was my oyster.

Thanks to Morgan Stanley, Alliance Capital, and Merrill Lynch—my clients at Price Waterhouse—I had started traveling and exploring foreign shores, specifically India, Netherlands Antilles, South Korea, and Türkiye. The travel bug had already bitten me.

I joined Morgan Stanley and was quickly sucked into their India plans via Luxembourg and London. It did not take too long to learn that large global financial firms like Morgan Stanley work in a very loose, dynamic matrix format, with multiple lines of reporting. I had two bosses in New York (they would not admit it), one in London and later, one in Bombay. This arrangement worked fine with me because I ended up becoming my own boss, and very soon, I also realized that controls and approvals for international travel were very informal. It was first class all the way!

Besides the signup bonus, Wall Street is all about the year-end bonus. There are four levels in investment banking: Associate, Vice President, Principal (Executive Director outside the US), and Managing Director. Everyone strives toward the goal of attaining one of these by the year end. Come fall season, "You scratch my back, and I'll scratch yours" becomes the norm. Consequently, the greedy, pathetic runup to that million-dollar bonus takes a serious turn. I remember one managing director (with whom I had interacted very briefly) taking me out to lunch and mincing no words in asking me to write a few favorable words about him. In turn, he promised to do the same. And then there are the first-generation Indians with a prominent presence in Wall Street firms, who excel at kowtowing to the power brokers to pave their way up the ladder. This game was being played all across the firm globally.

Vishnu was ready to shower His blessings on me. Little did anyone realize, not even me, that it was all just an aspect of *maya* that had turned everyone blind.

Along with the financial rewards, something far more rewarding came my way. I was sent to Bombay to kickstart the India operations in preparation for the launch of the first mutual fund by an international company. This was the beginning of the mutual fund industry in the nascent Indian market, and expectations were sky-high, mainly due to the complete ignorance of this product on the part of everyone involved. It was an ego-led initiative by a single Morgan Stanley employee of Indian origin, who did nothing to educate the investing public before launching this product. The frenzy leading up to the launch resulted in mile-long lines at banks accepting the applications. The gravity of the situation hit me not when my long-lost family members started calling me for favors, but when my chauffeur asked me, "Sir, may I give my application to you?" Vishnu was playing a strange Leela.

I ended up spending two years ensconced in a plush five-star hotel in South Bombay, a stone's throw away from where I was born and from Maa's lap. Unknown to me, this was the first indicator of what was to come. During this time, I also lost one of my nephews, Manish, due to the oppressive behavior of his parents, grandmother, and uncle. His *Vishuddhi* was locked shut, and he succumbed to it.

I quit Morgan Stanley, having milked them to the extent that they deserved, and joined Fidelity Investments in Boston, a conservative investment management firm that was a far cry from the freewheeling culture of Wall Street. It was soon clear that I was a fish out of water there. I lasted for a little over a year, during which I met my boss just twice: once, when he interviewed me over dinner, and the other time, when he moved to London for a Fidelity assignment. No one had time for anyone, and everyone was entrenched in their own set ways. Feathers were not to be ruffled, and Ned, the legendary one-man force behind Fidelity, was not to be challenged.

In the mid-1990s, Boston and Fidelity were the epitome of parochial conservatism ruled by the so-called old money Brahmin elite. Someone like me had no chance to infiltrate that tight circle. Three of us who came from Wall Street ended up elsewhere within a year. As core money managers, they minted money for themselves. Even so, to their credit, they did not hesitate to share it with their employees.

Vishnu and Lakshmi were not done with me yet.

Shakti Plants a Seed

The Reiki initiation from 1997 was kicking in forcefully. I had begun recognizing the chakras and their movement, and more importantly, their impact on my psyche. I started to withdraw within myself in a subtle manner. All sensory perceptions were becoming more refined.

I decided to take some time off from the corporate world.

The millennium was approaching, and I found myself in Asia, increasingly more comfortable there than in the USA. On December 31, 1999, I was in Bodh Gaya, sitting under the Bodhi tree at the stroke of midnight. And when I opened my eyes, there she was. My first glimpse of Shakti incarnate, sitting next to me, having come all the way from Brazil. When she learned I was from Mumbai, she asked me, "Have you met Ramesh Balsekar?" I had not even heard of him. But it planted a seed that was to sprout a couple of years later. Yet another Happening in the course of my journey.

Her name was Gabriela, and she was traveling with her mother. We ended up visiting Nalanda the next day. On the way, we stopped at a desolate temple, and she spent half an hour practicing her asanas in the courtyard, a cool winter mist enveloping us. The sight of Shakti in that courtyard in the early morning hours brought the temple to life.

Anjali had not accepted or reconciled herself to any of this and was clueless as to what was happening to me. It was futile trying to explain.

Kali in London

One day, I got a call from an ex-colleague asking if I would be interested in a position with J.P. Morgan in London. An opportunity to return to Wall Street, and that too in London, one of my favorite cities, reminiscent of my childhood introduction to English literature. I jumped at it. Surely, Lakshmi Narayan had something in mind to keep my sustenance going. It turned out to be a fiasco, with one boss in New York and three in London, none of whom spoke with each other. All of them were groping in the dark about my role and responsibility in the firm. One of them was Veronique, an incarnation of Kali, but a Shakti nonetheless. She could see that I was Shiva and was out for revenge of sorts. I was too busy enjoying London and England to pay heed to her. And then I learned my first Kali lesson: "Hell hath no fury like a Kali scorned." My short stint came to an end.

But Lakshmi Narayan were satisfied as I had added to my sustenance coffer.

More Shaktis Appear

I returned to Boston and Anjali, but deep within me, there was a nagging sense of Maa calling me. And then something called 9/11 happened. Two weeks later, I was on the flight to Mumbai on a six-week consulting assignment for Sunlife of Canada, which had an asset management joint venture with the Birla Group. The Universe was clear about its plan for me. One last blessing from Lakshmi Narayan before I would be ready for Shiva *Parvati* in all their glory.

The six weeks became two years. Once again, I was ensconced in a five-star hotel in the suburbs, away from Maa, yet close enough to be with her twice a week. I could feel the momentum building up. I also had to deal with one of the most toxic and egoistic individuals I had ever met in my corporate career, a character known as SK. Due to the nature of my assignment and reporting line, I was able to ignore him. Then I met Dipak, the general manager of the ITC Maratha (where I was staying), and Madhu, the executive chef. Dipak and I had a spiritual connection through *Kashmir Shaivism* and Reiki. Madhu and I had a food connection. With their blessings, the Maratha became my home away from home.

Shaktis started appearing in my life regularly. Through Dipak, I met Asmita, and then Ferzyn, Meher, Silvuska, Gabriela, Ruksana, and many more. The Raas Leela had commenced. The cosmic dance of Shiva Parvati was beginning to gain momentum. I started Reiki sessions at the hotel and ended up initiating Dipak and Asmita, and another couple, as my first students.

Career is one's indulgence and one's domain of expertise—something that fuels you enough to walk ahead. Nevertheless, the consulting assignment had taken a back seat. The Universe's plan was very clear: to top up my coffers, bring me into Maa's lap, and help me get a firm foothold in the world of Tantra, Advaita, and Zen, through Osho and Ramesh. I had no say in the matter and was a mute witness, with the first rays of bliss lighting up my life.

From Finance to Philosophy

I have spent my entire corporate career in the financial world, specifically, asset management. When I watch the gyrations of the stock market, I wonder, as some of them are brutal and nerve-racking. With a few exceptions, it is the same all over the world. So, it does not matter whether you are in the USA or India or elsewhere. It is just a matter of degrees. As always, conventional explanations for the stock market gyrations are a dime a dozen, ranging from technology downslide to geopolitical factors to economy slowdown, and so on.

I, too, have been affected by the stock market since I invested my first hard-earned $1,000 in the market through a mutual fund in 1984. But at the same time, I also had the good fortune to be an insider in this business and understand its intricacies. The individuals managing and controlling this business make so much money at the individual level even in a downturn that a common investor can never expect or hope. While the investor will be having sleepless nights, the money manager will be sleeping peacefully. I have since moved on to philosophy. The parallels I see between the guiding principles for life and the stock market are amazing. They have helped me deal with the stock market and manage my investments much more effectively. I would like to share some of these learnings here.

Taking "Stock" of Life

Instant gratification almost always causes pain sooner or later. Initially, it gives the senses a high, but subsequently, it numbs common sense. Ultimately, what matters is how we live our lives and what *karmas* and *sanskaras* are nurtured as we go along.

Short-term market movements can prove to be disastrous. This is an age-old and time-honored axiom in the investment world, yet it is completely ignored by the experts and the gullible common investor. The only strategy that works in the long term is a disciplined approach to investing. Assess your returns for the entire portfolio and your entire investment period.

Embrace everyone in life. We are all made of the same flesh and blood, and are nothing but different manifestations of the Supreme Self. Open yourselves to new ideas; there is no single path to nirvana. Be all-inclusive, and you will find it sooner.

Diversify, diversify, diversify! That is the key to sensible investing. Do not concentrate on one sector at a time. Fads come and go. However, the only factors that survive in the long run are thoughtful management, sensible products or services, profitability, and common sense. Concentrate on these, and you will be ahead of the curve. Warren Buffett never invests in a company he does not understand. He does not chase fads. He is the only legend in the investment world.

Indian scriptures emphasize the importance of a *guru–shishya* relationship and finding the right guru. This is not for nothing. The path to nirvana is strewn with obstacles, and only the enlightened or realized one, the guru, can help lead us there. The all-knowing guru is also within each of us. We have to recognize and nurture this guru principle, so that it can show us the path.

Follow the herd mentality in investing, and you will regret it. Find a genuine expert who correctly reads the pulse of the market over a long period and does not hesitate to speak the truth. Such an investment guru will ignore short-term peaks and valleys for long-term stability. Like a beacon of light, they will see their followers safely through the dark periods.

The Gita identifies greed, lust, and anger as the main obstacles to realization, as they feed the ego. The Gita also teaches us about being content with the basic necessities of life. Anything beyond that is a source of misery.

Stock markets can never sustain triple-digit or high double-digit returns beyond the short term. Only the speculators and the shortsighted mistake it for the real market. The investment guru and their smart investor see it as a red flag and act accordingly. If a stock tip or the investment returns are too good to be true, they probably are! Stay away.

There is no free lunch. As you sow, so shall you reap. Krishna counsels in the Gita that good company is as important as good actions. There is no good company in the investment world, only as good as the next tip.

No matter how many ways one tries to analyze or dissect, the only factor that determines the stock price of a company is its profitability. Everything else is nothing but a figment of the imagination of the investment bankers, brokers, and analysts, who all work for the same employer. The banker concocts the story and prices it, the broker sells it, and the analyst sustains it through reinforced fiction. The money manager is left holding the dud. If you or your fund manager buys the stock of a company with no profits, or worse, no revenues, you become the laughingstock. Whereas the banker, the broker, the analyst, and their boss laugh all the way to the bank.

Vedanta tells us that life is an illusion. The reality, which lies beyond what we can perceive with our senses or think with our minds, can only be experienced by the realized.

The stock market is, likewise, fiction. It is nothing but an amalgamation of individual perceptions. In short, it is a zero-sum game. Only the ignorant think they can swim in its turbulent waters and reach the other side safe and sound. If one lives by the stock market alone, they should also be prepared for a watery grave. I have seen numerous individuals lose their shirts in the stock market, just as I have seen them fall into the dark abyss of depression and ill health.

Lakshmi Narayan had gently passed me on to Shiva Parvati to complete the Trinity circle.

|| Aum Tat Sat ||

| | You Were Sleeping
Now You Are Awake | |

5.
|| The Teachings ||
|| Shiva ||

My formal education, that is, my high school and college graduation, as well as my chartered accountancy professional qualification, ended in 1979, followed by my CPA qualification in the USA a little later. It served a purpose and ended when its time had come. An active sense of doership prevailed during this process, though later on, I realized it was an illusion since I really did not have any say in the matter. My horoscope had clearly charted out my life.

The learning from observation continued, and does so to date. It serves to condition and mold me, moving me along the path meant for me. This is totally passive and subconscious, yet the sensory organs are involved. You see, you hear, you smell, you touch, you taste. It is close to impossible to shut off these sensory perceptions unless you are suffering from a physical ailment. The sense of doership starts to diminish. The chakras begin to open and vibrate. However, even though the sensory organs are involved, one may not register the perceptions if the mind is shut off. If you live your life with blinders on, headphones shutting out all external sounds, and your body covered with fragrances; do not experience the joy of a pat or a hug or a kiss, consume tamasic food all the time and shut off your brain using AI, you become a zombie or a robot.

The Teaching comes from deep inside, from a realm that is beyond the physical, the mental, and the emotional. A sense of equanimity is essential for the Teaching to rise from within.

I Am the Witness (Sakshi Bhava)

Being the witness was the first teaching that came to me through Osho. I never met him while he was in his body. But he was the realized Buddha who did not need to be in his physical body. He had started to touch me through his books, recordings, and videos, even before I moved to Pune, close to his ashram. His eyes had the luminosity of a million stars. His gaze penetrated me deep inside where no one had reached before, not even Maa. One of the reasons for moving to Pune in 2004 was to be close to his being and energy, even though it was fast dissipating from the ashram, thanks to the bunch of unscrupulous individuals who milked his legacy for their selfish purposes. I became immune to the shenanigans going on there and focused on imbibing his energy.

This is where yet another Shakti, Vrinda, appeared in my life. Soon after that, during a *Vipassana* meditation, Osho appeared to me and initiated me. That was my second initiation after the Reiki initiation. Thereafter, there was no more reason for me to be attached to the ashram, and I stopped visiting it. But Osho remained with me.

I Am That

Ramana Maharshi's down-to-earth, simplistic answer to "Who am I?" was one of the first seeds sown on the path of Advaita I had taken to. This was well before Osho and Ramesh. However, it was not until Ramesh's satsangs, focused on "You are not the doer," resonated with me that it all came together. If "I am That" is a reflection of the Higher Self, how can I possibly be the doer? For me, this Teaching is impossible to put into words, even though Ramana Maharshi did so. It came as a bolt of lightning at the feet of Ramesh.

I Am Not the Doer

From the first satsang I attended at Ramesh's feet to the last, over a span of over four years, he did not tire from repeating the mantra, "You are not the doer." It emanated from Ramana Maharshi through Nisargadatta Maharaj. It was the corollary to Ramana Maharshi's "I am That" in response to "Who am I?" If I am That, there is no question of my being the doer. It would be a contradiction. It was simple, yet very difficult. If one is firmly entrapped by the ego, it is impossible to let go of the perception of doership. Ramana Maharshi solved this conundrum by advising us to start with the answer to the question "Who am I?" It is a relatively easier climb on the spiritual ladder to grasp "I am That," and once that happens, then "I am not the doer" becomes more comprehensible. However, in both cases, as in all teachings, logic and the mind do not work. I have seen numerous spiritual adherents get stuck on the path because they insist on using their mind. No doubt, before long, they will want to use AI. They need to be inert to enable the teachings to sink deep inside before they erupt with a burst of joy and bliss and tears in the eyes. I was with Ramesh when this happened to me, right during the second satsang. The Teaching became alive in everyday life, just as Ramesh used to emphasize that it should.

The three core teachings converged into Advaita like the *Triveni Sangam*, effusing me with that indescribable feeling of Satchidananda. I was firmly anchored in my Satsang of One, with none other.

The Guru

Unlike formal education, where one seeks out the best school and teacher, and the best college and University, and unlike the witnessing that is passive and spontaneous, and requires no teachers, spiritual awakening can happen only through a guru. And a guru is not sought; he appears when you are ready, and not a moment before.

The concept of a guru is unique to India and has been so throughout its spiritual history and evolution. It starts with the *Adi Guru*, the first or primordial guru. The vastness, richness, and diversity of Indian spirituality allow one to choose one's own Adi Guru, if one is so inclined. Shiva is the most popular Adi Guru, followed by the sages Dattatreya and Dakshinamurthy. Even the primordial sound, Aum, resonates as the Adi Guru. An Adi Guru is for eternity. For me, it was Maa, that Devi who asked Shiva for me as a boon and sheltered and nurtured me for nine months before the orgasmic blast that brought me into this world in my three-dimensional form. She may not have been a teacher or guide, or shown me the spiritual path like a guru, but she was the Goddess who gave me the gift of life itself. If not for her, I would not be writing this today.

Then there is the *Ishta Guru,* the chosen guru whom you adopt as your own personal guide throughout your life. For me, that was my Inner Child with the innocence of *Bal Krishna* and the wisdom of Shiva. When I grew up and was firmly anchored in my spiritual journey, I discovered a picture of me taken when I was a toddler of six months, in the hoard of photographs at home. When I first saw it, I had goosebumps all over. The child in the picture was talking to me in silence, with joy and bliss radiating in all directions. I immediately adopted it as the child I never had. It was me, my Inner Child—pure, precious, pristine. I understood what Maa Yashoda felt while watching Krishna. I was already getting ready for the Raas Leela!

Osho was my first guru, but I never met him in his body. He was the Buddhahood, the realized Buddha, the *Bodhisattva,* who was the epitome of his teaching rooted in Zen. The ideas, thoughts, and vibrations underlying Tantra and Zen came alive through him. Lao Tzu entered my psyche thanks to Osho.

Bhagavad Gita Comes Alive

In August 2011, on Janmashtami day, I was at the Osho World Galleria in Ansal Plaza, New Delhi, attending a dance and talk by Sonal Mansingh on Krishna and His multidimensional roles. It was not a coincidence that I was attending this performance. Sonal and I had become good friends after traveling together to Kailash Mansarovar as part of a group. After the performance, I was browsing the shelves and came across a set of CDs titled *Gita Darshan* by Osho. Instinctively, I was drawn toward it, and before I knew it, I had bought the entire set of twenty-two CDs and walked out. I had not even bothered to notice that the CDs were in Hindi! That was the beginning of an eighteen-month-long journey through the world of wisdom.

It was March 2013, and I had just concluded my journey of listening to Osho walking me through the seven hundred verses of the eighteen chapters of the Bhagavad Gita in chaste Hindi. Hindi is my mother tongue, but it had not been my medium of education, upbringing, communication at work, or spiritual learning until then. Nevertheless, I was surprised how easily it became the language through which I embarked on this remarkable journey, listening to someone, for whom it was the language of his heart, just like the flute was the voice of Krishna. I do not remember a single word of English interrupting the Hindi spoken throughout the twenty-two CDs, lasting a duration of thirty hours.

Those who have heard Osho in Hindi have experienced something close to ecstasy. His own journey started firmly rooted in Hindi, and in his early days, all his discourses and talks were in Hindi, for the discerning Indian audience he spoke to, traveling all over India. This was well before the dramatic shift that took place in the late 1970s when his audience changed almost completely from Indian to non-Indian, and the language from Hindi to English. While he was equally successful in mesmerizing his audience in English, those who have been fortunate enough to have heard him in both languages know that the experience was as different as day and night. When he spoke in Hindi, his heart poured out, and it almost seemed like Krishna Himself was talking.

Since my school days, I had read many different interpretations of the Gita, both in its entirety and as individual verses and chapters. As I have said earlier, I consider myself very fortunate that my father had insisted

I choose Sanskrit as a "foreign" language in preference over French and German. The manifestation of this decision was starting to appear, and with it, one of the most basic yet deepest spiritual lessons of my life: Things happen for a reason as part of a plan for each of us.

The Sanskrit lessons in school made liberal use of excerpts from the Gita, and that was my first introduction to the pearls of wisdom hidden within each verse. The Boston Philosophy School experience cited earlier was my stepping stone to Advaita philosophy, and the Gita was the medium for this purpose. This was my first in-depth and serious introduction to Advaita philosophy. Without a basic knowledge of Sanskrit, it was very difficult to really gather the true wisdom that Krishna was expounding to *Arjun*.

Even though the Bhagavad Gita, along with the *Ashtavakra Gita,* was instrumental in keeping me focused on my spiritual journey, there were occasional gaps in my understanding, and some unanswered questions. Later, almost all of them dropped at the feet of Ramesh, my second guru. Osho's appearance in my life earlier, not in body but in spirit, engulfed me. The medium of learning was mainly his books (all in English), along with his talks (in English) at the white robe meditation at the Osho ashram in Pune. More than his words, his spirit and his energy dwelled within me.

But the *Gita Darshan* brought him alive for me.

The set of CDs sat in my car for eighteen months, and during this time, Osho became my companion whenever I was at the steering wheel. Whether it was a quick ten-minute ride, a three-hour drive to Mumbai, or a traffic jam lasting hours, his voice filled the car, and I became oblivious to everything outside: the chaos, the confusion, and the cacophony that used to bother me so much while driving around Pune and Mumbai. It all disappeared the moment Osho started talking. It was almost as if I was sitting right in his presence while he was talking live. It did not matter whether I heard him for just five minutes or an entire hour. Nor did it matter where I stopped listening or resumed. The energy was a continuum that lasted through the entire thirty-hour duration. Each word was chaste, crisp, and clear.

Osho explained each *shloka* as if Krishna Himself were explaining it. Each talk was interspersed with questions and answers, anecdotes, stories, and his favorite Mulla Nasruddin jokes. I never felt the need to rush to the next verse or CD. I wanted to savor each word uttered by Osho (Krishna) like a morsel of saatvik nutrition. It penetrated my heart. I had my first *Shaktipat* experience in the fourteenth chapter, where Osho leads the audience toward the same.

The Gita came alive as it had never done earlier while reading various books and interpretations. Even *this* was an interpretation. Osho's. As he himself says throughout the talks, anyone who talks about the Gita can only talk from their perspective. Yet for me, it was Krishna Himself who was talking. During the time the CD would be playing, the car would appear to run on autopilot. I honestly would not realize how and when I reached my destination. For someone who intensely dislikes driving in India, it seemed like Osho (Krishna) himself was navigating me like my charioteer. There was a certain calmness within me and in the car.

The icing on the cake was that my Hindi skills sharpened as never before, and not once did I have to seek help for any words or phrases used by Osho. For the first time in my journey, a workshop I conducted soon thereafter was almost entirely in Hindi. Of course, it helped that the audience, too, was mainly Indian. Just as *Sanjay* acquired *divya drishti* from Ved Vyas to be able to narrate the war to *Dhritarashtra*, it seemed like I had somehow acquired *divya shruti* to be able to listen to Krishna Himself. But was there ever a Krishna, or was it Ved Vyas who was expounding the Gita? A question that has never been asked or answered. After all, the Gita is enshrined in the *Mahabharat,* written by Ved Vyas.

This journey of eighteen months was a phase of my spiritual growth that is as remarkable as the five years I spent at the feet of Ramesh. Osho came alive for me finally.

Ramesh: "A Happening"

Albert Einstein wrote a tribute to Mahatma Gandhi on the occasion of the latter's seventieth birthday: "Generations to come, it may be, will scarce believe that such a one as this ever in flesh and blood walked upon this earth." When seekers and students of Advaita read about Ramesh in the years to come, they will scarcely believe that a man such as him was one of the last living masters of the twentieth century, during the peak of Kaliyuga.

And I still find it difficult to believe that I was one of the privileged few to have been touched by him, in flesh and blood. More often than not, spiritual knowledge is obtained secondhand, from books, hearsay, and interpretations. I got my teaching firsthand.

During my twenty-five-year-long search for the answer to the question "Who am I?" Ramesh's name popped up time and again, but it never stuck. I traveled around the world, meeting gurus, attending discourses, and visiting ashrams, besides devouring scriptures and books. But the answer eluded me. Upon my return to India in 2004, one day, I found myself in the Philosophy section of Oxford Book Store. Ramesh's *Sin & Guilt* was staring at me. Instinctively, I pulled it out, and before I knew it, I had read the book cover to cover, over numerous cups of tea at the Cha Bar at Oxford. I went back to the bookshelf and emptied it of every title by Ramesh. I contacted Zen Publications, got Ramesh's phone number, spoke with him right away, and found myself on the "hot seat" at his residence off Pedder Road in South Mumbai, the next morning at 9 AM!

That was the end of my long search.
That was the beginning of a new life for me.

I lived on Pedder Road before I went to the USA in 1982. How was I to know that the answer to my question, which took me around the world, was right around the corner from where I lived! It was not meant to happen a day earlier or later than that hot, sunny day in April 2004, when I found myself at Ramesh's feet. The Happening happens when it is meant to happen.

Ramesh was a Happening.
Blessed are we who experienced this Happening.
That itself was a Happening for each of us.

One of the first things that struck me from the time I called Zen Publications to get his contact details was the ease and informality with which almost everyone was addressing him by his first name. Even though I had lived in the USA for twenty-two years, where the first name is the norm regarding almost everyone except one's parents (in some cases even the parents), I had retained my Indian ethos and identity that disallows the use of the first name for anyone except someone younger than myself. And here was this guru, teacher, and master in his mid-eighties being addressed by his first name! But instead of revolting, I found it endearing, with no barriers of formality. The story goes that during the early years of Ramesh's daily morning satsangs, a gentleman from abroad asked Ramesh how he should address him. Ramesh replied, "Why, my name is Ramesh!"

Adi Sankaracharya wrote thousands of verses explaining Advaita. The Upanishads run into hundreds of pages. Lord Krishna took eighteen chapters to get it across to Arjun. Osho, the last living master and Advaita teacher of our times, along with Ramesh, was prolific to the point of being obsessive about explaining "You are the witness." Ramesh needed just forty-five minutes each morning to explain "You are not the doer." A teaching so simple that it completely floors you the first time. This cannot possibly be the answer to the question "Who am I?" But how could it not be? The question itself is so simple. How could the answer not be so! Simplicity begets simplicity. This frail man in his simple white *kurta pajama* was simplicity personified. From his simple self came this simple answer. And when it did, it resonated with the only words the Buddha actually uttered after his nirvana: "Events happen, deeds are done, but there is no individual doer." Zen at its simplest, profound best!

Whenever I mentioned Ramesh, his daily morning satsangs, and my own awakening to anyone, they would refer to him as my guru. I felt strange. Does one address one's guru by his first name? Does one feel like embracing one's guru instead of touching his feet? Can one think of enjoying a beer or a shot of whiskey with one's guru instead of accepting *panchamrut*? Does a guru crack jokes and laugh heartily like a child? Does one walk into a guru's bedroom unabashedly and have a quick chat? Ramesh turned the concept of "guru" on its head. No saffron robes, no beads, no ash, no mantras, no miracles, no *prasad* (only cold coffee sometimes!), no assistants surrounding him, no donation box at the entrance, no airs. He was like R.K. Laxman's common man, like any of us. Nevertheless, he shed the darkness for me, as the word "guru" implies. He lit the path for me with his simple teaching. No, he was not a guru to me; he was a friend, guide, and philosopher; he was like a child—playful, innocent, and funny; he was accessible to anyone in person, on the phone, and through mail. There were no expectations; only unconditional love and compassion. He was faithful to his wife for sixty plus years, to his employer for forty plus years, and to his teaching for thirty plus years.

People attending his satsangs from all parts of the world asked him questions about family, relationships, sex, business, and money. He talked about art, culture, politics, sports, finance, and religion. No topic was taboo. There were intense discussions on consciousness, rebirth, and free will. There were the typical inane questions also: "Ramesh, I do not get along with — —. What should I do?" He brought it all down to a common denominator in five simple words: "You are not the doer." It resonated and echoed constantly, until it became a mantra, like "Aum," part of one's breath. And there it sits with me too.

Ramesh, in his physical body, is no more. Who cares!

Ramesh, the Teaching, will always be there. I care!

Blessed by a Shakti Guru

In December 2015, I was in Rishikesh with Juliya, trying to recover from the heartbreak over my helpless situation with Migle. We visited various ashrams, including Santosh Puri, Swami Rama, and Swami Ved Bharti ashrams. I was blessed to have met Swami Ved Bharti at the first International Yog Festival at Parmarth Niketan in Rishikesh. He was the true Himalayan master in the Swami Rama tradition. Other than Osho, I have never been mesmerized listening to a master, as I have been with Swami Ved Bharti.

Juliya was on the search for an authentic yogic experience. She kind of found it in a Kriya Yog course near Lakshman Jhula on the banks of the Ganga. We were staying at the plush Neemrana Glass House on the other side of the Ganga on the road leading toward Devprayag. Basic comfort and an ultraclean functional bathroom were absolute necessities for me on my spiritual journey, and I made no compromises about that. Years later, Babaji and I would agree on this aspect. We both had Eastern ethos but Western sensibilities.

One day, Julia and I were walking down the road and saw a place with a sign outside saying "Satsang every day at 4 PM." It was just about that time, and we went inside. We were led by this charming young girl into the presence of Maa Gyaan Suveera, the first and only Shakti guru I have met on my journey. I was blinded by the radiance emanating from her and soothed by the calm and peace of the space, allowing you to hear the Ganga flowing below. I fell at her feet and said, "Maa." I felt I had come home. She quickly took us under her wing and told us about the Vashishta Gufa and the various Shakti Peeths in the area. Her story about her journey was as divine as she was. It was clear to me that I was in the lap of the Divine Goddess Herself. It was difficult to extract myself from her presence. On that day, I did not have the divine sight to foresee the future and know what that space had in store for me and what was to be revealed. The Himalayas, Maa Ganga, Rishikesh, the land of the *rishis*, *munis*, and realized souls, potent with divinity, was to be my true birthplace.

Babaji Appears

Babaji (Baba Harihar Ramji) appeared in February 2020, after which he initiated me into the Aghor tradition of Baba Keenaram in July 2020 in Sonoma, California. That was the first formal *deeksha* I received. Ramona got her deeksha the next year, and soon we were under Babaji's blessings.

In December 2020, I had gone to Rishikesh to immerse the ashes of Nirmala Jiji in the Ganga. As I was sitting there, surrounded by the Himalayas, I felt the presence of the Divine in that rarefied space and penned this letter to Babaji:

Dear/Respected Babaji,

As I am sitting by the Ganga, my heart and mind are flooded with emotions, thoughts, and visions that I need to pour out and share with you. All of these are at the mundane level mainly and represent Pradeep in this gross body. Yet I rise above this gross level and know "Who Am I" in an unwavering realization of the Eternal Truth. I am not yogi enough to ignore my physical body and the restless mind with all its *vrittis*. As I meditate and contemplate this, sitting by the Ganga, I feel the Mother Divine place her hand over my head, reassuring me, "It is OK." The occasional guilt feeling disappears, and I find myself merging with the Shakti energy completely.

Senses

I have always been a creature of my five senses, and as I have walked further along the spiritual path, these senses have become increasingly refined and saatvik. In my own way, they have brought me closer to the Mother Goddess. I consider my sharp sense of smell, touch, taste, sound, and sight both as an offering to the Goddess as well as a boon from Her. These senses manifest themselves in the form of fragrance, sensuality, food, chanting, and beauty all around me.

Food

I have been a foodie since I was young. This inclination has evolved over the years into the preference for natural, organic, and saatvik nourishment, but the fondness for diverse, varied, and flavorful food has not waned. Fasting regularly is inherent to my lifestyle, but so is having regular, balanced meals with an emphasis on the Indian style of cooking with herbs and spices. I am very conscious and mindful of what I consume, and I treat it as nothing less sacred than prasad for the Devi.

Comfort

Since childhood, I have been aware of the limitations of my physical body, and I have never tried to push those limits. I have compensated for a lack of physical strength by maintaining a healthy body, which I find more useful in my spiritual journey than a strong one. Along with a healthy body, I have always felt the need for creature comforts that are more than basic and find myself quickly agitated if they are not available daily, to the point that it affects my *sadhana* and spiritual quest. The best example of this is my trip to Kailash Mansarovar a few years ago, where I was totally miserable in spite of being enveloped by Mahadev Himself. I am not able to ignore my physical body at the mundane level, knowing that it is an instrument that allows me to move further along my spiritual quest. Extremes of weather bother me and create ripples of discomfort in the physical body. My body needs a warm and humid environment. No amount of yogic living helps to overcome this tendency.

Beauty

I need to see beauty and order in everything around me to be able to see Divinity. I cannot see Divinity in the ugly, filthy, dirty, chaotic, haphazard, and unorganized. I quickly move away from these since I cannot be away from Divinity even for a moment. *Durga Saptashati* eulogizes the Mother Goddess in Her resplendent, beautiful form, and I need to see that all around me to feel close to Her. Nature attracts me in all its glory. I see Her in everything in Nature, as a reflection of Her true Self, even though She is formless.

Creatures

Ever since I was young, I have abhorred all kinds of creatures, small and big: insects, bugs, birds, fish, and animals (except the cow, elephant, horse, and deer). I have both a fear and disdain of them, no matter how tiny they may be. I do not see any Divinity in them. I know this is some kind of a *karmic* carryforward, and I do not try to analyze or understand this aspect of me. I accept the reality of their existence as much as mine, but I have a huge mental and physical block against them being in my vicinity.

Sensuality

Ever since I can remember, I have felt a very strong attraction for the female form. It was only much later, when I was progressing in my Devi sadhana, that I understood the spiritual significance of this. The story of my birth, the passing away of Maa, and now the passing away of my sister have all been orgasmic Tantric experiences rooted in Shakti sadhana and Lord Shiva's presence in my being. My *kaam vasana* has always been elevated, and this is well documented in my *kundli*. This quest for the divine female form finally culminated in the form of Ramona appearing in my life as my Shakti, and the divine union I feel with her. I have never had any regrets about this aspect of my life and considered it a form of Devi Puja and complete surrender to Her.

As a *Jnana Yogi*, I have found the scriptures to be confusing and conflicting at times, especially when they relate to the above issues. I have relied more on my own Ishta Guru to guide me on this. As a *Hatha Yogi*, I have learned to take care of my physical body since that is the instrument through which I have to live my spiritual life. In the process, I have learned to enjoy the physical body with all its senses that have been given to us. I have always considered it to be the vessel through which we make our offerings to the Divine and surrender to the Higher Self. Hence the importance of keeping it healthy and hygienic.

I am a yogi, but not really.

I live a yogic life, but not really.

I follow the scriptures, but not really.

I live in my body and worship it as an idol that has been gifted to me by Maa.

Maa is the Mother Goddess.

I surrender to Her.

I am blessed to have Her as my Mother/Shakti.

I am blessed to have Babaji as my guru.

I am blessed to have Ramona as my Shakti.

Always seeking your guidance and blessings.

At your feet,

Pradeep

One Teaching

Rishi Ved, Rishi Dakshinamurthy, Rishi Dattatray, Ved Vyas, Krishna, Buddha, Confucius, Yashua, and Prophet Mohammad have all been my teachers, and their teaching has been simple and consistent: "We are One, without the other." I have not yet met Om Swami or been to his Ashram in Himachal Pradesh. He is that rare modern teacher who straddles Sanskrit, Hindi, and English with equal ease while imparting wisdom on almost any topic of Indian spirituality in the simplest manner.

Guru Dakshina: Donation From the Heart

I have tried to follow the age-old tradition of guru dakshina prevalent in India. It refers to the tradition of repaying one's teacher, guru, or spiritual guide after a period of study or the completion of formal education. This tradition is one of acknowledgment, respect, and gratitude. It is a form of reciprocity and exchange between the student and the teacher. The repayment is not exclusively monetary and may be a special task that the teacher wants the student to accomplish.

Guru dakshina has its origins in the guru–shishya tradition, or *parampara*, in India. It denotes a succession of teachers and disciples in traditional Indian culture and religions such as Hinduism, Jainism, and Buddhism. It is the tradition of spiritual relationship and mentoring where teachings are transmitted from a guru, or teacher, to a shishya, or disciple. Such knowledge, whether it be Vedic, *agamic*, architectural, musical, or spiritual, is imparted through the developing relationship between the guru and the disciple. It is considered that this relationship, based on the genuineness of the guru and the respect, commitment, devotion, and obedience of the student, is the best way for subtle or advanced knowledge to be conveyed. The student eventually masters the knowledge that the guru embodies.

A guru does not expect any benefit from sharing his knowledge and wisdom with the student. He does it from his heart. Reciprocally, the student is free to offer whatever their heart desires, after the learning is over, based upon the perceived value or benefit.

Deeksha and Shaktipat

In the spiritual dimension, the gift of deeksha bestowed upon the disciple by the guru is a very important ritual that brings the student into the guru's lineage and establishes that connection for eternity. Similarly, Shaktipat is an important ritual that helps to raise the student's consciousness to a higher level. Shaktipat may or may not happen alongside deeksha, and the two may even be received from two different gurus. I received my first deeksha by way of Maharishi Mahesh Yogi's Transcendental Meditation initiation, and then from Harihar Babaji. I received my Shaktipat from Osho.

The Teaching has happened. All questions have dropped, but the seeking continues.

|| Aum Guruve Namah||

|| Nobody Does Anything
It Is All a Happening ||

6.
|| The Awakening ||
|| Light ||

When you wake up from a good night's sleep, you feel rested and refreshed, and look forward to it every day.

When you wake up for a nightmarish sleep, you feel restless and disturbed, and hope it does not repeat the next day.

When you wake up from the sleep of darkness into the light of awareness, you are bathed in light, a light that shines on you all the time.

This is Satchidananda, the pure consciousness bliss, your true Self. When you are awakened, you go back to that pure, innocent inner child that emerged from your mother's womb. Your aura takes on a different color, and your chakras are all in balance, with the rainbow transforming into white light, as in the case of the Buddha. It is an experience like none other; one that is felt and cannot be put into words. The best I can do is to describe it as a million times more powerful than an orgasm. This is the Cosmic Orgasm, where Shiva and Parvati become one. They are one without the second, the very essence of Advaita.

The Awakening happens only once, but the ripples last a lifetime.

When I embarked on the spiritual quest at the tender age of seven, staring at the sky, the moon, and the stars, the question was, "Who am I?" After forty long years, I found the answer at the feet of my gurus Osho and Ramesh. I am That.

My love affair with myself started ever since, and it has been bliss, Satchidananda, all the way.

Relationship (with Others, God, and Oneself)

I had gone through almost half my life living through a myriad of relationships: those with my parents, siblings, spouse, friends, and extended family (some thicker than blood, some thinner than water). Almost all of them were conditional, expectational, or transactional in some way or the other. There was always "the other" involved; there was always give and take, joy and sadness, disappointments and fulfillments. It was only during my mother's last days that I truly experienced unconditional love with someone. She and I had become one; there was no "other." It brought to life the very teaching and awareness that had awakened in me. I am That. It was not coincidental that my experience with my mother came about almost immediately after the awakening. It was almost as if the Universe was putting its own seal on the Teaching!

We spend our entire life looking for love everywhere. Sometimes it is obvious, and at other times, not so obvious. There are as many shades and definitions of love as there are individuals. The mother–child love relationship is the most primitive and obvious, and spans the entire lifetime of either one of them. This was the love that Maa and I shared. The next rung down is the relationship with our father, siblings, children, and other blood relatives, which comes in a whole range of colors. This is what I had (and continue to have) with Babuji, my five sisters, two brothers, eight nephews, five nieces, and seventeen grandnephews and grandnieces.

I was the youngest of eight siblings, my father was the second youngest of eight, and my mother was the third eldest of nine. Of my four grandparents, only my maternal grandmother was alive at the time of my birth. I was surrounded by a vast extended family, and for the most part, it was a very loving family. However, under the surface, there were rivalries, conflicts, and ego trips, just as in most other large families. The strong sanskaras imparted by my parents held the family together. All members nurtured love for each other in varying degrees, despite the inevitable dramas and falling-out among them. The dynamics between each of the individuals in the family were interesting to watch. For the most part, I remained untouched by all this and was just a witness. As I grew older, I got more involved, especially since Maa had entrusted the responsibility of three of my siblings to me. I had a major falling-out for years with my brother who was immediately older than me. Subsequently, I was totally at peace when Maa orchestrated a reconciliation of sorts with him.

The generation after mine (my nephews and nieces) gradually moved away from the fold and started living their own lives. We still stay connected to a large extent, but some of them have started showing signs of disrespect for their elders. Respect for elders is one of the most cherished values we have inherited from our parents. But it is not so for the second generation, for whom the priority is attachment to their own children. And the third generation (grandnieces and grandnephews) is fast getting lost in the world of easy money, unbridled consumption, and instant gratification, and becoming thirty-second-attention-span zombies in the world of social media and artificiality. It is a sign of the ages. An interesting phenomenon of this generation is that they are influencing the older generation, who are starting to behave like their children and grandchildren.

Not having any children, I showered all my parental love on my nephews and nieces. I was barely older than my oldest nephew. I was six when my oldest niece was born. I did not feel a generation gap with any of them. It was as if I were the bridge between their parents (my siblings) and them. Later in life, this would turn out to be misplaced for the most part. With the third generation, my relationship is very tenuous, at best.

The next obvious love relationship is during the time we attain puberty, when our sex hormones start to play cupid. It begins with having a crush on our teacher or nanny, flirting with the opposite gender, engaging in boyfriend–girlfriend games, and finally, getting caught in the marriage trap for good or bad. Marriage is by no means the end game, and the hunt for "true love" continues right till our deathbed. We all want this elusive true love, and each new relationship promises to be that eternal love, until it lies shattered on the altar of commitment and monogamy. Such was the case with my relationship with Neelima and Migle, but I am still connected with them. I was destined for Ramona, whom I met in 2020.

I have never heard anyone say "I love my God" or "I love my guru." Instead, one always *fears* God and *respects* the guru. We have put them on a pedestal, and we can only look up to them. What has love got to do with religion or spirituality? Love is looking in the eyes. You do not look your God or your guru in their eyes. Love is primeval, sublime, intimate, all-encompassing, and intoxicating. We may be devoted to God and the guru, but we do not associate these feelings of love with them. Meera's feelings for Krishna were totally and purely devotional, unlike those of Radha, born out of unrequited love. But Krishna loved Himself, and thereby, he loved Rukmini, Radha, Meera, and all the gopis at the same time. He loved the *Pandavas* as much as he loved the *Kauravas*. His love knew no bounds.

But we never look at our own self, which we know best and is the easiest to fall in love with as there is no "other." It's quite the opposite. We wallow in self-pity, loathe our self, and are unduly harsh, critical, and negative toward it. Instead of counting our blessings and being thankful for our life, we complain, beg, plead, and pray for even more. Sometimes we almost wish we had not been born. We feel that the entire world is stacked against us and nobody loves us. But do we love our own self?

In Love with Myself (Finding My Inner Child)

When I fell in love with myself, I rose like a phoenix from the ashes. It was a new beginning, a new life, full of joy and happiness, brightness and clarity. The cobwebs of confusion from years of conditioning had cleared away. The sun was shining bright, and even in the darkness of the new moon night, there was always the knowledge that the sun would rise the next morning. I hugged myself like I had never hugged anyone, I smiled from ear to ear, and life became a blessing.

When I realized that I am connected to every being in this world and we are all connected to that one Consciousness, my love for myself radiated in all directions. I would still get angry in the moment, but the anger would drop soon enough. Ramesh called it a biological reaction, over which we have no control. We come back to awareness almost immediately. I was no longer the doer, nor was the other. Unconditional love poured out in the form of hugs and healing circles, workshops, and tete-a-tetes. The conflicts, the stress, and the tension had all melted away. I discovered that when you fall in love with yourself, even God falls in love with you. After all, I was His child, his alter ego.

Doors started opening, paths started getting cleared, and answers started materializing. It was almost as if I had progressed from the drudgery of day-to-day life to the bliss of Now. Each moment seemed eternal. My prayers changed from asking, to expressions of gratitude. Solitude became my best companion when my lover and I were one and the same. I did not need anyone else. The change was anything but subtle. It was Satsang of One.

When you are in love with yourself, you take better care of your body. You start noticing things about it you never did before. The signals you were always getting from your body now become loud and clear. You start treating it with more respect and love. You are in love, after all! Your mental faculties become sharper, and your observation, keener. Your spirit rekindles the long-dormant intuitive ability. You can now "read" yourself better, as well as others. Your love for yourself lights the path to reach out to others. You find your own inner child, the innocent self that came out crying from their mother's womb with not a worry in the world.

Once you fall in love with yourself, there is no getting out of it. Why would you? You have finally found your true love. One that is pure, pristine, and primeval.

The Path, Not the Goal

There are generally two kinds of individuals who come on the spiritual path. The first is the one who is running away from something and looking for an escape. The second is the one who has questions and is seeking something.

The first type is what I call the negative seeker. They seek out the spiritual path as a temporary retreat from whatever they may be trying to escape. Usually, as soon as they get respite, they are back to square one. For this individual, spirituality is like a balm to soothe frayed nerves or like a pill for a headache. But it is rare that they stay on the path and go further and higher. They are the weekend seeker.

The second type has a calling within themself that typically starts with many questions: Who am I? Why am I here? What is the purpose of life? What is this manifestation? And so on. When they are unable to get satisfactory answers from the usual sources (parents, school, college, teachers, religion, and others), they turn to the spiritual path. It is a positive seeking. It becomes a journey.

Along the spiritual path, one comes across various concepts such as *moksha*, nirvana, enlightenment, realization, salvation, and liberation. Depending on the specific path they are on, the teachers and masters they encounter, or the books and scriptures they read, one of these concepts becomes a goal to be achieved. Most of the time, the questions that arose at the start of the journey drop, and the only thing that remains is the single-minded focus on achieving this lofty goal.

If one achieves the goal, what comes next? What happens to them for the rest of their life? Is this goal for something after death or the next life? Is it for sharing with others through teaching? Is it for acquiring supernatural powers to be able to perform miracles? Or is it, plain and simple, an ego booster with a sense of achievement and accomplishment? And how does one know when one has achieved one of these goals? Is there a certificate conferred at the end that testifies to this?

It is the rare master who will help a student with this aspect. Most teachers guide a student along this path with the sole purpose of achieving the goal. After that, they leave them stranded along the way. Many students imagine sitting in the mountains or in the caves in constant meditation, or becoming a renowned teacher with hordes of followers. None of this may happen.

A true sadhak finds awareness along the way and realizes that it is the path that is important, not the goal. The path does not come to an end when the goal is reached. It continues until the last breath. An awakened individual will even stop thinking of those lofty concepts and goals. They will just focus on living their life from moment to moment. They will live in the Now. Life becomes *dhyana,* and dhyana becomes *Zazen.*

How does an awakened individual live their daily life? They start vibrating on a much higher frequency. The daily life goes on as always, but the higher frequency results in various changes that appear subtle but are very deep. What is this higher frequency?

Those who are familiar with the metaphysical world or those who work in the field of energy healing are aware that the human mind–body connection is nothing but a solidified manifestation of energy waves. It is a microcosm of the Universe itself, which vibrates at different frequencies. Each cell in the body is a microcosm of the entire Universe, and each mind–body connection is the sum total of these cells. Each cell is an energy wave that vibrates at a certain frequency, which is a function of one's acquired genes and up-to-date conditioning that is happening at each moment. Therefore, the mind–body connection itself is vibrating at a frequency that is the sum total of all these individual frequencies.

In energy healing, channels that have become blocked are cleared through various modalities like Reiki, *Pranic Healing, chakra cleansing,* sound therapy, aroma therapy, past life regression, and the like. These blockages affect the individual at three levels: physical, mental or emotional, and spiritual. Physical blockages manifest as various diseases. Mental or emotional blockages result in mental or emotional instability, such as outbursts, mood swings and interpersonal conflict. Spiritual blockages, which are mainly in the aura or subtle body, do not allow the individual to progress to their full spiritual potential.

Each of the seven chakras has a direct bearing on these blockages. The first three chakras (Muladhara, Swadhisthana, and Manipura) have mainly to do with the physical blockages. The next two (Anahata and Vishuddhi) deal with mental or emotional blockages. The highest two chakras (Ajna and Sahasara) concern spiritual blockages. When these blockages get removed gradually, the individual starts vibrating at higher frequencies. All the static in the form of impurities gets cleared. The vibrations are much clearer, just like a finely tuned radio or TV reception. With total awareness and awakening, a person vibrates at the highest frequency with total clarity. This is labeled as moksha, nirvana, enlightenment, realization, salvation, or liberation.

So what does it really mean to vibrate at higher frequencies? Is this a state to be achieved by itself? How does it translate into daily living?

Everyday Awareness

Daily living involves interacting with other individuals and with the environment in which one lives. This includes the food we eat, the home we live in, the activities we indulge in, and Nature. Once the awareness of "I am That" has been realized, one sees oneself not as an island unto oneself but as connected to the Whole, that is, the Universe and the entire manifestation. However, since this state of awareness means vibrations at higher frequencies, one becomes more sensitive and subtle, and vibrates in consonance with other similar higher frequencies. Higher frequencies reach out into the Universe and, at the same time, are received from wherever they may be emanating: from other individuals, animals, plants, food, space, and the environment. It is like being a transmitter-cum-receiver. As a corollary, one starts shirking away from anything that is transmitting a lower frequency.

We intuitively become more comfortable with people at the same subtle level as us and connect with them easily. We avoid people with gross tendencies and characteristics. We are able to see through people more clearly and, thereby, understand them much better. This is true of family, friends, and colleagues, as well as strangers. We enter a space and immediately back off, repelled by the lower frequencies vibrating there, either from the people in that space, the materials used to construct the place, or the shape and form of the place. We observe that "the vibrations here are not good" or the opposite. We are able to discern between saatvik and tamasic food, and our food habits change such that only saatvik food satiates our need for nourishment. We no longer indulge in frivolous activities that have no higher purpose. We are drawn more and more toward writing, reading, teaching, and the arts. We are drawn toward Nature and spend as much time as possible interacting with her. We are drawn toward the energies of animals and plants. Becoming fully aware that they are as much a part of the Whole as we are, we adopt a more nurturing attitude toward them. We cringe at the thought of any harm caused to them. Our attachment to people and objects disappears, and we observe without judgment as mere witnesses. We do not lose our emotions; we still feel sorrow and pain, joy and happiness, but we stop shedding tears. Knowing fully well that everything is transitory and an illusion, we move on to the next moment. The past has no more relevance. The future is not here yet. We savor each moment in the present.

During my spiritual journey, while traveling around the world, I have watched in sadness the havoc caused by the modern, "developed" Westernized way of life, which has made people zombies and robots reaching its nadir in the AI phenomenon. Their focus is on instant gratification and consumption, with little or no sense of awareness of any kind. But then, this too is a Happening, like Hitler was a Happening.

During my travels, I would increasingly seek out people and places of refinement that resonated with my own frequency. These would be museums, art galleries, dance and music performances, spiritual gatherings, cafés, restaurants, and quiet, pristine natural settings that were calming, away from the crowds and the chaos. The offerings at these places were elevated and would touch me deeply somewhere inside. Also, I would meet interesting people in such places along my journey. I became more aware of everything around me that would help me discern between the desirable and undesirable. My sixth sense and sensitivity would pull me toward that which would offer me sublime experiences (of which there were numerous), making them sharper in the process. Consequently, silence, equanimity, and nothingness become second nature.

When all the questions have dropped, one starts living in awareness. Life is beautiful. Life is grace. Life is grateful. It is meant to be lived to the fullest, with each moment full of awareness; of "I am That." Many masters have reached this state of full, blissful awareness, but only some of them continue to live their normal lives. Many other individuals have also reached this state, and they continue to live their normal lives, quietly and inconspicuously. This is living in awareness.

The Three Gitas

The Bhagavad Gita, the Ashtavakra Gita, and the *Avadhuta Gita* are the three Gitas that contributed to my awakening. They need to be read and absorbed, in that order. The Bhagavad Gita is read by most people. Once that is absorbed, the Ashtavakra Gita will appear in your journey at the right time to make your learning deeper. Once that is internalized, the Avadhuta Gita will provide the seal on the understanding and awakening. However, each of the Gitas is like a guru in book form and will not appear unless you are ready for it, and they will appear only in that order. You cannot just *read* the Gita; it has to be absorbed. Most people in India, including a family member, quote from the Gita regularly, especially verse 2:47 on karma. However, very few of them really understand what Krishna is saying. Anyone can read the Gita, but only an awakened person can grasp it.

|| Aum Tat Sat ||

|| Spirituality Abides
in
Silence, Solitude, Surrender,
Simplicity, Serenity ||

7.
|| The Happenings ||
|| Witness ||

Happenings are happening all the time.
They are not your doing.
Be the witness and revel in the divine play all around.

The concept of free will has been discussed since time immemorial, in all strands of philosophy, Eastern and Western, with no decisive conclusion. It tends to lean toward the Western socioreligious view that free will exists and a human being is free to do and act as they deem fit. They are the master of their destiny; they chart their path from birth to death and are responsible for the consequences of their actions. Indian philosophy centered around Advaita does not address this concept directly but arrives at the conclusion indirectly that there is no free will. The entire Indian thinking on life is based on divinity, destiny, and fatalism. This has been my experience.

We find ourselves faced with a dichotomy here.

The Western view of free will simply falls flat on its face. And here's why. The two most important events in an individual's life are birth and death, and the rebuttal to the existence of free will lies therein. One *does not choose* to be born, in the first place. Second, one *does not choose* to be born of certain parents in a certain place at a certain time. It just *happens.*

Each birth is a Happening, independent of the person taking birth. And likewise with death. No one chooses to die, even when they choose to take their own life. The taking of one's own life is just another Happening as a form of life coming to an end. It is determined as much by the Laws of Nature and the predetermination of someone dying of old age, of natural causes, by an accident, or by suicide.

The Western view on free will is dictated primarily by organized religion as a means of asserting its power over the masses and controlling them by introducing the ideas of Heaven and Hell, sin and guilt. This religious view instills a sense of shame and fear in those who do not follow their diktat, and a sense of righteousness in those who do. The sinful go to Hell; the righteous end up in Heaven.

Conversely, the Eastern view on free will is determined largely by the concepts of destiny and divinity, which govern daily life. However, organized religion in India in the form of blind faith and rituals has imprisoned the spiritual aspect of this issue behind locked temples. The Church of the West and the Temple of the East have caused more harm to mankind than all the wars combined.

My father got a horoscope prepared for each of his eight children right at birth, as is the general practice in India. There were three major revelations in my horoscope at birth (mentioned below), which became the natal chart. All three revelations have come true on my journey. The natal chart is fixed during the lifetime of an individual, based upon the planetary positions at the time of birth. As the planets, the sun, and the moon transit through different houses during one's lifetime, events happen. These are "Happenings."

In my case, the first Happening was my birth, based on the charts of my two mothers. From that point on, my life events have been determined and forecast by the transits in my chart. This has been decisively proven by getting my readings done regularly to date through many different astrological systems.

Astrology is broadly divided into three systems: Vedic (Jyotish), Chinese, and Western. The Western system is the weakest of the three and does not go deep enough to be accurate and specific; it provides general trends in one's life. Vedic astrology is part of the Indian psyche. A good astrologer, with the help of an accurately prepared chart, can lay out the entire lifetime of an individual. There are numerous examples from Indian scriptures to corroborate this, and most importantly, it has been my own experience. The Chinese system is deep-rooted as well, but difficult to access and understand for a person who does not speak Chinese. That said, a major revelation was made by an English-speaking Taiwanese astrologer, in my case. And then there are many other peripheral forms of prediction, the most common being Nadi Shastra, the *Akashic Records*, and the Tarot.

These were the three major revelations in my natal chart: One, I will become a teacher; two, I will travel the world; and three, my life will be surrounded by Shaktis. They have all come true.

"Teacher" is a generic word that suggests one who sheds light on something, or shares knowledge or wisdom. It does not necessarily imply a schoolteacher or one involved in some kind of formal teaching. Without being privy to my chart, my eldest brother was intuitive enough to suggest *"Pra" "deep"* as my name. The second revelation was even more direct. I have traversed the length and breadth of the globe, visited 130 countries to date, and spent more time traveling than grounded. I have already discussed the third revelation in detail elsewhere in this book.

Was this free will?

Free Will?

This is a true story of my friend Deepak, in his own words:

> I consider myself to be spiritual and enlightened, and aware of "Who I am." I am anti-religious to the extent that I consider all religions to be dogmatic, exclusive, and ritualistic. I was born in a typical Hindu family, not too conservative, yet rooted

in the traditions of basic pujas, superstitions, and beliefs. I shied away from them from my teen years onward, after my introduction to Bertrand Russell, Albert Einstein, and George Bernard Shaw. The question "Who am I?" first appeared before me when I was seven years old. But there was no one around to seek the answer from. I rebelled against all belief systems that appeared to draw strength only from blind faith or could not be explained by my logical mind. Intuition, ESP, and the sixth sense had yet to take root in my psyche. I was a rebel to the core.

I continued to abhor all religions, including the Hindu religion, in terms of everything that manifested in its name. The question "Who am I?" stayed with me right through my adult years. I found myself on the spiritual path, thanks to my Reiki teacher, and then there was no looking back. I knew that the long-sought answer to the eternal question was ahead of me on this path. I got introduced to Osho's teachings and my ultimate and only teacher, Ramesh Balsekar. And sure enough, the answer came in an instant.

The question: Who am I?

The answer: I am That!

The answer rested on the foundations of understanding free will, or its absence. In my search for the past and present masters, teachers, scriptures, and writings, I did not come across anyone who explained this concept so clearly and simply as Ramesh Balsekar. Even Krishna has various veiled references to free will in the Gita, but consistent with his very playful nature, he leaves all of them subject to interpretation by the reader, and there have been interpretations galore! Ramesh explained it in terms of its relevance in daily living, because that is all we are concerned with, and therefore, it struck the right chord. While the teaching and the understanding registered completely at the intellectual and intuitive levels, their validation also started appearing in daily happenings.

Little did I know that the biggest validation was to come soon.

My horoscope reading at various times by various individuals had indicated that I would be under the malefic influence of Saturn for seven and a half years, commonly known as the *Sade Sati* in India. I was also advised against buying land or any property during this time. My logical as well as my spiritual self scoffed at this, and attributed it to a creation of the indigenous and entrepreneurial mind of Indian priests, astrologers, and others, who gain directly from spreading such fear, because along with every malefic effect in the horoscope, there is a "remedy" for it as well! The remedy for Sade Sati consists of performing certain pujas, making certain offerings, wearing certain stones, and the like. The reason for my skepticism was that, in Western astrology, there is no equivalent of the Sade Sati, even though Saturn is very much part of the Western astrology system. Sade Sati can supposedly have a malignant impact on one's health, relationships, finances, and other aspects of one's life. In general, one is advised to "keep low" and be "on guard" during this period. In other words, be very careful of your free will! It could create havoc.

In 2007, I bought a piece of land, after a three-year-long search, with the intention of developing it into an organic farm and a healing center. When I saw the land, overlooking a lake and surrounded by hills, it was love at first sight. It was idyllic! After a year-long search, I narrowed it down to an architect and contractor, and the work began. Almost immediately after I signed up with the architect, it became clear that he was the wrong choice, and negative vibrations started emanating all around the project. The contractor also turned out to be inexperienced for the job. In July 2009, in an accident on the site, a newly raised slab came crashing down, and there was a fatality and injuries. The police descended on the site, more intent on making gains from the tragedy rather than on placing responsibility for the accident where it belonged. There was finger-pointing and passing the buck all around. The project came to a standstill, and I was in a state of shock.

What did I do wrong?

In 2003, I met my childhood sweetheart totally out of the blue, after a gap of twenty years! It was as if time had stood still. It was love at first sight and also the beginning of a very intense and satisfying relationship amid great odds on both sides. The relationship derailed in the summer of 2008, got back on track later in the year, and again derailed in the summer of 2009. It had a disastrous effect on me, emotionally, mentally, and physically. When the above-mentioned accident on the site happened in July 2009, I was seriously nursing the wounds of this broken relationship. I was devastated. My health started to deteriorate rapidly: I started suffering from bouts of high blood pressure, insomnia, and depression.

What did I do wrong?

My well-wishers (or so they thought themselves to be), comprising my family, friends, and even strangers, started rallying around me. Each of them had suggestions to offer. Sade Sati and *Vaastu* became the topics of discussion and advice. They started haunting me day and night. I lived in a beautiful apartment, had bought an idyllic piece of property, and was generally leading a quiet, spiritual life. Why then, all of a sudden, were such "bad" things happening to me? I discussed it with Ramesh during my interactions with him. Since the teaching had already gone deep down, I myself started explaining it to him (and thereby to myself) that this was all a Happening. At one level, the teaching helped tremendously in dealing with the situation. But at another level, I was restless.

I was scared and insecure with what was happening, but at the same time, I wanted to test the validity of this age-old belief system that was being imposed on me. Could *Shani* (Saturn) really play such havoc? Could bad Vaastu really have such dire consequences? Was the Devi really upset with me and needed to be appeased?

It was a conflict within my Self, the kind I had never faced in my entire corporate career. My entire being was in turmoil, and I felt shaken to the core. Everything that I believed in and considered sacrosanct was falling apart. My spirituality itself was being questioned. And I was getting pushed toward something that I did not believe in, and in fact, abhorred. Where was my free will?

Before I knew it, I had consulted with two famous astrologers, two Vaastu experts, a *pandit*, a psychological counselor, and my physician friend. Over the next two months, from July to September 2009, the following "happened" of my own free will:

> I had a Vaastu check done for my apartment. Various deficiencies were found, and remedies were put in place. I placed a shrine, pyramids, wind chimes, *Ganeshji*, flowers, water bodies, crystals, and mirrors in various places as suggested.

> I started performing a small puja at the shrine each morning. I also started chanting the *Hanuman Chalisa* each day, no matter where I happened to be. I arranged for a pandit to come each Saturday to perform a puja and chant for an hour to appease the Devi and *Hanumanji*.

I performed the *Kaal Sarp Yog Puja* in Trimbakeshwar, Nashik, to appease *Rahu* and *Ketu*. I organized a *mahajaap* over a period of two half days, with twelve pandits, to appease *Mangal* (Mars), Shani, Rahu, and Ketu. I started wearing the *pukhraj* stone (yellow sapphire) in my right hand.

I had a Vaastu check done at the land. It turned out that the south side needed to be made heavy, so I started planting large trees on that side.

I made certain sankalps with the blessings of Lord Krishna at a shrine I visit in Haridwar.

I had three counseling sessions with my counselor, and followed the advice given by her.

The results were almost instantaneous. My relationship came back on track; in fact, it got elevated to a much higher level. Even though the project did not start again, I managed to get the architect and the contractor off my back, and organic farming continued at a steady pace. Most importantly, I acquired total equanimity and peace of mind, and never felt better emotionally, mentally, and physically. During this entire period, the rebel and rationalist in me were still kicking and alive, and I refused to indulge in certain other remedies suggested to me: I refused to go to the Shani temple every Saturday. I refused to make an offering of black sesame seed and oil every Saturday. I refused to take antidepressants and sleeping pills, strongly advised by a famous psychiatrist who prescribed the same to me after diagnosing me with manic depression within five minutes of seeing me!

So where did free will end, and where did destiny take over? What happened to my abhorrence of all rituals, blind belief, and faith? What happened to my spirituality?

I have known Deepak since childhood. He is almost an alter ego. The dark phase that he encountered, the conflicts and the turmoil that he faced, and the questions he has raised regarding free will are genuine. I have seen and felt his pain very closely. Ramesh was a teacher to both of us. As Ramesh used to say, "Yes, we have free will, but it is worth nothing. It is like a fake currency note." A thought gets planted in the mind (not in our control), a biological reaction takes place based upon genes and conditioning (not in our control), free will is asserted, and an action is performed, but having done that, the results are not in our control.

Deepak's free will caused him to fall in love at first sight with his childhood sweetheart, and the land, and there was a biological reaction in both instances. Thereafter, the results of those actions were not in his control, because his destiny, as determined by the stars, had something else in mind for him. His destiny kept pulling him toward performing actions of his own free will, which he would hitherto never have contemplated. As Deepak says, little did he know that Ramesh's teaching would get validated in such a major way for him and for the benefit of others.

Family Happenings

I have seen eleven marriages in the family (besides my own), seven divorces (besides my own), numerous births, and ten deaths. All of these were Happenings, but not spiritual Happenings that had any impact on my journey. Births and deaths are an inherent part of the life cycle, being the most euphoric from a spiritual point of view. However, most people see these two events as anything but. Natural birthing has long given way to artificially induced birthing to give rise to any euphoria. It has become just another appointment in the calendar to keep. Breastfeeding has long given way to formula milk to create any excitement around the baby suckling a mother's breast. Death has become an event for mourning rather than a celebration of the person's life, with cliched obits and meaningless rituals dictated by the religious powers and deeply ingrained superstitions and beliefs.

Osho's death was celebrated with joy, dance, and music to celebrate his rich life and carry out his wishes. I wish mine to be the same.

I was at work in New York in September 1986, when I got a call from India, which was very rare. Right away, I intuitively knew it would be ominous. Babuji had had a stroke while watching a very exciting cricket match and was in a coma in the hospital. Dilip Bhaiya and I were on the next flight to Bombay and reached late in the night. The next day, we were allowed into the ICU where Babuji was lying. We both held his hands, and I felt an instant tug. Tears started flowing. I had kept the first part of the promise made to him to return to India, and he knew it. Redemption had taken place. He knew Maa would be fine after he was gone.

On October 3, 2020, I got a call from Manju that Nirmala Jiji had tested positive for Covid. I was in the USA, but I swung into action with phone calls to Dr. Suhas Shah and Jitendra Pandya, got her admitted to Bhatia Hospital, and left for Mumbai in the midst of all kinds of travel restrictions related to Covid. I had resolutely decided not to get vaccinated, and the travel protocol was even more onerous for those who were not vaccinated. I managed to reach Mumbai relatively easily and rushed to the hospital. I was not allowed to see her. I camped out in the hospital lobby for the next week until she tested negative and was subsequently discharged. She didn't seem to be overly emotional on seeing me. I took her home, where Manju and the staff were waiting. The next few days, we were monitoring her regularly with the help of Dr. Pandya, and she was well on the road to recovery.

Soon after, she slipped and fell, breaking her thigh bone in the process. It was night by the time we discovered that the bone was broken. She had endured the pain all day long without a word. It was back to Bhatia Hospital with surgery scheduled two days later. This time, I was with her in the room. When they wheeled her to the operating room, I cried profusely.

It was a successful surgery, and we took her home in a week, where she remained bedridden for the most part and soon developed a UTI. Dipika, the nurse, was an angel during this entire time, along with Sheila, her maid. Manju was also there all the time. Gayatri Mamiji was next door. The entire contingent of Shaktis was with her. I felt reassured, yet did not leave her side. I asked Dr. Pandya if I could take a break and go away for a few days. There was no sign of anything untoward happening. But it did. And I was not next to her at that moment.

Nirmala Jiji was my eldest sister, and I was born after she got married. She could not conceive, so she doted on all her nephews and nieces. She had lost sight in one of her eyes. Despite tremendous challenges in her married life, she was a pillar of support for my parents and everyone else in our family, as well as her husband's.

Sushil Jijaji, her husband of sixty-two years, passed away in 2017, leaving an empty bank account. I rushed back to India and quickly organized her finances and support system, with many in the family pitching in financially and Manju in charge under my guidance. Things quickly got back on track, and from then on, she retreated into a shell and assumed a quiet demeanor. With Manju at her side, I managed her affairs from the USA, with regular visits.

I was in Istanbul on November 19, 2020, when Manju called to say that Nirmala Jiji had passed away that morning.

Later in India, when I took her ashes to Benaras for immersion in the Ganga, Maa immediately appeared and gave her blessings. Her divya drishti of years ago had come true.

I was at the funeral home in Queens, New York, on March 8, 2019, delivering a eulogy for Bhaisahab. He had breathed his last two days earlier, after a three-year-long gallant battle with leukemia. When he was diagnosed, he was given three months, but he went on to be with us for three years. He was a fighter. During this time, I visited him regularly in New York, and we got close. Ayo, he, and I would visit the hospital for his periodic checkups. I was familiar with the efficacy of Tibetan and Chinese medicine in cancer and sourced it from Dharamshala for him. I had discovered the power of cordyceps mushrooms and got a packet for him from Bhutan. We would have no-holds-barred talks, primarily about the family.

Unfortunately, Bhaisahab had the tendency to alienate people he interacted with, be it family, colleagues, or strangers. This continued throughout his life and affected his relationship with Babuji, his wife Sneh Bhabhi, his son Anuraag, his sisters, his brother-in-law, his bosses, and many others. Sneh Bhabhi divorced him, instigated by her own children, after over forty years of marriage. It was the first divorce in the family, and it broke Maa's heart. However, it did not affect my relationship with either Bhaisahab or Sneh Bhabhi. We were close to each other since my birth. He had chosen my name with his foresight. I just stood witness to his relationships melting around him. Maa was sad about it and occasionally asked me to help him financially. I did whatever I could.

Sneh Bhabhi always had a soft corner for me, and we stayed in touch. She even invited me to Anuraag's wedding in New Delhi, which I attended. Anuraag and I had become estranged a few years ago, but he apologized and invited me himself. Anuraag became a father soon thereafter, and Bhaisahab became a grandfather. However, Anuraag refused to allow his father to meet his son. That is when Maa intervened. Pramila Jiji and I were visiting Bhaisahab in New York after his cancer diagnosis. Events happened very fast during that week, and soon, I was driving Bhaisahab and Ayo to Anuraag's home to meet Aahan, his grandson. The three generations were finally together, albeit for a short time. Bhaisahab and Anuraag were soon tearing each other apart, and this continued till the end.

Bhaisahab's end was nearing. Ayo was by his side. She had told him I was on my way, and he smiled. I got the call from Ayo when I was at Charlotte airport, while connecting to my flight. It was too late. Ayo had been the Shakti who had stood by him throughout this ordeal. I was merely fulfilling yet another of Maa's responsibilities given to me. I was just a witness to the sad ending of my brother, whom I loved very much.

I moved to Pune in November 2004 after Maa passed away. Hari Jijaji, my youngest brother-in-law, who lived in Pune, said to me, "You are our insurance." It sounded like an echo of Maa's words to me regarding Sunila Jiji, my youngest sister, who had endured breast cancer at a young age, had not been able to conceive, had other health issues, had adopted Ankur, and was also dealing with Hari Jijaji's health challenges. She was one of the most stoic people I have met in my journey. There was a time when each of my first six siblings got married and left home. Sunila Jiji and I were left alone. I could not stand her, and we fought a lot. Things changed completely once she got married and Hari Jijaji came into our lives. Both became my support system in Pune. I cannot imagine how I would have survived my fourteen years of *vanvaas* in Pune without them. However, Maa's foresight was validated, and Sunila Jiji became the third of my responsibilities.

Ankur and Nupur got engaged in July 2012, and the wedding was scheduled for later in the same year. However, a couple of months later, Hari Jijaji suffered a heart attack and had to undergo a bypass surgery immediately. He was in no position to handle anything, and Sunila Jiji was helpless. Maa appeared. I stepped into the picture and organized everything in a span of four months. I wanted to give Ankur the most memorable wedding ever in the Darooka family, and it veritably turned out to be so! Maa was happy.

It was 2:30 in the afternoon in South Carolina when I got the message from Hari Jijaji: "Ankur is no more." The day was November 15, 2023, two days after Diwali in India. He had just collapsed, leaving Nupur, his wife of ten years, and his daughter Aanya, barely a year old. That message shattered me as no other. I had witnessed the deaths of many family members (near and distant) at close quarters, and none had caused any emotional turmoil. Each of those deaths was inevitable and expected, and I was calm and collected, again, a witness to life playing out. Ankur's passing, too, was life playing out, but I could not just be a witness. The thought of Hari Jijaji, Sunila Jiji, Nupur, and Aanya did not allow me to be one. In the Indian psyche, *putra shokh* is considered the highest form of mourning, as characterized by Dhritrashtra and Gandhari mourning the slaying of their hundred sons, the Kauravas, at the hands of the Pandavas. I had never seen Hari Jijaji ever emote for any reason. His mourning was largely internal, and it corroded him deeply. Ankur was the second of my nephews to fall victim to overprotection by their parents, blocking their Vishuddhi.

Nupur called me on July 17, 2024. Hari Jijaji was no more.

I rushed to Pune, albeit after his cremation. During my eulogy at the prayer meeting, once again, Maa's words and foresight echoed in my mind. He had taken seriously ill a year ago with a cardiac arrest. Doctors had given up and advised us to take him home. I had arrived and was by his side. I witnessed a different side of Ankur this time, unlike the past, when he would be a quiet witness whenever Hari Jijaji had to be hospitalized. Now, he would not let go of his father. He extended himself in ways I had never seen before to ease his father's pain and make him comfortable at home. I receded into the background but stayed by his side. It was an uphill battle against all odds, but a miracle of sorts started happening, thanks to an Ayurvedic doctor in Jaipur. His remedies started to revive Hari Jijaji's heart, and very soon, he was walking and sitting at the dining table.

Having witnessed this miracle, I decided to return to the USA, but before long, I would be back, as destiny would have it.

Other Happenings

In 2007, I had my kundli reading updated, and it suggested that I needed to be careful of driving and being on the road in February 2008. One does not live one's life by reading the horoscope each morning or week or even month, no matter how detailed and accurate it may be.

On February 17, 2008, I was driving early in the morning to drop my niece at Pune airport. There was not much traffic at that time, and I was driving at a normal speed. Suddenly, a pedestrian darted in front of my car, and I swerved to avoid hitting him. Instead, I hit the divider with some impact, and the front of the car burst into smoke. Both airbags inflated on activation, and my niece and I were trapped inside, unable to open the door. Just then, a bystander (seeing what had happened) smashed the side window with a large stone, allowing us to get out. Seconds later, the front of the car exploded in flames.

The last few years of Maa's life were intrinsically interlaced with mine. In more than one reading, including the palm leaf reading of Naadi Shastra, I was given the period of *Kartik Shukla Paksha* in October 2004 for her passing away. It helped me to prepare for it mentally and emotionally. True to the reading, Maa departed on October 24, 2004, in Brahma Muhurta on Kartik Ekadashi, considered a highly auspicious moment.

In numerous readings, I was told about my one offspring. It made no sense since I had none. When it kept recurring, I contemplated, and then it all made sense! It took me back to a happening in 1984 that posed a huge dilemma at that time. But the Happening was determined by the Universe in consonance with the plan laid out for me, which I was obviously not aware of, until much later. Nothing happens at random.

In 2001, I was visiting Mahableshwar, a hill station near Pune. As I got out of the car near a park, I heard a voice calling me by my name. It was a simple-looking man who appeared to be a sadhu. Before I could respond, he went on to tell me about my life and my situation then, including intimate details that no stranger would ever have known. I stood there dumbstruck before he walked away.

The above episode repeated in 2006 in Kodaikanal, another hill station in South India, as I was walking by the lake.

Yet again, it repeated in 2011 in Rishikesh by the Ganga. This time, it was a properly dressed sadhu who crossed my path a few times over two days.

The Guru Appears

In January 2019, I was staying at the Brijrama Hotel on the banks of the Ganga in Benaras and had my horoscope read by Vidyasagarji Upadhyay, a *jyotish*. He told me that Babaji was waiting for me at the ashram and went on to describe him. I was scheduled to return to the USA soon and did not have the opportunity to meet Babaji then. Babaji has an ashram in Benaras and in Sonoma, California. Next year, I was back in Benaras, and Vidyasagarji took me to meet Babaji at the ashram. I fell at his feet, tears welling up. The Guru had finally appeared! I was ready for my deeksha.

My True Shakti "Happens" in My Life

It was January 2020, the start of the Covid pandemic, and I was in India. While checking my phone, I saw an email in my inbox. Something told me I needed to open it right away, which I did. It was from a woman in Dallas, Texas, thousands of miles away. Her name was Ramona. A look at her picture, and I knew it was her!

In 2018, a Chinese astrologer in Taipei, Taiwan, told me I would meet my true Shakti in 2020, and she would be from a different country. That Shakti had appeared. The next three months, we meditated together daily via WhatsApp. In one of the meditations, she had a vision of an elderly Indian woman giving her a purple velvet box and a red scarf. I later showed her a picture of Maa, and she instantly recognized her as the same woman in the vision. I then showed her the purple velvet box Maa had left me, containing some jewelry. I also showed her the red *chunri*, the traditional scarf worn by a Rajasthani bride. She recognized that, too, from the vision. She was fed up with Dallas and wanted to move to Michigan. Shiva rescued this lost Shakti, and she moved to Asheville from Dallas a month later. Maa had sent her to me. Babaji took care of the rest in his Sonoma ashram. And what unfolded thereafter was for the Divine to take care of.

Sri Sukta to the Rescue

Swami Rama, from the long lineage of the Himalayan Masters, had established the Himalayan Institute in Honesdale, Pennsylvania, in the 1970s. From the time I lived in New York and then Boston, I used to visit the institute regularly for retreats. Pandit Rajmani Tigunait was the spiritual head after Swami Rama's samadhi. I was not particularly close to Panditji at that time. There was a long gap before I found myself again in the sacred presence of Panditji in December 2017 on the occasion of the ten-day-long study of *Sri Sukta*. Panditji immediately recognized me. I was with Maria, another Shakti who had appeared in my life that year.

I was staying in a duplex loft, and one morning, as I was coming down the stairs, I missed a step and sprained my ankle. I screamed as the pain was excruciating. It was snowing and icy outside, and I needed to walk across the campus to reach the auditorium for the morning class. I somehow limped across with the help of Maria. It was New Year's Day, and we were in a remote area with no possibility of a doctor or hospital in the vicinity.

We had completed seven days of the *Sri Sukta* teaching, and it had started to touch my core being. Devi had gradually gained asana in my Anahata. I went to sleep, still in pain, reciting the *Sri Sukta*, not able to move my foot. I woke up in the morning and gingerly tried to twitch my toes and feel my foot under the covers. I felt no pain! I then started flexing my foot. Still, there was no sign of any pain. Tears welled up, and I reached out to Maria, who was equally shocked. I quickly got out of bed, got ready, and walked over to see Panditji and tell him what had happened. He had a smile on his face, and he blessed me as I touched his feet. Later that morning, Panditji had me describe the entire experience to the audience, and I was emotionally overcome as I started talking. At the end, people came over and started hugging me. *Sri Sukta* had come alive, and Devi had given her *darshan*.

In 2018, I bumped my head a few times. The first couple of times were in the foyer of my sister's apartment building in Juhu, Mumbai, which had a very low ceiling for a six-foot-plus person like me. I almost had a concussion, and the pain lasted a few days.

After a few weeks, while visiting Kathmandu, I again bumped my head (the same spot as before) on a protruding beam of a building. There was no external sign of any injury. I had started having intermittent shooting pains after the Mumbai incident, but this time, they persisted. I did not want to visit a hospital in Kathmandu. I was on my way to Rajah Ayurveda in Kerala for a ten-day retreat. Neelu was with me, and I accompanied her to Bangalore, where her daughter lived. We visited a neurologist at the hospital there, and the MRI revealed a hairline fracture on the left side. The pain was still persisting in the form of a constant headache. According to the doctor, it would hopefully heal itself, and the pain would subside, or I would need surgery. That was not an option I wanted to contemplate. I decided to continue to Rajah Ayurveda as per my plan and discuss my problem with the doctors there.

Dr. Jayarajan, my personal doctor there, prescribed some herbal medicated potions on the affected part, along with some pain-relieving herbal remedies. But there was no change, even after four days. On the afternoon of the fifth day, I was lying in bed due to the constant headache, looking out the window in front of me. Suddenly, a beautiful golden deer darted out in front of me. It was too sudden to grasp what had happened. And then I sat up in bed and realized that the pain had gone! Before I could blink my eyes, the golden deer appeared again and darted away in the opposite direction. *Sri Sukta* had once again come alive; Devi had appeared just as described in *Sri Sukta*, as a golden deer.

Life is a Happening

Happenings are not random. Our life is a continuous series of happenings in accordance with our genes and conditioning. As I said earlier, we have no control over our birth and, therefore, no control over our genes. From before our intelligence starts to develop and our ego begins to raise its ugly head, we start getting conditioned each moment by the food we are fed, the clothes we are made to wear, the environment at home, the love (or lack thereof) we get, our first school, our first friend, and so on. The combination of our genes (hardware) and conditioning (software) propels us forward in life in accordance with the plan that the Universe has laid out for us.

Each moment is a Happening.
Each breath is a Happening.
Be grateful for this gift.
It is all a Happening.

||Aum Guruve Namah||

|| Less Is More
We Are All Connected
Simplicity Is Serenity ||

8.
|| The Spirit ||
|| Self ||

The spirit is all there is.

And *TanTien* took form.

TanTien is Universal Energy. It came into being, inspired by Osho, the Zen teachings from China, and the tranquility of Japan. It is deeply rooted in the Chinese and Japanese languages and cultures. TanTien became my motto, my calling card, my avatar.

As a three-dimensional object, the body withers away, the mind goes astray, but the spirit lives on. It is that *prana shakti*, the life force, the Universal energy, the *chi*, the *ki,* that cannot be experienced by the five senses; yet there can be no human life without it. Each breath we take is full of this energy. The first breath that we take, coming out of the mother's womb, is full of potential in this physical world of maya, and the last breath we release relieves us from this world and takes us back to the Source.

This spirit can be experienced in many ways, and the entire journey of spirituality is about experiencing this spirit and connecting with the Source.

Dhyana or Meditation?

Is meditation the same as dhyana? If yes, does one "do" dhyana as one "does" meditation? If not, which came first?

I was introduced to yog over forty years ago, mainly through asanas and pranayama. During this time, I experimented with various forms of yog from different traditions all over the world. I have read various books and scriptures on yog by many teachers and masters. It became increasingly clear that yog, as I had learned in the beginning, was not just asanas and pranayama. It was a way of life. There was an element of meditation built into each yog teaching I attended. Some of the more traditional ones gave greater importance to it. Many ignored it altogether. One thing that stood out consistently throughout my yog practice was my inability to sit in meditation for more than a few minutes. It was not because my body was not flexible and supple (I was able to perform various asanas quite well). It was not because I was not used to sitting on the floor (I grew up in a household where it was common to have meals on the floor, and to date, I prefer sitting on the floor instead of a chair or couch). I tried all kinds of meditation: Transcendental Meditation (TM), Vipassana, Kundalini meditation, and simply sitting cross-legged in *Padmasana, Ardhapadmasana,* or *Sukhasana.* Nothing worked. So what was it that was missing? Or what was it I was doing wrong? The only answer I would get from the teachers was to keep practicing.

I got my answer only when the answer to the eternal question "Who am I?" was understood by me. "I am That."

Yog, as a way of life, was taking deep roots within me well before I got the above answer. While it did not bother me much that I was not able to do meditation, it did rankle me a bit since meditation as a technique to achieve certain results (better health, lower blood pressure, a calm mind, the ability to focus deeper, hidden answers to eternal questions, etc.) was being talked about everywhere. So why was I not able to meditate?

Patanjali's *Yog Sutras* and the Bhagavad Gita were my guides as I learned and adopted yog as a way of life. Patanjali is the source of all yog teachings. Even Krishna refers to this in the Gita. Dhyana is the seventh of the eight limbs mentioned by Patanjali. "Dhyana," a Sanskrit word, has been translated into "meditation," an English word, and interpreted to mean, for the most part, sitting in meditation and focusing or concentrating the mind. It became an action to be done. Whereas dhyana, in Sanskrit or Hindi, is a state of mind. From dhyana comes *"dhyanachitt,"* which means mindfulness or awareness. In Hindi, we say "dhyana se," which means "with awareness." When Krishna talks about dhyana in various parts of the Gita, He is talking about performing action with dhyana, that is, with mindfulness and awareness of Him all the time. In fact, Zen, the philosophy that alone represents the Buddha's teachings in its purity, is derived from dhyana, and in Chinese, its pronunciation is very similar to that of "dhyana."

So how did dhyana become meditation, and how did it get lost along the way? The problem was the English language with its limitations. Just as various other concepts from the Indian scriptures (karma, *dharma*, yog, etc.) have been loosely translated into English and interpreted according to the English meaning of that word, or using other English language words, so also dhyana. The English language does not have the richness and depth or the nuances and subtleties of the Sanskrit language to do any justice to these very rich and meaningful phrases and concepts from the Indian scriptures. It is not for nothing that Sanskrit is called the mother of all languages. Hindi and various other Indian languages that are a direct offshoot of Sanskrit are equally rich. Unfortunately, those who are responsible for translating words from Indian languages tend to do a word-for-word translation; for instance, the single word "dhyana" would be translated as "meditation," a single word in English. The fact is that even an entire paragraph in English may not suffice to bring out the full and proper meaning of a single Sanskrit word. It has been said that a language can be understood only by living its words, not by uttering them.

In modern times, meditation as a technique first took root through Maharishi's Transcendental Meditation, which quickly became all the rage with his followers. The focus was on quieting the mind using a mantra. When I got my TM initiation, I was never told what the deeper purpose of this technique was, if any. It was presented as a mechanical exercise that would give results. It never stayed with me for more than a few weeks. After TM became popular, many more teachers and gurus in India started teaching how to "do meditation." The audience was mainly the Western world, and the medium of teaching was English. It was a rare teacher like Swami Muktananda or Swami Chinmayananda who tried to weave meditation into their teachings, not as a technique but as something that carried a deeper meaning. Osho offered many forms of meditation (Kundalini, Vipassana, Dynamic, Naada Brahma) for the uninitiated. He gave seekers what they had heard about and had come to expect. But he made even these forms of meditation playful and fun to do. He wanted them to be aware of the entire body during meditation while dancing, swaying, walking, and humming. However, for the initiated, he said, "One cannot *do* meditation. One has to *be* in meditation."

Zen uses *koans* and *haikus* to get the message across. A common haiku says, "If you are chopping wood, chop wood." Do whatever you do in the moment with total focus and attention. That is true meditation, or dhyana, as Patanjali meant.

However, the image of the Buddha sitting in Padmasana has become so ingrained in the minds of most students of Indian spirituality that it becomes a posture to be attained and maintained for as long as possible to achieve whatever they are seeking.

So what is this deeper meaning of meditation? "Dhyana" is "being in a state of mindfulness and awareness." This can be reached only when a certain discipline (*niyam*) and way of life have been achieved. This is achieved by purifying the body and mind through *pratyahara*, asanas, and pranayama. Having purified the body and mind, the path is now open for one to rise higher and seek the answer to the eternal question, "Who am I?" Having obtained the answer to this question through Advaita, Zen, or some other teaching, and having fully understood and accepted it, one has reached the state of awareness, or dhyana. It is the awareness of "I am That." One then remains in this state until one is ready for samadhi.

So dhyana is awareness of the Truth, "I am That," and living moment to moment with that awareness. This is also called mindfulness in Zen.

Meditation as a technique is merely a physical action resulting in futility. To "do" meditation is an action and therefore requires physical effort, the effort of sitting in a certain posture with eyes closed and without moving for a certain period of time. Meditation is taught and done with the help of many aids like verbalization (chants, mantras), visualization (focusing on an image or a candle), or *malas*. My own experience showed me that the focus remains mainly on the correct use of these aids rather than the meditation itself. What happens when one completes "doing" this meditation? Has it created any awareness or taken you to a higher plane? Most of the time, the only awareness it creates is that of physical pain in the joints and whether the stipulated time for "doing" meditation is over or not. Those who are able to sit for long periods without much agony do so primarily because of their excellent physical condition, similar to maintaining any asana for a long time.

None of the Advaita masters, such as Adi Shankaracharya, Ramana Maharshi, Nisargadatta Maharaj, Osho, or Ramesh, talked about the need for meditation as a means to spiritual growth. Nor does meditation feature in Zen. Zen talks about mindful sitting, mindful walking, and mindful eating; in other words, every action and every moment is to be done mindfully, that is, with dhyana.

So when I finally realized the eternal Truth of "I am That," the agony and misery of trying to "do meditation" finally dropped and was replaced by dhyana, a state of bliss from moment to moment all the time.

The simple truth is that one cannot *do* meditation. One has to *be* in meditation all the time.

Full moon meditation

Full moon meditation has become an inherent and important part of my spiritual journey and practice. It has become particularly more regular and interesting in the last few years as I travel the world as part of my ongoing spiritual journey. The very first full moon meditation I experienced was at Bodh Gaya in 2000, on the terrace of the Root Institute guest house. I will share two of the more recent experiences here. But first, what is full moon meditation?

Every full moon occurs when the sun shines the brightest in the night. Yes, this appears to be a paradox, but it is true, and therein lies the significance of full moon meditation. As we all learned in school, the moon has no light of its own. It is the sunlight reflecting off the moon's surface that we call moonlight. This moonlight changes from total darkness on a new moon day to full brightness on a full moon day, as the moon goes through the different phases with respect to its relative position to the sun. So the Creator, in His myriad magical ways, has given us this wonderful gift of light even in the darkness of night. We think the sun has set and darkness descends on us. But, lo and behold, it comes back on the opposite side, reflecting its light through the moon. Even on a new moon day, our experience tells us that we will start seeing the crescent of light from the next day, giving us hope and something to look forward to. This play of the sun and the moon is extremely symbolic and totally reflective of our own lives as we go through the ups and downs. There is never any reason to give up hope, because we know the sun is shining even when it is dark.

There is another aspect of the moon and its phases that has a very important impact on the human body. Again, from our science lessons, we are familiar with the fact that the phases of the moon give rise to high and low tides. The human body is made up of almost seventy percent water, and the brain alone has a relatively larger percentage of water. This water in our body is subject to the same gravitational pull from the moon as the oceans, which manifests in the form of mood swings and various health-related issues. There are many folklores, fairy tales, and even personal anecdotes of strange things happening on new moon and full moon days. Some may be true, some may be mere imagination. But there is a valid basis for it.

In my workshops and meditation sessions, which are predominantly attended by women, it is very easy to quickly determine the impact of the moon's phases on a woman's menstrual cycle, and if she is lactating, the impact on the flow of milk from her breasts. Many women who keep a diary of their monthly cycle also correlate it with the lunar calendar and find a very interesting relationship between the two. Men are quick to claim they do not have to go through any of this "womanly" stuff. But that is not entirely true. It manifests in men differently, through their mood swings and energy levels, especially sexual energy. I have noticed this myself and also challenged many men to maintain a diary to establish this correlation. They are all surprised when they see the results. Men have "periods" too!

So, if the moon has such a profound impact on the human body and wellbeing, what could be better than harnessing this wonderful energy on a full moon day, trying to remove the blockages that clog our energy channels, and synchronizing ourselves with the discipline and regularity of the moon's phases? The moon, like everything in Nature, works like clockwork: never late, never behind schedule, no sick day, no excuses. There is no reason why we, who are also gifts of Nature, should be any different. Meditating in the full glory of the moonlight, absorbing the moon rays full of cool, soothing energy, allowing them to melt away all the darkness within ourselves, is one of the most powerful practices in spirituality.

In many tribal and traditional cultures, there are numerous rituals that take place on full moon days. In the world of Tantra, Shiva performs his *tandava* on a full moon day to woo Shakti, and the ecstasy of the male and female energies coming together helps them transcend this mundane world to the highest level of existence. Some of us have already experienced the sensual pleasure of a simple walk in the forest, or by a shimmering lake, or on the beach on a full moon day, and reveled in it for hours later.

Each of the twelve full moons (sometimes thirteen) correlates with one of the zodiac signs, and the significance of each may vary for individuals, depending on their zodiac sign and the moon sign. On October 28, 2012, I was in Vilnius, and it was the Scorpio full moon day, and we organized a full moon meditation. Full moon meditation is ideally done outdoors, basking under the moonlight. But it was chilly at that time of the year, so we had to be indoors in a beautiful tea house with tatami mats, cushions, and lots of hot tea of all kinds. If it is tolerably chilly, I organize a bonfire. Only if it is unbearable do we hold the meditation indoors. Nevertheless, the benefits are the same, whether inside or outside. There were fifteen of us that night.

I start with a healing circle, holding hands and giving thanks. We share deep hugs all around and then sit comfortably on the floor, warm and cozy. I start with a short talk on full moon meditation. This being the Scorpio full moon, I talk about the Warrior and the Disciple, urging the fighting spirit within us to come through and accept the leadership and guidance of our teacher or guru and surrender ourselves as disciples, totally and unconditionally, just as the moon surrenders itself to the gravitational pull of the sun and then shines in its radiant light every full moon day. The guru never lets his disciple down.

I chime the gong by my side to start the quiet period. Lights are dimmed; there is only candlelight. Everyone is now visualizing the beautiful moon shining bright outside and drawing its energy within themselves. The energy permeates every part of the body, as we draw it in through the Sahasara Chakra and see it flow down the spine, touching each chakra, and then back again to the top, forming a full circle. We let it wander a little longer on the Anahata Chakra, where it energizes our heart, and we feel it bursting with love and compassion. We feel the pull in our hara and lower chakras as our energies align with the pull of the moon. We experience a sense of upliftment as we try to reach out to the moon shining brightly in all its glory. A sense of calmness descends upon us, a smile flutters on our lips, and we want to stay in this reverie forever. But I strike the gong again. We look around and see smiles everywhere.

We now take a piece of paper and write an affirmation on it, something we want to share with the Universe. We gather around a small fire set up in the middle of the room. Each of us, one by one, offers the affirmation to the fire and lets the Universe take care of it. We again hold hands and sit quietly for a few minutes. It is bliss. We do another round of energy healing, this time keeping the affirmation in our attention. We close with another healing circle and lots of hugs all around. There is complete silence. No one wants to say a word.

After the full moon meditation in Vilnius, one of the women in her mid-twenties came up to me and hugged me tightly, tears in her eyes. She confided that she had not had her monthly cycle since she was eighteen. She said that now, after the meditation, she felt this surge of energy inside her, as if she were rising like a balloon. She had never experienced anything like it. I asked her to continue the meditation and the ritual every full moon. Four months later, she called me up on Skype, crying, barely able to talk. She finally calmed down, and with a huge smile on her face, informed me that she had just had her period last week after eight years! She was Juliya.

A few years ago, I led a group of twelve people for full moon meditation at the Sun Temple in Konark, Orissa. No location on Earth could perhaps be more appropriate for full moon meditation than the Sun Temple. The symbolism is just awesome. However, for our group, the logistics were a bit of a challenge. The temple is open from dawn to 8 PM each day; no one is allowed to stay after that. The Universe was with us; we managed to convince the guards to allow our bunch of crazy meditators to stay after the crowds had dispersed. We had packed some snacks and flasks of hot lemon and ginger tea, and brought our mats and blankets. We did not need any candles; the beautiful moon would be our guide.

We sat on a porch under this beautiful banyan tree on the North side of the temple. We got a small fire going in the center as we gathered around it. The ritual followed the same pattern as described above, except it was more drawn out. This was the Capricorn full moon. It was about grounding and being with Mother Earth, with our self firmly planted there, as we gazed at the moon in the beautiful infinite sky. It was cool, but nice and cozy under our blankets. The energy was amazing and enough to keep us all warm. The warm yellow glow of the rising moon belied the cool energy it emanated, as it gradually bathed the entire Sun Temple in its radiance. This was irony at its peak. The Sun God was being bathed in its own light and energy through this luminous celestial body, slowly rising in the sky. It was almost as if the moon was reciprocating the sun's gift of light. There could be no bigger tribute or offering to the Sun God. It was a full circle. We stayed till midnight, enjoying the eerie silence all around. No one wanted to leave. By now, the blankets were not enough to ward off the chill. Slowly, we gathered ourselves and walked back in meditative silence. This was the most powerful full moon meditation I have participated in.

Spiritual Nutrition: Sattvic Aahaar

As one progresses on the spiritual plane and reaches higher levels of consciousness, many hardened practices and habits drop off naturally. The chakras open up, energy starts moving more vigorously, and the body-mind-spirit synchronicity starts to take firm shape. In order for it to continue its momentum and take us to still higher levels, the body needs *aahaar*, and it has to be as sattvic as the rest of our being has started to become.

Sattvic aahaar is food made with loving care and awareness, from the freshest, purest ingredients, without the use of any animal products. Each morsel has to be accepted and consumed with full awareness, recognizing and relishing the taste of each ingredient used in the preparation. Sattvic aahaar is ideally eaten with hands, so that one can enjoy the food using all our five senses, including the not-so-obvious one of hearing. Yes, hearing the sound of food. As a Zen koan says, "When you are chopping vegetables, chop vegetables." The next time you are cutting, chopping, and cooking, or near someone who is doing that, or when you are eating, become fully aware of the experience of hearing. You will be surprised to notice the various sounds of peeling, cutting, sizzling, boiling, simmering, and finally, chewing and biting. They form as much a part of our sensory experience of food as aroma, taste, touch, and sight.

Mantras

Like most people, the first mantra that came to me was the *Gayatri Mantra.* It was many years later that Pandit Tigunait revealed the impotency of the Gayatri Mantra in modern times. This mantra is blared out over loudspeakers and devices at home and outside, devoid of any potency. The same is true of the *Mahamrityunjaya Mantra.* The rishis knew this would happen, so they added secret keys to unlock the core mantra, which were to be revealed only to the true sadhak. This became true of many other common mantras. These keys are hidden in the scriptures but cannot be deciphered by the average reader. Only a guru can reveal them to an adept seeker.

Mantras are the backbone of spirituality, and I learned this rapidly along my journey. They opened doors and paved the path for me to walk on, and became a *kavach* to protect and bless me. They became my internal singing melody. I wake up with Aum and go to sleep with Aum. In between, the chanting happens spontaneously any number of times. Mantras are sound vibrations tuned to the highest frequencies and have the power to connect your spirit to the higher Self. At the initial stage, I started with *Vaikhari,* then moved subconsciously to *Upamshu,* and finally, the chanting became *Mansika.* There is actually a fourth stage where one does not even realize that chanting is happening. This brings you closer to the Samadhi or Turiya stage. When mantras are resonating internally, I have often seen them turn into visions.

Mantras are written in Sanskrit as well as in Pali because they were the medium through which the mantras were revealed to the sages. However, the vibration within the mantras can be felt only if they are pronounced correctly. Even a slight flaw in the intonation will change the vibration. I find that non-Indians are incapable of chanting mantras correctly. Mantras are as ingrained in Indian culture as *dal* and *roti.* As a student of Sanskrit, I learned to recite various words and names repeatedly until my teacher, Mr. Shukla, was satisfied with the pronunciation. At that time, it seemed very tedious. It was only years later that I would realize the importance of that foundation. Swami Purnachaitanya is that rare non-Indian I have heard who has mastered the art and science of mantras. But then, his mother is of Indian origin, and that possibly explains his command over Sanskrit. If you would like to listen to a pure, perfect, chaste recitation of mantras and shlokas, listen to Swami Purnachaitanya.

An important milestone for a serious seeker is to get deeksha from his guru. This is the spiritual initiation into the guru's lineage with the help of a mantra that is held sacred between the guru and the seeker. I got my first deeksha from Osho in my dream, along with Shaktipat. Then I got my next deeksha from Maharishi Mahesh Yogi through a TM teacher. My last deeksha was from Babaji in Sonoma Ashram. The deeksha mantra connects you to your guru, who then assumes responsibility for your spiritual progress and development. Receiving it is one of the most sacred rituals in Indian spirituality and is generally not granted to everyone.

Another lesser-known mantra ritual is that of receiving the *Ishta Mantra* from your Ishta Guru, if you have one. I received mine from Shiva. I have created a *mantra mala* (a sequence of mantras) of my favorite and powerful mantras, which I chant all the time. Mantra chanting is also a very powerful remedy for insomnia.

Mantras are different from shlokas, though they are interchangeable at times. Mantras have to be activated to unleash their power. Shlokas are recitations from scriptures, but still need to be recited with a pure heart and mind. During fire ceremonies, I use a combination of mantras and shlokas to invoke the various powers and make offerings. I chant mantras when I am under stress or feel threatened in any way. I also chant them every time I am on a flight, before takeoff. There are also various *stutis* that are longer than mantras and shlokas. While mantras and shlokas are always in Sanskrit, stutis can be in various dialects. The most common one is the Hanuman Chalisa. It has never failed me.

Malas

A mala (a string of prayer beads) is a useful aid in the chanting of mantras. Chanting a mantra a specified number of times (e.g., 125,000 times) to activate its inherent potency is called *purushacharan* and is said to grant the sadhak certain spiritual powers, known as *siddhis*. Obtaining siddhis on the spiritual path is considered a very important milestone. These are extremely rare, and once obtained, they are not to be trifled with. Usually, the guru who guided you during the purushacharan will guide you further after you obtain the siddhi. There are numerous interesting stories and anecdotes surrounding this, and some of the most interesting ones I heard and read were about Swami Rama. Pandit Tigunait had a very humorous way of describing these events, some of which were witnessed by him.

I received my first *rudraksha mala* during the International Yog Festival in 2002 and the next one during the Kailash Mansarovar *Yatra,* both from Swami Chidanand of Parmarth Niketan. Since then, I have received many rudraksha malas and *tulsi* malas. One of the most cherished ones is the *siddha mala,* consisting of fourteen rudraksha beads, ranging from one to fourteen *mukhi,* including the *Gauri Shankar.* A mala received from the guru as part of the deeksha is very powerful. The rudraksha mala is intricately connected with mantras, with its 108 beads to facilitate the chanting 108 times. It is a divine number enshrined in the Indian scriptures. There are 108 mudras, 108 names for Krishna, and 108 names for Shakti. While there is a certain significance attached to this number, I have never allowed myself to become too dogmatic about it. For me, the free-flowing process of life itself has provided the momentum for my spiritual journey.

Mudras

A mudra is a hand gesture using the fingertips and the thumb. As mentioned earlier, there are 108 different mudras. When combined with certain mantras, they help move the energy in a certain direction in the body. Each mudra has a specific purpose and activates that particular energy center in the physical and subtle body. The hand and the fingertips are a powerhouse of healing. The *nadis* in the fingertips get activated when a mudra is formed, and each nadi is connected to an organ of the body in the physical realm and with a chakra in the *Sukshma* body.

I discovered the power of mudras first during the Reiki initiations, and as I progressed on the journey, mudras appeared frequently in Hatha Yog and various scriptures. Krishna has referred to the *Jnana Mudra* as the highest. The Buddha is typically depicted in the *Abhaya Mudra* or *Dhyana Mudra*. Yeshua used mudras for healing purposes, no doubt learned during his stay in India and Tibet during his formative years.

Mudras are an essential part of the Indian psyche. The next time you watch an Indian classical dance program, watch the dancer forming different mudras.

Mandalas

A *mandala* is a sacred geometrical symbol or image. Just as in mathematical geometry, in spirituality, too, a mandala follows certain rules of drawing that are not always easy to understand, unless you are very evolved.

At the macro level, the entire Universe is a mandala, and at the micro level, each cell is a mandala. The Sri Yantra is considered the highest mandala in Indian spirituality, depicting the Mother Goddess Herself.

Mandalas are common across both Hinduism and Buddhism, and therefore, it is not surprising that they overlap. Mandalas have great significance in Tantra, and, in fact, originated as part of Tantra philosophy.

The Borobudur Temple in Indonesia is the largest mandala ever built. It takes the form of a Sri Yantra with its layers and gates. One of the most powerful spiritual experiences I had was to be on top of this mandala at sunrise, slowly being bathed in the golden light.

The *chakravyuh* in which *Abhimanyu* was trapped was a mandala with specific ways for getting in as well as out. Hindus draw mandalas in the form of *rangolis* at their entrance doors to attract the right energy. Tibetan monks draw sand mandalas and sweep them away as soon as they have completed them. The act symbolizes the ephemeral nature of this manifestation. I remember watching one such mandala being created on an entire floor in the Met Museum in New York, by eight monks, two on each side. After painstakingly crouching on the floor for hours to draw it, they immediately swept it away as soon as the last grain of sand was in place. The onlookers watched aghast.

Mandalas also cross paths with sacred numerology. In Indian scriptures, numbers play an important role, with certain numbers being designated as cosmic numbers, such as three, seven, and eleven. What science has discovered in the last two hundred years by way of numbers and calculations was revealed to the sages thousands of years ago. Seven is one of the most powerful numbers in cosmology and has appeared in my life regularly.

In my interactions with various Shaktis, I noticed that many of them had a natural inclination to draw mandalas, with the form taking shape from the depths of their Anahata. After all, it is their abode! Migle and Ramona are two of the most powerful Shaktis in my life who have brought mandalas to life through their sketches, drawings, paintings, and henna.

Minerals

Minerals are as ancient and alive as Mother Earth Herself, having solidified from the rivers of fire flowing at the time of Creation. Being part of the earth element (one of the five), they are all about grounding and come in an infinite array of colors and textures. Some of these minerals in the form of hard stones carry vibrations from millions of years, perhaps even from the origin of life itself. These vibrations resonate with our own vibrations, which, in turn, are determined by the Sun, the Moon, and the planets, as charted in our horoscope. So, a direct correlation can be established between stones that emanate a certain vibration and one's own chakras and nadis, which, as we know, are energy centers and channels that carry these vibrations.

Astrologers can identify the stones that are appropriate for each person, based on their horoscope. By using or wearing these stones on the body, one is able to enhance positive energy and diminish negative energy. My various Jyotish readings recommended that I wear a yellow sapphire, an emerald, a coral, and a pearl. I have been doing this ever since. Whether or not their efficacy is happenstance or superstition is all a matter of belief, and I do believe that these stones have helped me to be in this state of Satchidananda.

Some of these stones, called crystals, are used for healing as well. I have been using them right from the time of my Reiki initiation. One of my favorite crystals is the lapis lazuli, a vibrant turquoise blue stone found only in the Afghanistan mountains. It is "my crystal." I have walked by a crystal shop many times and have been pulled inside by the strong vibrations emanating from a lapis somewhere inside, waiting to be adopted by me.

There are innumerable ways for a healer to use crystals in their healing practice. Bhaisahab used a quartz pendulum to seek an answer to a question that was puzzling him. Each time he went with the answer he got from the swinging pendulum, he found that it was correct. The power of the thought, the purity of the intention, and the immense nature of the vibrations all around us transcend the doubts and skepticism of all those seeking proof in the laboratory. As I tell my other brother, Dilip Bhaiya, who is of a closed, scientific mind, "the entire Universe is one big laboratory" and has been functioning nonstop as such. It does not work on the basis of "testing a sample." However, just to allay the skeptical nature of scientific minds, quantum mechanics and physics came into being in the last hundred years to confirm everything that the sages, astrologers, and healers have known for thousands of years. The proof of the pudding is in the eating, not in the recipe.

Meditation, mantras, malas, mudras, mandalas, and minerals are all links that create the chain we hold on to while moving forward in this Satsang of One.

Family Constellation

Among the various healing and spiritual modalities that came my way was Family Constellation. It is a therapy introduced by Bert Hellinger for healing multi-generational issues and traumas within a family. Dorota from Krakow introduced me to this very powerful therapy that helped me personally to deal with issues related to my father, brother, and certain other family members. I then included it in my repertoire and started helping others. Once again, it was a Shakti who took me down this path.

Spirituality on Call
(Take a Pill, Call Me in the Morning)

Spirituality is now a billion-dollar worldwide business.

Yes, you read it right. Spirituality, the essence of the human spirit, has become a business, and one of the fastest-growing at that. It comes in all colors and shades, all shapes and sizes, all languages, and all media formats, and now even the AI version. The Buddha, Patanjali, Shankaracharya, Dr. Usui, and all the other original teachers must be wondering what the knowledge gathered by them after years of penance and contemplation has come to. What does Buddhism today have to do with the Buddha's four noble truths? What does Hot Yog have to do with Patanjali's Ashtanga Yog? What do theta, karuna, and other forms of Reiki have to do with the traditional Reiki of the Medicine Buddha, as rediscovered by Dr. Usui? What has happened to the four *maths* set up by Shankaracharya to propagate and protect the Advaita teaching of Hinduism?

Well, let me give you the answer to that. It is the emergence of the so-called New Age and the Zombir World. I have never really understood what it is that is "new" about this age. To me, it means "capitalism meets spirituality." Religion had become the biggest business in the world long ago, and now spirituality is fast following in its footsteps. Just as God was kidnapped by religious zealots and made into a universal currency of organized religion, the human spirit (the backbone of what separates spirituality from religion) is at the same risk of being hijacked and sucked dry by the New Age teachers and Zombie adherents. Organized religion was more blatant and direct, and worked directly on the most potent of human fears. Death, sin, karma, heaven, hell, reincarnation, and purgatory were all used to instill the sense of fear in the human mind, such that instead of living their present life in full glory, humans were more concerned about the next life and the previous life. New Age teachers are far more opaque, talk mumbo jumbo, and prey primarily on the second main insecurity of the human mind—health. Zombies are only interested in getting thirty second answers to everything in life without having to lift their finger except to push a button on their device.

The human being suffers from four main insecurities: death, health, relationships, and money. Religion deals primarily with the fear of death, but touches upon the other three as well, and promises succor if certain rites and rituals, accompanied by lots of donations, are undertaken. Spirituality is more subtle and deals primarily with health but also touches upon relationships. The human mind, riddled with fear, becomes very gullible and vulnerable, and falls easy prey to anyone who offers solutions. Human psychology is such that the value of something is determined in terms of what it costs, rather than the other way around. This creates obvious and immediate barriers and classes, and runs totally contrary to the very concept of spirituality. When money becomes a factor for "acquiring" spirituality, it also sets up expectations and, therefore, disappointments.

Today, it is possible to attend workshops, seminars, and courses, all for a price. You take your pick with what suits your calendar and your budget. However, these "events" rarely touch upon the depth of Indian scriptures and the vast knowledge of the Indian sages and masters. The wonderful tradition of Indian oral wisdom rarely comes through. There is more of a sense of instant gratification and quick answers than in-depth sharing and dissemination of sacred knowledge and experience.

Instant coffee culture

The land of the rishis, masters, and realized souls, known and unknown, has descended to the land of self-styled godmen. India has now become famous for these godmen with sprawling campuses. They peddle the shallowest of the shallow versions of spirituality to the gullible masses who assume they will attain nirvana. These godmen are raking in millions through the sales of products, with their brand firmly etched on the labels. It is the great mall of spirituality. One such yogi from North India has become a multibillionaire promoting his brand of products, which have reached every corner of India and have given the multinationals a run for their money.

These godmen survive and thrive due to the patronage of those in power who can clear obstacles for their spirituality business. A few years ago, a jamboree was held on the banks of the Yamuna in Delhi by a godman from South India, damaging the already fragile ecosystem. The authorities turned a blind eye. Land has been grabbed from adjoining areas in Coimbatore by another godman. Again, the matter was hushed. Environmental laws and concerns have been flouted in Rishikesh, right in the lap of Maa Ganga, by yet another godman in the area, who hosts VIPS regularly at his ashram. They come here to see the giant Shiva statue in the middle of the Ganga. Black magic and sleight of hand have been used to deceive people by yet another such person in South India. Sexual abuse has taken place in so-called ashrams all over India, all in the name of religion and spirituality.

These godmen have become the modern era cult figures who offer false hopes to the gullible, innocent masses. Television and the media have opened up avenues for more of these spiritual teachers to reach out to even more people. When you watch these gatherings of thousands, neatly segregated into men and women, it could well be an election rally. A diluted version of Hinduism is on offer so as to reach the vast majority who are looking for instant gratification and validation outside of the religious ramparts of society, but who will never have the opportunity to find their own spirituality within themselves. These peddlers of spirituality and those who flock to them serve each other mutually, and no matter how many stampedes and tragedies take place at these gatherings, it is a nonstop activity across the length and breadth of India.

At one of these gatherings in Puttaparthi, my shoes got stolen, and when I complained to the organizers on site, I was admonished for having come in shoes! At yet another gathering in Rishikesh, my companions and I were jostled by the organizers' staff because there was a VIP approaching. Every famous temple in India has a deeply entrenched VIP culture and entry ticket system. If you are a well-heeled devotee, you get preference for the darshan of the resident deity over the common folks who may be waiting for hours. One such temple in South India requires online registration, which needs to be done days in advance. This temple is considered the richest in India and rivals the Vatican. The only difference is that instead of various arts, sculptures, books, and the like, this temple is sitting on piles and piles of gold, besides the hoard of precious metal, jewels, and cash. At another gathering in a famous ashram in Mount Abu known for its women adherents, I was asked, "What is God?" I replied, "I am That," and I was kicked out. Almost the same thing happened in a beautiful and very famous mosque in Muscat, Oman, and at the Vatican. My happening at the Jagannath Puri Temple is related elsewhere in the book.

Chalk and cheese

Each of these episodes and observations has reinforced the stark difference between religion, cultism, and spirituality. Paganism that prevailed in the West in the Middle Ages, which was totally secular and nondenominational, was trampled upon by the later idol worshippers of the Church. Paganism, along with various native cultures and belief systems, has existed since time immemorial in different parts of the world and has been the reflection of spirituality, until it was gradually attacked and destroyed by the Church and its followers.

I have attended shamanic and other Incan and Mayan ceremonies in Guatemala and Peru. Since these cultures are primarily matriarchal, the ceremonies are typically led and conducted by women. The power of the Shakti could not be more apparent here, as it is not confined to the Indian culture alone. No major religion, except Hinduism to some extent, has allowed women to be ordained as a priest, an imam, or a lama. Such is the stranglehold of men over religion. Some of the so-called gatekeepers of their religion even go to the extent of ostracizing women for menstruating, totally oblivious to the Divinity that oozes out during the lunar cycle that is considered *Somras* in Tantra. Spirituality, on the other hand, is predominantly a dimension for women. Over ninety percent of attendees at my workshops are women. And why not? Spirituality starts and ends with the Mother Goddess, and men run scared from this highly potent energy.

Of course, there are exceptions, and many. But they are not advertised and, for the most part, are known only by word of mouth and accessible to only a handful of serious seekers. They have their humble ashrams and abodes tucked away remotely in the mountains and forests. If your heart is pure and your yearning is sincere, you will find them. Sometimes, these realized souls are right in the middle of where we live, such as Nisargadatta, Ramesh, and many Tantra masters who live right in our neighborhood but below the radar, or Om Swami, who inconspicuously maintains his presence at the foothills of Himachal Pradesh.

Superficial seeking

The New Age fad is likely to cause more damage than good. It gives false hopes and raises unrealistic expectations. Any kind of esoteric practice that is rooted in some sort of mysticism can only be imbibed by personal experience and practice. While a teacher is necessary for guidance, that is all he can do—guide. He cannot "sell" anything since there can be no price attached to something so sacred and personal.

As far as the media talks are concerned, they are nothing more than "blah, blah, blah," the kind that can now be heard 24/7 on various TV channels. I meet and talk with some of the attendees of these talks, seminars, and workshops, and find that they go about their life in the same aggressive manner, devoid of even a ripple of awareness, flouting traffic rules as they head home, abusing people verbally, littering garbage all around, and heading to the nearest fast-food place to satisfy their pangs of hunger from the long sessions. At the same time, they start sharing their newly acquired knowledge with all and sundry as newly anointed experts on the subject matter. Osho rightly said, "It is very difficult to get through to most Indians; they think they know everything." Half knowledge is worse than ignorance. In Zen, "no mind" is the beginning and end of all seeking. In the final chapter of the Gita, Krishna exhorts Arjun (and thereby all readers) never to share the secret knowledge revealed in these verses with certain people (simply, people who are not ready, will not understand, or will not value).

My own experience has been exactly the same. People approach me wanting to be initiated into Reiki over a weekend or to be cured of something or the other. They always point to many others who promise this, and I politely ask them to go there.

Intuition, awareness, awakening, and consciousness come in an instant. But it takes years of penance, practice, and patience before that moment arises. In India, spirituality, like religion, is taking on the herd mentality, bordering on fad mania. Superficiality and shallowness surround it. A true sadhak never follows the crowd. He makes his own path and has his own experience.

Keeping the Sacred Tradition Alive

Indian spirituality is deeply rooted in the *ashram pranali,* which refers to the sacred relationship between the guru and the student. There is no solicitation or monetary exchange of any kind. At the end of the teaching, when the guru is satisfied that the student has learned what he came for, the guru will accept guru dakshina. It is an offering. It is not a price. Indian mythology and scriptures are replete with examples of a guru declining any guru dakshina for some reason or the other, or accepting it in kind, or accepting or extracting a promise to redeem it in the future. When it came to sharing their knowledge with the students, the guru made no compromises or exceptions. It did not matter what the student's background was or whether he could afford the teaching since there was nothing to afford. However, a guru was intuitive about whether a prospective student was worthy of his teaching, and he declined those whom he felt were otherwise.

There are still many ashrams and other institutions in India that religiously follow this tradition. Many individuals also do the same. This is the noble path. In the past hundred-odd years, Swami Muktananda, Swami Sivananda, Swami Chinmayananda, and a few others have kept this tradition alive. Spirituality cannot be a profession, business, trade, or a means of livelihood. Those who offer it on that basis are best avoided because their motivation can never be selfless service. It will always be dictated by monetary needs, no matter how good the teacher may be or how sacred the teaching may be. Offerings received by voluntary donations are far more satisfying for the true teacher than earnings from tickets to his talk, that too of different denominations, depending on how close you get to sit to him!

Ayurveda

A clean, healthy body is the temple where the spirit dwells. So affirmed the Indian rishis ages ago. Over two thousand years ago, Rishi Charaka compiled the *Charaka Samhita,* which became the foundation of the Ayurvedic medicine system in India. It details the medicinal use of herbs, plants, and barks found in abundance in the foothills, mountains, and forests of India. The tradition has continued to date and has become very popular in certain parts of the world outside India, especially in Russia and Eastern European countries.

The West is wedded to the toxic allopathic system offered by mercenary Big Pharma and their willing and ignorant dispensers, who are constantly brainwashed and manipulated with largesse of all kinds. Of course, this is all facilitated by the pliant regulatory authority. I grew up in a household where my father would call a *vaid* in case of illness, who would check the pulse, the tongue, the eyes, and the skin; ask about your bowel movements (constipation is a big indicator of problems); make a diagnosis; and give a prescription, along with dietary dos and don'ts. When I was afflicted with various childhood illnesses such as jaundice, chicken pox, typhoid, and mumps, I was completely on Ayurvedic treatment administered by our family vaid, Sharmaji.

My relationship with Rajah

So, it was not surprising when I found myself at Rajah Ayurveda Center in Kerala in 2002 for the first time and met Dr. Sreeraj. It was a short stay (more out of curiosity than any medical reason) and would be the first of my annual visits thereafter. I started spreading the word, mainly to my students, Shaktis, and others, during my workshops. Many of them ended up accompanying me or visiting on their own. Grudgingly, a few of my family members came as well. Ramona came with me in 2022 and was instantly captivated. She returned to Asheville, North Carolina, to become an Ayurvedic therapist and started working at Sohum, an Ayurvedic center.

Sohum was set up by Dr. Vasant Lad from Pune forty years ago, when Ayurveda was still unknown in the USA. It is still not mainstream, thanks to the restrictions imposed by the US Government, instigated by the medical establishment. Like many other Happenings on my journey, this too was a homecoming of sorts. I had visited Dr. Lad's center when he was in New Mexico many years ago, and now Ramona was treating clients at his clinic. We also set up an Ayurvedic treatment facility as part of the healing and spiritual center at The Sanctuary, where we live.

Rajah Ayurveda has been a balm for me in many ways. As soon as I arrive there, my energy shifts in the calmness that prevails and the warmth and support I get from all the doctors, therapists, and staff, who have now known me for over twenty years. I have never had any chronic medical issues, yet I feel healed, rested, and healthy, allowing me to move further along on my spiritual journey of One. In 2015, when I was at a low ebb, I came here with Juliya for ten days and felt instantly uplifted. In 2018, the Devi herself appeared here in the form of a golden deer and healed me from my head injury. In 2020, during the Covid pandemic, I came here with four of my family members. As per the protocol then, we were all tested upon arrival, and I was the only one to test positive. I was immediately isolated and moved to a local hospital. It was a false positive, but rules had to be followed. Dr. Sajeer took me under his wing. He was one of the most compassionate doctors I had met. I could not eat the hospital food, so arrangements were made for my meals to come from Rajah, thanks to Dr. Deepa, an angel in disguise.

Osho said that we need to worship our body; it is a temple in which the spirit resides. I have done that continuously along my journey.

Vipassana Demystified

In the early and middle stages of my journey of One, I wanted to experience all the known and unknown ways in which spirituality was being sought in the modern world. One of these was the ever-popular, ten-day Goenka Vipassana course offered all over the world. I had attended Osho's Vipassana Meditation already and wanted to experience what was different about Goenkaji's course. I attended the one in North Fork, California, with Ishwar Jijaji, my brother-in-law, who was a devout and regular follower.

Let me make it clear at the outset that I have never been a believer in any form of spirituality that imposes restrictions and confines the student to one of the most restrictive environments. Here, at the time of registration, you are asked whether you follow any other spiritual practice, and if you answer yes, you are required to leave that practice at the door before starting Vipassana, just like you leave your shoes outside before entering a place of worship. I was a Reiki Master and also followed the Medicine Buddha, who was a progenitor of the Buddha. I was also an Advaita and Zen student, a yogi, and a Tantra student. How do I leave all this at the door?

Let alone being a believer, I had not even wanted to try it out until then. Being similar to the Sudarshan kriya "breathing technique" of a godman in South India who offers it as a panacea for all ills, the idea of using a "technique" to learn spirituality of any kind simply did not resonate with me. On my long spiritual path of twenty-five plus years, which finally culminated at the feet of Osho and Ramesh, my search took me to many teachers and masters, many retreats and ashrams, many teachings and writings, and various traditions all over the world. But not once did I get drawn toward Goenka's Vipassana until then, well after my search was finally over and I was at peace with myself.

This is the way it was meant to be. I do not believe I would have gained or learned anything if I had taken up Vipassana as part of my search. It is confusing and convoluted, and gets increasingly so, as one progresses from day one to day ten. If I had not already got an insight into Advaita and Zen philosophies and understood them, I would have come out of the ten-day course as confused and as much a zombie as most students did, and do all over the world. This is reinforced by the fact that the percentage of those who return to the Vipassana course is less than five percent. To be fair, one could argue that it is because the majority of the students have "got it" the first time and do not need to return. I doubt!

This is not meant to be a critique of the Vipassana course. It is an attempt to help simplify a philosophy that has been made unnecessarily confusing by straying from the simplicity of the teachings of the Buddha to the dogmas of Buddhism. Buddhism has nothing to do with the Buddha, just as Christianity has nothing to do with Christ, or Islam with Prophet Mohammad, or Hinduism with Krishna. All the isms belong to the world of organized religions with their attendant dos and don'ts, precepts and rules, and concepts of sin and guilt, Heaven and Hell. Vipassana, at its simplest, was meant by the Buddha to be about learning and understanding awareness.

At a time when India was caught deep in the shackles of the *Puranic* interpretations of the Hindu way of life, as portrayed by the self-imposed keepers of morality and order, Gautam Buddha got his insight into the eternal question, "Who am I?" The insight was deep, yet very simple. Awareness and acceptance of existence and manifestation as it is. He had experienced it himself. When people around him asked him to share it with them, he had no words to describe what he had experienced. For the most part, he chose to remain silent. Occasionally, he would use examples and real-life incidents to explain his own experience. Those who understood this well enough became Zen teachers and masters, and moved to China and other places in the Far East. Those who did not understand the Buddha took it upon themselves to come up with interpretations and solidify them in writings and books. This then took the form of rules and precepts, which became the basis for

Buddhism. *Dhammapada* came into being, along with the Eightfold Path. Buddhism spread far and wide, and very soon overtook Zen in its popularity and following. Why? For the simple reason that the simple human mind is far more willing to accept the written word, especially words that are attributed to a Godhead or a renowned individual. The human mind is also constantly looking for ways and means to lead a meaningful, wholesome life as an antidote to the day-to-day misery that it experiences. So, if a set of rules is provided, it will readily accept them as gospel truth and start applying them in their daily life. This is the typical success story of any organized religion.

"Vipassana" means "to observe." Osho called it "to be a witness." Ramesh called it non-doership. This is the basis of Advaita as well as Zen teachings. Not to be involved or get attached to whatever may be happening. Just observe, and let it pass from moment to moment, as intended by Nature. Eckhart Tolle calls it the power of Now, or living in the present moment. To this extent, the Vipassana course starts on the right note. However, Goenka's use of a "technique" to get this point across is where it becomes a mechanical exercise and diverts from the Buddha's teachings.

The technique involves sitting for long hours, observing the sensations in the body. It starts with the breath (Goenka calls it respiration) in and around the nostrils, and as the course progresses, it moves to other parts of the body. It requires sitting in a particular posture for an hour at a stretch, multiple times each day. It is not conducive to creating the right environment for learning to take place. Combined with the requirement to adopt the five precepts (no killing, no stealing, no sexual conduct, no lies, and no intoxicants), segregation of men and women, silence, and frugal saatvik nourishment, his technique creates an environment far removed from the reality of daily life. For an uninitiated student, this is a very restrictive environment in which to absorb a very powerful teaching meant to be used in daily living. As a result, the typical student spends the first day or two more concerned with finding the right posture, figuring out the right number and mix of cushions, and generally looking for ways to mitigate the intense stress and pain that their body starts experiencing from hours of sitting cross-legged, trying to focus their mind, and "doing meditation." This environment is monastic in nature and is appropriate for those who are on the path to renouncing their worldly life and adopting the life of a monk living in a monastery. It is not appropriate for those who wish to continue with their worldly life and yet have a yearning for the answer to the eternal question, "Who am I?"

Goenka's introduction of *shila*, samadhi, and *panya* as part of the Noble Eightfold Path on the second day only adds to the confusion. Various concepts from Buddhism, such as reincarnation, the art of dying, salvation, renunciation, and liberation, are introduced gradually. Monks and nuns are introduced for reasons unknown, even though the Goenkas themselves are a married couple. By day nine, it was mental torture with repetitions all the time. You are expected to start feeling some sensations in your body by now, which I did not. The only sensation I was feeling was hunger pangs and a strong desire to get out of there.

This is the typical response of most students who have completed the ten-day course and are asked about their experience: "They *make you do* meditation all day long for ten days!"

The spirit does not need techniques. It needs to be free from all shackles to soar high like a bird, to find its own nesting spot.

A Zen master once said, "Of the hundred people who take the tentative first steps on the Path, only ten continue. Of the ten that continue, only one makes it to the end." To that extent, the New Age teachers are playing an admirable role in getting people to take the first tentative steps. However, a real sadhak needs to wait for the right guru to provide them with better guidance to continue further.

Stop Playing God

In the beginning, there was the Word, The Sound, Aum, *Naada Brahma*.
This was the potential energy that got activated.
It became a vibration and took the form of kinetic energy.
Prana was unleashed.
This became Ether or *Akash*, the First Element.
Ether gave rise to Air or *Vayu*, the Second Element.
Air gave rise to Fire or *Agni*, the Third Element.
Agni gave rise to Water or *Jal*, the Fourth Element.
Water gave rise to Earth or *Bhu*, the Fifth Element.

The entire manifestation is an illusion, or maya.
These Five Elements are perceptions of this illusion.
Air, Fire, Water, and Earth give it an illusion of physicality.
Ether, which is prana, glues them all together.
Every living cell has these Five Elements.
All of these Five Elements are interconnected.
One cannot be without the others.

Everything is perfect.
Everything came out of perfection.
If you take away something from it, what remains is perfect.
If you add something to it, what becomes is perfect.
Nature is perfect.

The human being is also a product of Nature, but is saddled with intellect and ego.
And therein lies the imperfection.
Mankind has used this imperfection within himself to play God.
Stop playing God.
Let Nature take its course.

India was the cradle of civilization.
India was a land of riches.

India was a land of wisdom.

India was where the *saptarishis* were sent down by Brahma.

These seven sages carried with them all the knowledge contained within the entire Universe, the entire manifestation, without a beginning and without an end.

The Five Elements form the basis of this knowledge and wisdom.

This is the oral tradition of India.

It made its way to every corner of the world.

The Five Elements helped disseminate this knowledge, just as the Ganga and its tributaries spread water all over India.

It spread because it was simple.

It was simple because it was intuitive.

It was intuitive because it could be experienced.

It did not require proof and laboratory tests.

The falling of every leaf from every branch of every tree is predestined.

The leaf can only flutter until it falls.

Fluttering is its nature, its *swabhav*.

We can only act and behave according to our nature.

Be that individual self with full awareness of your connection with Nature.

Be the change that you want to see happen.

Do not try to change the course of Nature.

Stop playing God.

|| Aham Brahman Asmi ||

|| No Space, No Time, No Self
Just Tantra ||

9.
|| Tantra ||
|| Sacred Sexuality ||

All Life is *Sambhog.*
All Sambhog is Tantra.
All Tantra is Life.
Life, Sambhog, and Tantra are inseparable.

I was initiated into Tantra through the Shaktipat I received from Osho. At the same time, I was also guided to his *Book of Secrets* based upon *Vigyan Bhairav Tantra*, perhaps the oldest of the Tantra texts still available. Parvati, sitting in Shiva's lap, with His *lingam* firmly planted in Her yoni, listens intently as He reveals the secrets of Tantra. Although Parvati is the Mother Goddess who has manifested the entire Universe through Her powers, during this Teaching, She is nothing more than Shiva's student, learning the secret, esoteric lessons about life itself from Him. In the process, She has totally surrendered Herself to Him. It is the acme of the Cosmic Dance, and one of the many paradoxes in Indian spirituality. This Sambhog between them has been symbolized in the form of the *Shivaling,* which is worshipped all over India, yet most of the so-called Shiva adherents are oblivious to the significance and symbolism of this idol. This is perhaps the prime example of how religion and spirituality have divorced from each other.

Decline of Tantra

Tantra is the mother and the source of all other scriptures and, therefore, precedes them. It originated and was revealed verbally; only much later did it get transcribed. Even then, just a fraction of this vast body of sacred and secret knowledge is available to us today. On one of my visits to Babaji in Benares, he sent me to meet Bettina Baumer, an Austrian woman who lives for the most part in Benares and the foothills of the Himalayas, north of Rishikesh. She is as mysterious and secretive as the Tantra knowledge she imparts to her students, who are primarily non-Indians. She has, perhaps, the most comprehensive collection of Tantra texts found today anywhere in the world. My own collection of Tantra texts is primarily from Motilal Banarsidas, publisher and bookseller of Indian spirituality books, and Vak, a small, intimate bookstore in Pondicherry.

Tantra has long disappeared or gone underground, away from the mainstream of Indian spirituality. It now exists primarily in the arcane texts and teachings of the Tibetan branch of Tantra. Unfortunately, it is also misrepresented by a handful of misguided and ignorant Westerners who hijacked it from Osho to serve their shallow needs and offer it as a sexual panacea to the West. Consequently, the Osho ashram quickly declined, turning into a farce.

Osho was the last true, realized Tantra master of the modern world. His books and his discourses are a testament to this. When I moved to Pune in 2003, I lived close to the Osho ashram and would go there almost daily to participate in one or more of the meditations. As the vibes started to turn negative, I would do it just once a year on my birthday. On one such visit, I was denied entry. Upon inquiry, I was informed by a pompous, self-appointed caretaker of the ashram that the reason for this was that I was pimping for Ramesh Balsekar to attract the Osho followers to his fold. Instead of being shocked or angry, I had a hearty laugh and realized this was Osho himself advising me to stop going there, and I never entered the ashram again. It was no longer even called an ashram but a resort. Yet another Happening.

Due to the sexual undertones in Tantric teachings and the Shiva Parvati connection, Tantra began to be misunderstood and misused. Very soon, it was treated as a taboo subject and went underground. The few masters and teachers adept in Tantra kept the knowledge to themselves and imparted it very selectively. The texts started to disappear. The West went along on its own mission of misrepresenting Tantra, and very soon, it became synonymous with free sex. It was sad to see this ancient, sacred body of wisdom degraded by certain misguided and ignorant individuals.

Unfortunately, the depth of Tantra has morphed into the shallowness of religion, with ignorant rituals and practices perpetuated by the greedy and power-hungry keepers of society. This has created a hoard of wealth for temples across India, and if it were to be all added up, it would rival that of the Vatican. A classic case of the blind leading the blind toward untold riches, which will be used to pave the way to Heaven with gold, glorified by all religions.

But Tantra is life itself, and life cannot be extinguished in this manner. Tantra is also about polarity and the opposites, the male and female, Shiva and Shakti. It does not support any happening that does not follow the Laws of Nature. There can be no creation or manifestation without Tantra. The polarity exists within each human being, the male and female within the self. There is the concept of *Ardhanareeswara* in Tantra, where Shiva and Parvati share the same physical body. The law of polarity governs everything in Nature, and that helps maintain the natural order of things.

Propagation of Tantra

Pandit Rajmani Tigunait of the Himalayan Institute is perhaps the last living Tantra master today. Thanks to his mastery over this ancient body of wisdom, gathered over the course of double doctorates in Sanskrit and decades of teaching and practicing, he has created a vast storehouse of Tantric knowledge and its practical use. I have attended some of the most profound discourses conducted by him, supplemented by powerful havans. Sanskrit is alive in him, and Sanskrit and Tantra go hand in hand.

The Aghor tradition, rooted in Benares and originating with Baba Keenaram, is still alive in the by-lanes of its place of origin and continues to be kindled by Babaji of Aghor Foundation and Sonoma Ashram. The Lalitadevi Temple on the banks of the Ganga vibrates with the ancient Tantra energy. Devi worship is an inherent part of Tantra, and it is vibrantly thriving in the hills of Himachal Pradesh, Uttarakhand, and Manipur, albeit in a form that appears mainstream but is, in fact, rooted in Tantra. Similarly, Shiva worship is also prevalent in many parts of India. This is evident from the unbridled attraction of women adherents to Shiva, including my mother. The fifty-one Shakti Peeths and fourteen *Jyotirlingas* spread across India are all highly esoteric and potent Tantric sites.

Tantra is alive in various Indian arts, namely dance, music, sculpture, painting, literature, and poetry, which depict the *navarasa*. The classical dance forms of Bharat Natyam and Kathak are replete with references to and depictions of Shiva Parvati and Radha Krishna, two of the most famous amorous deity couples in the Indian psyche. M.F. Hussain depicted them in his paintings, because of which he was banished from his own country by religious zealots. Tantra is alive in the *thali*, a type of Indian meal common all over the country, where people relish it by using their fingers, which they lick clean after they are done! Tantra is alive in the love poems, *ghazals*, and *shayari* in various languages, where love and alcohol are both used as metaphors for intoxication.

Tantra: The Essence of Life

Tantra is life itself. Each breath is the *So Hum* mantra, the beej mantra for this manifestation. In Sanskrit, "Tantra" means to bring together; in the spiritual context, it is the bringing together of the two basic forces of the Universe, the polarity of male and female. Shiva and Shakti have become symbols of these forces. There can be no life without Tantra. The lingam sitting inside the yoni, forming the Shivaling, is the most potent symbol of this union. At a deeper level, the Kundalini rising from the Muladhara to meet its consort in the Ajna is the ecstatic orgasm experienced by certain yogis and yoginis. This is the microcosm of the Cosmic Orgasm that created this world. Sexual orgasm pales in significance when compared to the Kundalini rising and mating in the Ajna. It requires the grace of a guru to experience this. It is also akin to the orgasm between the mother and the child during birth. A natural childbirth is a highly spiritual experience that most modern women are deprived of. Breastfeeding, a rarity in the modern world, is another Tantric experience between mother and child. A huge price is paid later in life by the child who is deprived of these natural orgasmic experiences.

Somras is the nectar of life, and those who have access to this from the yoni and lingam are bathed in Devi's blessings. Performing havans, *homas*, and *yagnas* with the chanting of appropriate mantras and the offering of appropriate ingredients is another way to connect with the Tantra energy. A pure mind, a clean and healthy body, and a sattvic lifestyle are essential to follow the Tantric way of living.

Tantric meditation for couples, leading to Cosmic Orgasm, is one of the most powerful meditations one can experience under the guidance of an adept. The space and the body are adorned with flowers, fragrance, lamps, and music, thereby creating a Temple of Love. Sensuality flows like water. Time stands still. Sometimes, this takes place outdoors with a fire lit on a moonless night. Sometimes, it happens in a cemetery, for the very advanced adepts. Menstruation is a Tantra celebration.

The Shiva tandava is an inherent part of Tantra where Shiva is performing the Cosmic Dance and goes into raptures of ecstasy and trance. Listening to the music (during Tantric meditation) is enough to send me into the same trance. Shivoham itself is Tantra. For the initiated, Tantra is the highest form of spirituality. For the uninitiated, it can spell disaster.

Living Tantra

Tantra is vast and infinite. It is the manifestation itself. This is evident from the array of texts on Tantra, known and unknown, perished and existing. The brevity of this chapter is symbolic: Tantra is complex if you read the texts; Tantra is simple if you live it.

I was blessed to have experienced all the orgasms with Maa: a natural birth, an extended period of breastfeeding, and Sambhog with her energy at the end. This is the ultimate bond between a mother and her child.

I was born a Tantra child and have lived my life as a Tantra Yogi.

||Aum Namah Shivaya||

|| The Whole World is My Oyster
Vasudhaiva Kutumbakam ||

10.
|| Wanderings ||
|| Hanuman ||

In the epic *Ramayana*, Hanuman was sent by *Rama* to get the *sanjivani* herb from the Himalayas to help save *Laxman's* life. In the present epic, the Mother Goddess sent Shiva all over the globe to help rescue Shaktis.

One Hundred Thirty Countries and Counting

I hiked up a mountain in the Alps with Flurina in the summer of 1994. It was my first hike in the Alps, just outside of Zurich, where she lived. We had been invited for breakfast that Saturday morning by her parents at 8 AM. When we arrived at 8:05 AM, they had already started their breakfast. I could feel the quiet, chilly welcome. Flurina had earlier mentioned her father's disciplined approach to life in contrast to her mother, who seemed more laid back. He got up and left before we finished breakfast. In my early years of wandering around the globe, this was my first experience of Swiss discipline. It led me to understand why you could set your watches to the Swiss train schedule. Coming from a land where the concept of time is floating, and you are not expected to apologize if you show up late, this was an eye-opening experience. Among the many Western sensibilities I imbibed on my journey, this one has stayed with me throughout.

Later in the afternoon, I showed Flurina's mother how to cook dal, rice, and Indian *sabji*. This marked the first of many upcoming demos and workshops, showcasing the cooking skills I honed while living alone for extended periods in New York, London, and Luxembourg.

When I first arrived in New York in 1982 and set up home, I was homesick for *Maa ka khana* (Mother's cooking) that I had been brought up on, and I would write to her to ask for her recipes. Her *sabudana khichadi* was one of my favorites. In the 1980s, options for vegetarians to eat outside were few. Anjali came armed with a handwritten collection of her mother's recipes, a testament to her mother's culinary skills. To Anjali's credit, she hated cooking, but she still managed to cook up a proper Indian meal almost every day.

My natal chart had indicated I would be traveling the world. Babuji had inculcated a strong passion for travel in all of us children, which continued throughout our lives. Geography was my favorite subject in school, and I topped the class. But I took this enthusiasm much further by traveling to 130 countries to date. And plans for seven more major ones are in the pipeline. There are many more, of course, but I am not aiming to cover all the 193 member countries of the United Nations. Besides China, the other six are all Arab and Islamic countries that I am barred from or made very difficult to travel as a US citizen, thanks to the animosity of Uncle Sam. When I obtained my US passport in 1989, it was for the sole purpose of making travel easy, with no visa requirements to many countries. Gradually, the US passport became an albatross around my neck. Many people have obtained a second passport to get around country-specific restrictions, and I may do that, just so that I may visit Iran, Iraq, Syria, Libya, Algeria, and Lebanon, before the US and its stooge destroys them all. These countries are among the richest repositories of Islamic architecture and culture, rooted in Sufi philosophy, an important strand of my spiritual journey.

Spiritual and Physical Journeys Merge

My spiritual journey of One is inextricably interwoven with my physical journey around the globe. Some of the most profound experiences and Happenings have occurred in some remote corners of the world, and most of the Shaktis in my life have appeared on these journeys. My spiritual experiences have been shaped to a large extent by what I observed and experienced in these lands of myriad cultures, languages, and food.

Except for having to be rescued and airlifted from Lake Mansarovar during the Kailash Mansarovar Yatra, or having to abandon the Leh and Ladakh trip due to altitude sickness, I have never felt endangered or vulnerable anywhere. Getting lost and finding my way back, managing a vegetarian meal in the land of carnivores, and communicating in an alien language (before the advent of Google) were all challenging yet learning experiences. Anjali and I were hiking in the hills in France and got lost. An elderly man appeared from nowhere, and he walked us down to where we needed to go. He didn't speak English, and we spoke no French. In Bogota, Colombia, a land as carnivorous as it comes, and before the advent of all the apps to guide you, I walked for miles before I found a hole-in-the-wall dining place run by native women cooking vegetarian meals. Again, we couldn't communicate in each other's languages. It did not matter. The aromas and the smiles on their faces were enough for me to enjoy one of the most sattvic meals I have ever had.

The Italian Connection

I was with Francesca in Milan. On a Saturday morning, her mother had invited us for lunch at her sprawling house just outside the city. It was a beautiful, sunny spring day, and the table had been set outdoors. There were six of us. The dishes kept coming and coming until there was not an inch of space left on the table. The wine kept flowing. Francesca's Mama was one of those typical Italian mamas who loved to feed their children, just like Indian mamas. She knew we were vegetarians, and there was not a shred of meat on the table. This is when my love for Italian cuisine took a serious turn. I used to think that only Indian cuisine could boast of an array of dishes until I discovered Italian cooking. I do believe that

Francesca appeared in my life briefly, just so I could experience that divine afternoon.

The Romanian Connection

I did my first workshop in Bucharest, Romania, guided and supported by Anina. The venue was a vegan restaurant run by a woman who was a chain-smoker. The workshop was a sellout, comprising a group of twenty, where I met an elderly gentleman of Russian descent who had brought a very interesting machine for me to see later. It was a Quantum Resonance Diagnostic machine for checking a person's complete health status, which works with just the insertion of a finger, displaying various diagnostic parameters on the screen. Although they were in Russian, he was able to print the report for me in English. Finding it to be pretty accurate, I was amazed but not surprised. The Russians are well ahead in these matters, where they have been able to combine the intuitiveness of Nature with technology. I was to discover and learn more about this device on my trip to Russia a couple of years later.

In Bucharest, I discovered myriad teahouses that served varieties of teas from all over the world. The word for tea in Romanian and other Slavic languages is very similar to "*chai*" in Hindi. One teahouse was named Ganesha Tea House, and another, Ramayana. They both had motifs and decorations from Indian scriptures.

I soon discovered the connection between Romania and India, built up over centuries. The nomadic Banjara tribe of Rajasthan had started to migrate to the West about three to four hundred years ago, settling in various parts of Europe, but primarily in Romania and Bulgaria. They brought their language, attire, music, dance, food, and other traits to these foreign lands. Some of these aspects of their cultural and geographical identity made their way into the Romanian lifestyle, but unfortunately, the Banjaras themselves never fully assimilated into the local socioeconomic fabric. They came to be called the Romas. They are still considered outcasts and live in a ghetto-like environment. Every time I passed by them on the street, they would quietly stare at me, wondering whether I was one of them, but none of them ever reached out to talk.

Years later, in 2020, to be specific, a Romanian Shakti with Roma roots was to come into my life to complete the Shiva Shakti circle. As I have mentioned earlier, life is not linear but a random series of Happenings, all connected. I had been to Romania six times, including Brasov, the hometown of Ramona, but I did not meet her there. And after she came into my life, I have not visited Romania.

The Hungarian Happening

In Budapest, Hungary, I came close to being the victim of a gay assault in one of the iconic bathhouses, which are also known for gay encounters since the genders are segregated, unlike in Japan. I managed to extract myself from one of the most unpleasant situations I found myself in. It brought back memories of being sexually assaulted when I was a preteen by a male family member. And it had happened a couple of times. I was barely thirteen and did not know what was happening to me. I have since forgiven the perpetrator but not forgotten the episodes.

The World Becomes My Teacher

I quickly learned that it was a small world and it was round. No geography lessons in school could have ever taught me this. It was my own observation and discovery. Nothing I learned in school, college, and the corporate world comes close to what I have absorbed like a sponge as a traveler. Despite all the traveling, one's wanderlust is never satiated; there is always the desire for another experience around the corner.

In the earlier part of my travels, during my marriage, Anjali was a willing travel partner and enjoyed traveling as much as I did. However, it was clear that what she was absorbing was different from what I was absorbing. She wanted more of the conventional tourist experience, whereas it was just the opposite for me. Gradually, we went our own ways. Other Shaktis joined me on my journey to different lands, but mostly, it was a solitary journey of One.

The Islamic Connection

It is an unfortunate thing that most people around the world, especially in the West, look down upon Islamic culture and history, equating it only with violence. It is anything but. I would not have discovered the richness and depth of this culture had I not been to Türkiye, Morocco, Tunisia, Oman, the UAE, Brunei, Indonesia, Malaysia, Jordan, Palestine, and Azerbaijan.

The connection and impact of Islamic culture on India has been immense through Urdu, one of the richest and most lyrical languages in the world. It is the language of lovers, just as Sanskrit is the language of the gods. The connection may be subtle but direct. You see the Higher Self Itself in your lover. It is known as *ibadat* in Urdu, which is the origin of Sufism. Watching the whirling dervishes transports you into a world of trance, with nothing but ibadat. I had seen these dervishes perform in the Islamic world so often that the Osho Whirling Meditation started to make sense. Much as the Hindu zealots in India may wish or proscribe, the Hindu Muslim cultures are inextricably woven in the Indian ethos based upon harmony, amity and tolerance.

The awe-inspiring museums on Islamic culture in Istanbul, Muscat, Abu Dhabi, Kuala Lumpur, and Jakarta are a testament to the immense knowledge, wisdom, and depth of art, dance, music, and cuisine, which is the thread that connects these countries. One of my most memorable visits was to Yemen, rife with civil war and violence. Nevertheless, I managed to see some of the most stunning honeycomb tower houses made of sand centuries ago.

The conservative women in these countries cover themselves from head to toe, with just a slit to see the world through. One look at those doe eyes is enough to suggest the immense beauty hiding behind the veil. Movies such as *Mere Mehboob* have been made in India, glorifying this veiled look. Verses and odes have been written on this by Rumi, Kahlil Gibran, Amir Khusro, Faiz, Mirza Ghalib, and numerous other poets and writers, no less mesmerizing than Saundarya Lahiri by Adi Sankaracharya. The Muslim apsaras were no less divine or beautiful than the Hindu devis.

The Balkan Foothold

My next series of workshops was in Zagreb, Croatia, one of the seven ex-Yugoslavian countries. When I was growing up, India, Yugoslavia, and Egypt formed a triumvirate of nonaligned nations, and Nehru, Tito, and Nasser were their heads, respectively. Babuji took a deep interest in world affairs and would have loved to visit Yugoslavia or what remained of it. He did not get to do it, but here I was, thinking of him as I arrived in Belgrade, Serbia, and then Zagreb. In Zagreb, I met Marina, an English schoolteacher trapped in a dysfunctional education system. We hit it off, and very soon, we were conducting workshops in Zagreb, and Belgrade in Serbia.

The full moon meditation in Belgrade was held outdoors and was a sellout. In keeping with the common factor in all my workshops, it was Shaktis all around. Among them was a face that kept staring at me. She was Ivana, a TV journalist and a flamenco dancer. It was uncanny. On my next visit to Belgrade, she recorded a talk given by me on "The Concept of Time" and featured it on Belgrade TV. This was followed by an invitation to speak at the Belgrade Congress of Life Sciences in the company of highly evolved individuals from this part of the world. It was an experience unlike any other.

Alexandra, yet another Shakti in Belgrade, who was the owner of Radost, a wonderful vegetarian restaurant, organized a cooking workshop, where twenty-five people showed up. The chef, Maja, was my lifeline. She belonged to the ISKCON movement. This is also where I met Nela, a Russian transplant living in Belgrade. She ended up visiting the Osho ashram and KARE Ayurvedic center outside Pune. I introduced her to Kumari, who had moved to Pune from the USA. They hit it off. Kumari was a gift of solace for me during a time I was at my lowest. She was an accomplished artist, and like all creative people, full of love and compassion.

I had established a foothold in the Balkan countries, ravaged by war and yearning for a healing salve. The Shaktis of this land found themselves trapped in an economic mire and male chauvinism. There was no sign of Shiva anywhere. They grabbed any opportunity they saw to interact with Shiva. Zagreb, Belgrade, Sarajevo, Ljubljana, Mostar, Tirana, Podgorica, Skopje, and Pristina were part of my itinerary. In Mostar, Bosnia, a small, ancient city famous for its unsupported stone bridge, I met two sisters who insisted I teach them yog.

Besides Romania, I found an uncanny connection with India in the Balkan countries as well. Names of people over there had their roots in Hindi and Sanskrit. Most of the Shaktis who crisscrossed my path during my wanderings had a connection with Mother India in some way or the other. When they met me, I was just the *sutradhar* validating their connection.

Maja ended up in Mathura and Vrindavan; Marina, in Benares; Maria, in Benares and Pondicherry; Nela, in Pondicherry; Juliya, in Uttarakhand and Nepal; Migle, in Benares; Igle, in Rajasthan; Laura and her daughter, Akvila, both accomplished photographers, in Agra and Konark; Margo, in Shekhawati; Sandra, all over India; and Maria, in Puttaparthi. Akvila attended a family wedding with me in Pune, and, happily for her, it turned out to be a photographer's delight. She had gotten her hands and feet painted with henna for the ceremony. Her mother wore the saree effortlessly, as did many other Shaktis.

Marina introduced me to the Bosnia pyramid near Sarajevo. It is the largest natural pyramid of its kind in the world. Like all pyramids, natural or manmade, it is a vortex of energy so strong that it is impossible not to get drawn into it as you approach it. This is one of many vortexes and energy centers spread around the globe. They are similar to the chakras and nadis in the human body. Mother Earth has created Her own healing centers, prepared for the times when Her children plunder and rape Her. India is, of course, the largest vortex on the face of the Earth.

Russia Happens (along with Other Countries)

Russia was among the top countries on my list of places I wanted to visit. In Pune, I lived close to the Iyengar Yoga Institute, which was visited by many yoginis from Russia regularly. Some stayed with me, and the connection deepened. This is how I met Olga from Saint Petersburg.

As a US citizen, I needed a visa to visit Russia, and their strict rules specified that I could get the visa only from the country of my citizenship. My sixth sense prodded me to go to the Russian Consulate in Bombay, where I pleaded my case. I need not have worried too much. Unlike the Americans, the Russians love Indians, even if they hold an American passport! I left the passport at the consulate for endorsement and booked my ticket. But until the morning of the flight, there was no sign of the visa being issued. I again camped at the consulate with my bags. The same gentleman who had accepted my application appeared with my passport and grinned at me. I grinned back in gratitude and rushed to the airport, in possession of my coveted visa. My dream of watching Swan Lake at the Bolshoi Theatre in Moscow had come true.

Russia is a cold country with warm people. I was to experience the same in other ex-Soviet countries: Moldova, Georgia, Belarus, Estonia, Latvia, Lithuania, Armenia, Azerbaijan, Uzbekistan, Kazakhstan, and Kyrgyzstan. The ex-communist countries of Poland, Bulgaria, Slovakia, and the Czech Republic were equally warm and embracing. They were all part of the West, but the decadence and shallowness of Western Europe and North America had not touched them fully as yet. I have had some of the most lively and rich arts and culture experiences in these countries. Upon entering a cab, the driver would spontaneously put on a Raj Kapoor song.

Shaktis from the Catholic World

I met Dorota in Quito, Ecuador, while watching a folk-art performance in the square. She clicked my picture, took my number, and sent it to me a few days later. She was a research scientist from Krakow, Poland, and a regular exchange professor at Pune University! The coincidences were endless, yet none were random. She was a Shakti in hiding under the veneer of science, which she propagated, and was also a devout Catholic, like most Poles. We had endless discussions and arguments on religion vs spirituality. Nevertheless, the connection was deep. I ended up cooking an Indian breakfast for her in Krakow, while she drove me around Poland, including visiting an ayurvedic center that turned out to be a disaster. They were serving non vegetarian meals.

A few years later, I would have a similar spirituality vs religion disagreement with Kathy from Atlanta, who was visiting Bombay for work. I have always felt that the purpose of these Shaktis to become part of my journey was for them to get a taste of Shaivya and compare it to the false image of Jesus they were carrying with them. Whether it made a dent in their belief system is irrelevant. I was just the observer and sutradhar watching this incessant Leela happening all around me.

India Resonates Everywhere

As I traveled around the globe sharing my spiritual experiences while facilitating workshops, satsangs, and individual sessions, I came across people who are far removed from India physically, yet connected subconsciously with Indian culture and philosophy. Most of the Shaktis who joined me on my journey had an Indian connection of some kind and a yearning for India. This is a testimony to the depth and spread of ancient Indian wisdom in all parts of the world. My first profound experience of this was at The Philosophy School in Boston, mentioned earlier. As I traversed parts of Eastern Europe, the reverberations from the Indian ethos became palpable.

One such congruency happened one summer on the beautiful island of Iž, off the coast of Croatia. I was facilitating a weeklong workshop on "Self-Discovery and Self-Healing," where I met Nježna and her lovely young daughter, Camille. Camille was a swimming champion of sorts in her hometown, and when she heard that I did not know swimming, she insisted on teaching me. She was eleven years old! Her mother attended portions of my workshop, and we also did some personal sessions. She ended up sharing with me the piece she had written recently on "Economics and Spirituality."

When I read her article on integrating spirituality into economics, I was spellbound for two reasons: First, she was echoing a lot of what I had fought for when I was in the corporate world. Second, and more importantly, many of the concepts cited by her while referring to spirituality were similar to those found in Indian scriptures; for instance, her theory on the whole and its parts is similar to this well-known mantra:

Aum Puurnnam-Adah Puurnnam-Idam
Puurnnaat-Purnnam-Udacyate |

Puurnnashya Puurnnam-Aadaaya Puurnnam-Eva-Avashissyate ||

Aum Shaantih Shaantih Shaantih ||

Aum, That is Full, This also is Full,
From Fullness comes that Fullness |

Taking Fullness from Fullness, Fullness Indeed Remains ||

Aum Peace, Peace, Peace ||

It is also revealing that many of the Western philosophers cited by her are on the same wavelength as Indian philosophers and masters when they talk about Universalism (Advaita), Human Nature (*Prakriti* or Swabhav), Self-actualization (Karma), Parents as Godheads (Shiva and Shakti), and the role of the State (*Chanakya Niti*). Maslow's famous pyramid of human needs corresponds to the chakras and their role in human evolution.

Nježna's discussion of the importance of knowing the right kind of food and environment for each of us corresponds to the concept of the three doshas in Ayurveda.

All of these references could not have been mere coincidences, nor could my meeting with Nježna itself. There are no coincidences in life because there are none in the Universe. Everything is a Happening as part of a well-orchestrated plan. As I experience these Happenings every day in my life, I continue to be grateful for this beautiful life and all the abundance that comes with it.

Latin America, Portugal, and Spain

The Latin American world of South America and Central America was the least connected with India for reasons that had more to do with geography and distance than anything else. Yet the Mayan and Incan cultures flourished there for centuries, with pagan and other practices very similar to those found in India. Except for yog that has become the binding force around the globe (despite objections and discouragement from the Church), I have always felt a sense of aloofness here. Besides, I found it pretty disturbing that cows are slaughtered in these lands ruthlessly for consumption.

Portugal colonized a part of India, which established a connection of sorts between the two countries. I could find samosas on the streets of Lisbon.

On my various trips to Spain, I got fascinated by flamenco, the Spanish gypsy form of music and dance, performed by dancers attired in colorful dresses, tapping their shoes to the vibrant rhythms. By then, I had already become a connoisseur of sorts of Indian classical music and dance, with one of the forms, *Kathak*, being my favorite. The similarities between Kathak and flamenco were uncanny. I have attended flamenco performances in various parts of the world and soon realized that it was an improvised version of Kathak itself, combined with folk music and singing brought to Spain by the Banjaras, some of whom had settled there.

Asia

The vibe in the East is totally different. There is a homogeneity across all the countries of Asia in terms of values, food, culture, family life, attire, and many other aspects, as well as a strong religious connectivity through Buddhism and Hinduism. Angkor Wat in Cambodia, the nomenclature in Thailand, the rituals in Bali, the large Indian diaspora in Singapore and Malaysia, and the geographical proximity of these countries to India are all indicators of the strong Indian presence in Asia.

Japan is the cradle of Zen and Reiki, my spiritual underpinnings. China is the birthplace of Confucius, whose philosophy is a blend of Advaita and the Buddha's purest teachings. I have yet to explore the spiritual richness of China in depth. In its physical vastness is hidden as much wisdom as that of India, or perhaps more. This lifetime may not be enough for this purpose.

I find it very interesting that I have yet to interact with any Shakti from the East. Perhaps there is a reason behind it, one that is inexplicably woven into my destiny. It is no coincidence that Ramona feels a strong connection with Asia. She and I feel very attracted to Thailand and Vietnam, and to some extent, Malaysia and Cambodia. Singapore has become too sterile with its Western-style development to offer any spiritual richness. However, that is where I met Harmeet, though she was of Indian origin and one of those rare Indian women who are not stuck-up.

The Ayurvedic Connection

I visited the home of Abdul Salam, the owner of Rajah Ayurveda in Kerala, surrounded by his vast collection of vintage cars. His family has a royal lineage dating back to the British era, as well as various business interests. He started the Rajah Ayurveda centers across Kerala, initially as a philanthropic effort to offer treatment to the poor. Now, it draws people from all over the world.

I first came here in 2002 with some of my family members, including my teenage nephew Ankur, who is no longer with us. I have been coming regularly since then. I brought Ramona here in 2022, and she got hooked on Ayurveda. She returned to Asheville to become an Ayurvedic therapist, adding to her vast repertoire of healing and bodywork skills, such as Reiki, Thai massage, reflexology, hypnotherapy, Tarot, Theta Healing, and ear candling. She joined Sohum in Asheville, run by Dr. Vasant Lad, the renowned Ayurvedic doctor from Pune.

Ramona and I started bringing groups of people to Rajah from the USA and Europe for *panchakarma* retreats, which have become very popular. Abdul Salam is one of the most unassuming, simple, and humble human beings I have ever met, and Rajah Ayurveda has been one of the most precious Happenings along my journey. The team of doctors headed by Dr. Sreeraj, namely Dr. Jayarajan, Dr. Achuthan, Dr. Deepa, Dr. Thushara, and Dr. Soni, all the therapists, and the entire staff comprise the single best team of health workers I have met anywhere, full of humility, compassion, love, and care.

Meeting the Mystics

In May 1995, Tanja (from Denmark) and I were in Manali, Himachal Pradesh. One day, as we were walking along the village roads, we reached Naggar and spotted this beautiful, red-colored traditional Himachal house. As we approached it, I saw the sign "Roerich Art Gallery." At that point in my life, though I was not yet firmly entrenched in my spiritual path, the sight of that name immediately took me back to my early days of Bertrand Russell, Annie Besant, Gurdjieff, and theosophy, when Roerich had made inroads into my budding spiritual self. The seeds were planted early to sprout later in my life. As a Russian mystic, philosopher, writer, and painter, Roerich, along with Gurdjieff, touched my Anahata at a very tender age. Little did I know that one day, I would be standing in front of his house, that too in India, where he passed away.

Gurdjieff was a favorite of Osho, and that is how I first discovered him and took him seriously. A mystic (just like Osho) of Russian-Armenian descent, he traveled the East and the West, and spread the Fourth Way, his philosophy of life. He crossed paths with Sufism in Georgia and Turkey, and the entire connection between Osho, Gurdjieff, and Sufism came alive when I moved to Pune. I discovered the local Gurdjieff Group, one of many, spread around the world, and started participating in the meetings. His "movements" became the means to understand his philosophy. As coincidences would have it, when I moved to Asheville, North Carolina, in 2017, a Gurdjieff Group was waiting for me there.

In April 2021, Ramona and I were hibernating at Myrtle Beach, South Carolina, during Covid. One day, we lost our bearings while driving and found ourselves at the entrance of Meher Spiritual Center. I could not believe my eyes. Meher Baba had been in my consciousness for a while, ever since I lived in Pune for a few years. Pune was his home for many years, and many places there were associated with his life. But the Happening did not happen in my backyard. It happened in Myrtle Beach, of all places, in a very regressive and backward state deep in the Bible belt.

The center was an oasis of peace and serenity, nestled by a lake. I entered the cottage where Meher Baba lived for a while, and sat silently in the chair opposite his chair. His presence was palpable, and my sitting there was not an accident. It was the manifestation of my consciousness in yet another Happening along my journey.

When I mentioned this Happening to my dear friend JJ (Sir Cowasji Jehangir), he immediately pointed me to the various landmarks in Pune associated with Meher Baba. And they were all within a stone's throw of where I lived for fourteen years as JJ's neighbor, without realizing it. My wanderings were continuing to unfold in tandem with my spiritual path.

Shaman Experiences

In June 2024, I was sitting in Sandra's garden by Lake Atitlan in Guatemala, surrounded by native Mayan women from the nearby villages, some of whom were pregnant. Many of them had walked miles to come to this regular gathering for the spiritual enrichment of pregnant women and their unborn children. Everyone was gathered around a fire made from fallen tree branches. The lead female shaman invoked the spirits with the help of vapor emitting from raw tobacco and cacao leaves gathered from the forests. I was the only Shiva in this circle of empowered Shaktis connecting with Nature and praying for the soon- to-be-born child in the womb of its mother. The energy was intoxicating. We went around the fire and ended up hugging each other. This was my first shaman experience after a brief one I had in Alaska many years ago. That too was with a female shaman.

I got exposed to the ancient Mayan culture firsthand as I traveled across Central America, with Guatemala being the focal point. This was a continuum of the amazing Shiva Shakti connection in which I am the only Shiva surrounded by Shaktis dancing around me. I ended up doing a cooking workshop at a local vegan café, with Sandra by my side.

Sandra is a wounded Shakti from El Salvador. I first met her in Antigua, a very atmospheric, colonial, cobblestoned town in Guatemala. I was there with Anjali on our trip to the seven sisters of Central America: Belize, Guatemala, Honduras, El Salvador, Panama, Nicaragua, and Costa Rica. Sandra owned a café with an Indian touch. We connected instantly. Many years later, we reconnected, and I invited her to India, where she belonged. I then visited her in San Salvador, and she drove me around her country. She inherited this rustic cottage by the lake from her partner of many years and converted it painstakingly into a perfect abode for a Shakti.

Parsi Connection Continues

As mentioned earlier, I could not visit an agiary in Mumbai, but I did manage to visit the Ateshgah in Baku, Azerbaijan, in September 2018.

The Ateshgah is a very unique place that has an eternal flame burning. It is sacred to the Zoroastrians (Parsis), Hindus, and Sikhs. Similar to discovering Meher Baba in South Carolina, this was another instance of discovering something of interest in a faraway land.

Most of the places I have wandered around have had a deep purpose and meaning beyond being just a tourist destination. I have always been a seeker and never a tourist. It was not for nothing that my natal chart had alluded to wanderings throughout my life.

Rumi and Turkey

I have visited Turkey numerous times and ignoring its violent historical past, I have been awestruck with its rich tapestry of Islam culture and Sufism. After Osho's whirling dervish meditation, I discovered and experienced live this trance inducing display of ibadat in Istanbul train station. Thereafter I became a regular at any Mevlana event any time I was in Turkey. Mevlana was the first name of Rumi and the whirling dervishes were the connection with him. This then took me to Konya, where Rumi lived and died. His mausoleum there is an essential pilgrimage for any Sufi adherent.

Dargahs

Dargahs are the equivalent of shaktipeeths in the sufi tradition. Unlike shaktipeeths that do not emanate the energy of a human person but are cosmic in nature, dargahs are the burial places of a mystic that roamed the earth, and the mystic's energy has been imbibed in that place for eternity. One can experience the palpable energy in these dargahs just as in the shaktipeeths, provided they have not been taken over by the religious zealots. Besides the Rumi dargah in Konya, Turkey, some of the most powerful dargahs on my journey have been the Haji Ali in Bombay, Salim Chisthi in Fatehpur Sikri, Moinuddin Chisthi in Ajmer and a relatively unknown Darvesh Dargah near Pune, all in India. The Darvesh Dargah is known for the levitating 90 kilo stone that can be lifted by a circle of men (no women) using their one finger tip. It is a Happening I have experienced.

Shekhawati: A Journey Back to the Roots

Ever since I can remember, I have been ashamed to be a Marwari. The hypocrisy, double standards, flagrant display of wealth, dowry system, *sati* tradition, and emphasis on appearances that symbolize this community were all anathema to me. It took me a long time to distinguish a Marwari from a Rajasthani. I was enchanted by the vibrant and colorful Rajasthani landscape, the Rajput tradition, the awesome architecture, beautiful costumes, *sufiyana* folk music, earthy cuisine, and hardy people. I fell in love with Rajasthan, but was still ashamed to be a Marwari. Marwaris and Shekhawati seemed like an aberration in the Rajasthan landscape. But it was not long before my roots beckoned me to come and discover Shekhawati and the real Marwari.

Having grown up and lived among family, friends, neighbors, and acquaintances with names like Nevatia, Roongta, Poddar, Todi, Ruia, Makharia, Singhania, Kanodia, Goenka, Kedia, Dalmia, Parasrampuria, Dharnidharka, Jhunjhunwala, Khetan, Khemka, and many more, I was curious to see where these had originated. Most importantly, I was keen to discover my own roots, those of a Darooka.

Jasrapur (a tiny, remote hamlet on the periphery of the Rajasthan desert), along with Karachi, was a place that was mentioned regularly by Babuji, Maa, and all the elders in the extended Darooka family. There were many stories about Jasrapur narrated by Maa, and most recently by my cousin Omprakash Bhaisahab and Ramriksha Bhabhi. It seemed a distant place in a distant era. I decided to find it.

In December 2006, I journeyed through Shekhawati, starting with Nawalgarh, one of the larger towns in the area. I had heard from friends and travel books about Apani Dhani, an eco-resort in Nawalgarh, run by Ramesh Jangid. It also happened to be the ancestral hometown of Neelu's family.

Apani Dhani is sublime and as beautiful as it is reputed to be. It is a perfect example of how life can be sustained and lived beautifully, even amid scarcity all around. The huts are made of *khus* (vetiver grass), which grows wild all over. The walls are reinforced and disinfected with a mix of local mud and *gobar*, painstakingly painted over every year by local artisans with vegetable, flower, and mineral dyes. All the required energy comes from solar heating. Vegetables, fruits, and grains are grown by organic farming in the backyard, sufficient to meet the needs of the resort. Cows and goats provide milk. Vermiculture and recycling take care of all the waste. Rainwater is stored and provides a third of the total requirement. Ramesh and his assistant Kishan (Krishna, but pronounced "Kishan," as in my brother's case) are walking encyclopedias of Shekhawati. I could not have asked for a better place to start my journey.

In Nawalgarh, the highlights were the Anandilal Podar Haveli (which has been converted into a museum managed by Kantikumar Podar of Podar House on Marine Drive [Mumbai], and Podar Mills) and the Morarka Haveli (which has been lovingly restored by Kamal Morarka, a family friend, whose bungalows we stayed in, in Lonavala and Ooty on our trips there). I also came across the Dharnidharka Road and a set of Dharnidharka havelis owned by Neelu's ancestors.

For those who are not familiar with Shekhawati architecture, suffice to say that havelis were huge mansions built by the rich merchants of the region for their large joint families, and their hallmark was that all the walls (inside and outside) were painted with murals in vibrant, natural colors. Religion and mythology were the main themes of these murals. But increasingly, many of the artistes borrowed from the English Raj and depicted their lifestyles, mostly sight unseen.

With Apani Dhani as our base, Kishan helped me discover Dunlod (full of Goenkas), Parasrampura (home of the Parasrampurias, of course), and the *chhatri* of Raja Shardul Singh (after whom the region is named Shekhawati), Singhana (home of the Singhanias), Sethon ka Ramgarh

(Ramgarh of the *seths*), and Fatehpur. The highlight of Singhana was Sone ki Dukan (Shop of Gold), which is the name for the *pedhi* in the Podar Haveli there. The walls and ceiling of the pedhi are painted in gold, hence the name.

I had one of the many interesting interactions with the local people in Singhana. As I was walking down the street, I heard someone calling me in chaste English. I turned around to see that it was a shopkeeper. For the next thirty minutes, the shopkeeper, Major Sharma (retd), gave me a wonderful insight into life in Singhana and Shekhawati, and the strong connection of Shekhawati with the Indian Army. This was a revelation.

The next stop was Sethon ka Ramgarh, home of Vishnu Jijaji's family and Tarachand Ghanshyamdas, whose pedhi in Kalbadevi, Mumbai, is where Kunjbehari Krishnakumar (my father's business firm) dwelt for so many years. Without any prior intimation or knowledge, Kishan and I went around inquiring about the Poddar havelis. By now, it was very clear to me that in all the towns and villages, it was very easy to ask your way around, especially if you spoke Marwari. Boy, was I glad to still know a smattering of Marwari! Almost everyone knew the famous seths and their havelis. We found the Tarachand Ghanshyamdas pedhi. After further effort, we found Vinod Chajjad, their munimji (accountant). After I introduced myself and expressed my interest in seeing the Poddar havelis, he was quite lukewarm. I decided to call my sister right then and there, and after she spoke with him, his entire attitude changed 180 degrees! He gave me a personal guided tour of all the various havelis belonging to the extended Poddar family, including Chachaji (my brother-in-law's father) and his brothers. Even though they were in a bad state of disrepair, I could imagine their erstwhile beauty and glory. The highlights were the chhatris and the beautiful gardens, which were still well maintained.

From Ramgarh, we proceeded to Fatehpur. If Ramgarh is known as Sethon ka Ramgarh, Fatehpur should be called Gutteron ka Fatehpur (Fatehpur of the gutters). It was filthy beyond imagination and acceptance, even by the low Indian standards of hygiene. The roads (or so-called roads) were submerged in sewage to the extent that the driver was scared his car might get flooded. It was inhuman, to say the least. If the Fatehpur seths could divert just a fraction of the millions and crores of rupees that are spent at Rani Sati Temple each year, this blight on the face of Shekhawati could disappear. But the seths have different priorities.

Despite my urge to flee from Fatehpur, I could not do so without fulfilling the two reasons I had come there for. The first was to visit the Nadine la Prince Haveli, known locally as the Angrez ki Haveli. This haveli belonged to the Deoras and was purchased by a French woman, Nadine la Prince, in 2001 for ₹32 lakh. She spent another ₹1 crore to restore it to its former glory, and has now converted it into a private residence, guesthouse, and art gallery for Indian and French artistes who flock there every winter. It is a sight to behold, like a jeweled lotus in the middle of a cesspool!

The other reason, of course, was to visit the Nevatia Haveli. Even though Sushil Jijaji and his extended family had sold the haveli some years ago, I was curious to see it. I called up Jijaji, and he gave me directions to find it. He also asked me to see the silver doors engraved with the Nevatia name, which were donated to the local Laxminarayan Temple. The haveli had been bought by a Goenka family, after which it was restored beautifully. I managed to find the temple as well and saw the Nevatia name etched on the silver doors. Right outside the temple was a *churan* shop, where I gorged on forty different kinds of churan, and almost ended up buying the entire shop! Right across from there, I bought a nine-meter-long *bandhej* (locally dyed cloth) for my *saafa* (traditional headgear).

The next day, I started with Mukundgarh and stumbled upon the Saraf havelis, two huge ones, one across the other. As I walked through one of them, I saw names inscribed on the doors to various rooms, and I noticed Chiranjilal Saraf's name. Immediately, it rang a bell, first as him being someone who was Babuji's close friend, and then as Hari Jijaji's masaji.

Later, I found out from Sunila Jiji that the Choudhari Haveli was also near the Saraf Haveli, but that it is known as the Indoriya Haveli since they were from Indore. I did not manage to see it, but I met Mr. Sahal, a local journalist, and his family. It turned out that he knew Uma Jiji very well, and before long, he was interviewing me and clicking my pictures. It appeared in the local newspaper the next day!

The next stop was Mandawa, the most touristy place in Shekhawati. The highlight was the Bansidhar Neotia Haveli, now converted into a bank. The exterior of the haveli is painted with all the major inventions of the late nineteenth and early twentieth centuries: airplane, telegraph, telephone, motor car, bicycle, and the like. I was told that these were all painted sight unseen. Quite remarkable!

From Mandawa, I proceeded to Lakshmangarh, known as the snooty town, according to Kishan, who refused to go there with me! My stay was short; hence, I could not verify that perception. The town had two highlights: the Lakshmangarh Fort (which has been purchased by a Jhunjhunwala family of Delhi and converted beautifully into their personal residence) and the Ganeriwala Haveli, known as the Char Chowk Haveli since it is the only one of its kind with four (char) courtyards. It was in a decrepit condition.

I then moved on to Jhunjhunu, the de facto capital of Shekhawati, where Satnarayanji Poddar was eagerly awaiting my arrival, thanks to a prior intimation by Satish Jijaji. They are relatives. It also turned out that Satnarayanji was related to Balaramji Parasramka, our neighbor in Sadhana (my childhood home in Bombay), and he knew Babuji very well. Poddarji is a local journalist, and he had collected some other local people to felicitate me on the return of the prodigal son to Shekhawati. Of course, it was in the local newspapers the next morning.

It was getting late in the evening, and I wanted to visit a few places on my list before I headed to Bagar for the night halt. Rani Sati Temple, the one single symbol of the Marwaris and Shekhawati, is a gold mine that is reputed to be the third richest in the league of temples in India that are in the temple and religion business (the top two being Tirupati and Siddhivinayak). It is a place that reveres the practice of sati, outlawed in India. (There is a board outside the temple, which states, "We do not support the practice of sati," perhaps to cleanse their conscience of any wrongdoing.) To start with, it was not on my list of places to visit in Jhunjhunu. I was, instead, keen on visiting the *dargah* and Khetri Mahal, two well-known architectural and historical places. But the locals would have none of it. It was almost as if I had committed sacrilege by even suggesting that I could leave Jhunjhunu without visiting the Rani Sati Temple, and God forbid, visit a dargah instead! What kind of a Marwari was I! Little did they know that I was not a typical one. But in the interest of being politically correct and polite, I agreed to visit the temple and forsake the dargah.

I quickly made my exit from Jhunjhunu and headed to Bagar to spend the night at the Piramal Haveli. The Piramal Haveli belongs to the Piramal (Makharia) family, which is Vishnu Jijaji's maternal grandfather's family. Half of the haveli has been converted into a boutique hotel managed by the Neemrana Group, which was set up by two men (a French and an Indian) and is known for restoring heritage properties all over India and managing them as boutique hotels. My wanderings across India have taken me to some of their beautifully restored properties in Alwar, Pataudi, Rishikesh, Patiala, Pondicherry, Tranquebar, and the flagship property in Neemrana.

The Piramal Haveli is a beautifully maintained and relaxing place with huge rooms and bathrooms, tall ceilings, and period furniture. The highlight of Bagar, of course, is that it is Satish Jijaji's hometown, and he had pulled out all the stops to ensure a warm welcome for me. The Roongta family's retinue was in attendance and gave me a wonderful and insightful three-hour tour of Bagar from the Roongta perspective. I had tea and snacks at the Roongta Haveli, saw their little museum, which included a corner for Satish Jijaji and his family; the school and hostel for girls; the training institute for women; the Ayurvedic clinic; and the temple. These are all either funded or managed by the Roongta family.

Bagar has been a name that has resonated with me for years, thanks to its biggest proponent, Satish Jijaji. I had finally seen for myself the strong connection and the bonds between the Roongta family and this town, which is now the second most important educational center in Shekhawati after Pilani. I think, next to Jasrapur, Bagar is the most heard name in the Darooka family.

I was finally headed to Jasrapur, the purpose of my trip, to discover my roots. At the request of Satish Jijaji, Poddarji's son from Jhunjhunu had joined me in Bagar to accompany me to Jasrapur. I was very reluctant at first to have a stranger accompany me on this very personal journey. But soon, I realized what a help he was, and how fortunate I was to have his company. I would have still discovered my roots and experienced Jasrapur, but it would have been totally different without the help of Poddarji's son.

On our way to Jasrapur, we passed through various places: Chirawa, Islampur, Suhasara, Khetri, and Sultana. All of a sudden, I remembered the vivid descriptions Omprakash Bhaisaheb had given me some months ago about Jasrapur and its environs, and how it used to take them hours and days to reach these places on camel, which I was now traversing in minutes by car. The first pangs of nostalgia crept up. As we passed the Khetri copper mines, I started noticing the low hills looming on both sides. This was the first indication that Jasrapur was really secluded as we started entering the low valley between these hills. The vegetation became denser and lusher. Yet there was no sign of water anywhere. It was as arid as the rest of Shekhawati.

As I was busy taking in this unexpectedly eerie yet serene scenery, we found ourselves outside a small shop, and Poddarji introduced me to Kediaji, who was related to him. The streets were narrow and cobbled, the structures were mainly of stone, the people were few, and my first impression was that I had come to a medieval place. My car was the only car I saw in Jasrapur all day that I was there. It aroused curiosity, and before long, everyone had connected the news item in that morning's newspaper with the car and its occupant. There was no mobbing or anything of the sort; just quiet staring and curiosity. Kediaji turned out to be a very informative source about everything concerning Jasrapur. My alternative contact and resource was Gokulprasadji Sharma's family. But due to a death in the family, it was not appropriate to bother them, though I did visit them to offer my condolences.

We started with the girls' school. Had I not been introduced to the principal, I would have taken her for one of the students! Before long, I was surrounded by giggling girls who were shooting questions at a speed I could not cope with. They looked pretty excited about my digital camera and cell phone. Right opposite the school was the old school hall, outside which I saw a plaque with various Darooka names inscribed on it. The school, which is now run by the government, was originally started by various Darooka members.

Shortly, we proceeded to the boys' school, which was more spacious and better laid out than the girls' school. Dilip Bhaiya had donated ₹2 lakh some time ago, and they were waiting for me with a garland and the works. It was in the morning newspaper once again. Having visited and taught in many rural schools in India, this seemed no different. The principal and teachers were very simple and down-to-earth, and being a government school, it focused more on ceremony and hierarchy than on teaching. We had an animated discussion about their inability to use the ₹2 lakh donation and their alternative plans. As far as they were concerned, it did not matter that I was Pradeep Darooka and not Dilip Darooka. For them, one Darooka was as good as another. After all, the entire village belonged to them.

From the schools, we proceeded to the Darooka *Mohalla*. I had already been in Jasrapur for almost two hours and had yet to catch a glimpse of the Darooka Haveli. Everywhere I went, I was straining my neck to see if I could spot it. I remembered from the stories that it was perched on a slight elevation surrounded by hills. I was getting anxious to see it, when Kediaji finally led me up a cobbled path on a slight incline, away from the main village. As we turned the corner, there it was.

Even without being told, I knew this was it. My heart skipped a beat. I had never set foot here before, but nostalgia overtook me. Every minute detail I had heard about this place flooded my mind from the remotest part of my memory. I could visualize Maa arriving up the walkway after her wedding, without a *ghunghat* (veil), a sacrilege in those days, just as Gokulprasadji had described.

Actually, the haveli was a complex of four or five separate havelis belonging to different Darooka factions. However, one that stood out as being in better condition than the others had a lock on the front gate. I knew that was the one. Kediaji sent someone to get the keys from the local *Thakkar*. Meanwhile, I entered the other havelis very cautiously, since they seemed like they might collapse at any moment, whatever was left of them. They were all stripped bare, with barely a sign of anyone ever having lived there. From one of the top floors, Kediaji pointed out the *nohra,* which was common to all the havelis. A nohra, as I had learned earlier during my trip, was an open courtyard where cattle were kept, and where the outhouses (toilets) were located.

A young boy came back with the keys, and he gingerly opened the door. As soon as I entered, I was overcome by an unbearable stench, and I noticed that the entire floor of the front courtyard was covered with goat droppings. Apparently, a goatherd was using this place to keep his goats at night after they were done grazing in the daytime. This was exactly what I had heard from Bimal Bhaisahab. I knew I was in the Bashesharlal Darooka (my grandfather) Haveli. It was not grand by any stretch, compared to the numerous ones I had already seen. Yet it seemed huge and spacious, with three stories. Like the others, it was stripped bare. As I looked up, I noticed that some of the walls on the first floor were colored blue. I decided to go up the rickety stairs, which were barely holding together. Considering that no one had lived in the haveli for over sixty years (it is over a hundred years old), the blue color was surprisingly vibrant, with various animal motifs still visible.

I wanted to explore every nook and cranny, imagining which room belonged to Maa and Babuji, where the children used to play, where the *taujis* and *taijis* lived, and so on. I did recognize the kitchen and the water storage room, since they were pretty standard fixtures in all the havelis by now. I wanted to know when exactly "Dwarkadas" evolved into "Darooka," a name that has been my essence and identity ever since I can remember. Was it here or was it in Karachi?

By now, the stench was getting unbearable. Besides, we were all hungry. I took one last look at the courtyard, locked the door, and walked down the cobbled path back to downtown Jasrapur, to have lunch at Kediaji's home in a sit-down fashion on *paatlas* (short wooden stools). As I crisscrossed Shekhawati, one observation stood out from the rest: there was a close connection and familiarity among all those who still lived there or hailed from there. It seemed like every family was either related to or knew each other.

After lunch, Kediaji led me in a different direction, this time, uptown Jasrapur. We left the cobbled streets behind, and I saw some of the largest trees I had ever seen anywhere, looming ahead of me. For a second, I forgot that I was supposed to be in the middle of one of the most barren parts of Rajasthan. The entire energy changed. I saw a large sunken, open area, which looked like a dry lake surrounded by walls painted blue. We entered through a large gate into an open courtyard. I knew I had entered Jasrapur, the *siddha peeth*. It was Babaji's Ashram, more than three hundred years old. Kediaji introduced me to Babaji (not to be confused with my guru, Babaji, mentioned earlier). Generically, "Babaji" refers to a saintly person. He said he knew who I was and why I had come here. He led me to the inner courtyard where I saw a chhatri overlooking the dry lake. Babaji showed me the writings on the chhatri that indicated when it was built. I sat there for an hour breathing in the cool, sweet air while listening to various stories about Jasrapur from Babaji. I could imagine how much more magical this place would be when the lake, nestled amid surrounding hills, would be filled with rainwater. On top of one of the barren hills, I spotted a single *neem* tree, which, I was told, was one of the many mysteries about Jasrapur.

I did not want to leave this place. In all the stories and anecdotes about Jasrapur, no one had ever told me it was a siddha peeth. But then, a siddha peeth is something that is experienced and resonates within the heart. One could have lived one's entire life here and not realized it. Or one could have never set foot here, and yet got drawn toward it like a calling. The mystery of the sole neem tree on a barren hill was so simple. The huge verdant trees inside and outside the ashram made so much sense. The greenery and vibrancy all around could only be explained in one way. If Sheryl Benson, my Reiki teacher, had been here, she would have known what I was experiencing. After all, Dr. Usui experienced something similar on Mt. Fuji. Tears welled up in my eyes as I thought of the connection, and once again, it hit me what Reiki has meant to me. It truly is universal.

This discovery of a siddha peeth (akin to a Shakti Peeth) was well before I had firmly established relationships with all the Shaktis in my life. In hindsight, I realized this was the first formal introduction to the Devi, and that too in my hometown, where I had never lived and where Maa had come as a newly married bride. It was clear that the Universe was laying out the path for me to walk on, and the seeds of my spirituality were sown right here through the genes and sanskaras of my ancestors.

I had come to discover my roots.
Instead, I rediscovered my Universality.
It did not matter anymore whether I was a Marwari or not.

Child of the Universe

I was in Jaisalmer, Rajasthan a couple of years later. As I was walking the cobbled stone streets with Igle, I saw a sign in Hindi saying, "home cooked meal by Maa." I stopped in my stride and followed the sign up a couple of flights in a dilapidated stone house. There was this half bent, toothless, close to 80 years old woman with a smile who beckoned us inside her one room home with an Indian style kitchen on one side. She started talking with me in Marwari and was happy I could understand. I had to translate everything for Igle. She perched herself on the kitchen floor, asked us to sit on the mattress alongside, got the fire going, started talking and asking questions nonstop, and before we knew the time, our thalis were in front of us with a simple meal of dal, roti and subzi and raw onions. The rotis were coming hot from the griddle. This entire scene and experience took me back to Maa who used to cook similarly. Tears swelled up as I felt I was back in her lap. The Devi Goddess had again appeared in the form of this woman who had just served us one of the most sublime and saatvik meals of my life.

As I traversed the globe, it was clear that the human spirit is universal. The physical body with its attributes is a function of geographic location and conditioning, the mind is a product of socioreligious conditioning, and this is what has given rise to animosity and divisions among mankind, with untold misery inflicted on each other. The only way to experience and see this reality is to step out of one's comfort zone, whether it comprises your electronic devices, family, community, or religion, and explore the big, wide world with your eyes and heart, observing and grasping every moment of that enriching journey.

I would not trade my journey for anything else.

||Jai Hanuman Namah||

|| The Sound of One Hand Clapping
If You Want Enlightenment,
Go and Wash Dishes ||

11.
|| Zen ||
|| Nothingness ||

When we remember we are all mad, the mysteries disappear, and life stands explained.

We know that a bit of cruel ice resides in our hearts.

We know that we limply fall into our bed after a day's tiring work.

We know that we could smile more than we do.

We know that tears of glass stream silently down our pale faces once in a while.

We know that we often feel that no one understands . . . Do we?

We know that we, too, ignore the wounds of the person next to us.

We know that anger boils inside us, but we hide it well.

We know that we wish someone heard our soundless screams.

We know that we wish someone would notice the silent torment in our voice.

We know that we are waiting for someone to detect our hidden hell.

When we meet the enemy and realize that it is within us, our troubles end, our life brightens.

We know that we are all born to love, to nourish, to heal, to see the beauty of life every single moment, and to experience the essence of life.

We know that we yearn for happiness; we search for its path outside our being, when it is within us, unimaginable bliss arising from love.

Loosen your senses to regain life in its purest form.

Liberate your self to wander and explore the beatitudes of life.

Lost in loneliness, we feel like beggars; finding our aloneness, we become Buddhas.

You cannot travel the path before the path itself. Walk on.

A cold rain falling, and me without a hat. On second thought, who cares!

We do not practice to become enlightened; we practice as an expression of enlightenment.

Zen is to have the heart and soul of a little child.

These are not random thoughts. It is Zen philosophy itself.

A Zen master will give you a koan such as "What is the sound of one hand clapping?" and wait for you to respond with an answer. It may trigger instant realization, or it may take years. The master will not accept you as a student unless you have the right answer. And if you have the right answer, you will not need the master anymore! That is Zen.

Zen captures the essence of the Spirit even more directly and simply than Advaita.

Zen and Osho

Osho was also the last of the modern Zen masters, besides being the last of the modern Tantra masters. This is not surprising. Tantra and Zen are but two sides of the same coin joined at the hip by Advaita to form the trinity of the highest spiritual philosophy. As one gets deeper into each of these philosophies individually, one realizes that they start to morph into each other through the concept of One without the Other, resulting in *Shunya* (Nothingness).

Zen originated in India as part of Buddhist teachings, which were culled by the Chinese to represent the purest of the Buddha's teachings. Unlike what is propagated in Buddhism, Gautam Buddha spoke very little after his nirvana under the Bodhi tree. Most of the *sutras* and other teachings attributed to him are the writings of various monks and others who chose to spread his teachings through their own words. This is obvious from the different branches of Buddhism that sprang up after he left his body: Theravada, Mahayana, and Vajrayana. Mahayana became popular in Tibet and talks mainly of arcane Tantric rituals and practices. The Buddha never touched upon Tantra.

A few centuries later, Christianity would follow the same route. Just as Buddhism has nothing to do with the Buddha's teachings, Christianity and its centerpiece, the Bible, have nothing to do with Yeshua's teachings. The twelve apostles chosen by Yeshua to spread his teachings chose to add their own words to his humble teachings after his Resurrection and after he made his way back to India, where he had obtained his spiritual lessons earlier. Just as the Buddha's teachings are culled in Zen, Yeshua's teachings are culled from the philosophy of the Trinity in Indian scriptures, namely Brahma (the Creator), Vishnu (the Sustainer), and Mahesh (the Destroyer), and known as the Father, the Son, and the Holy Spirit.

Yet another realized soul's teaching got corrupted after his passing away. This was Prophet Muhammad and his divine and simple teaching of ibadat. The Sufi tradition that originated in the Middle East and spread further East, including the Indian subcontinent, is the only true reflection of his teaching of complete surrender to the Higher Self.

Every major organized religion has its origins in the realms of spirituality, which then quickly descended into the abyss of ignorance, greed, and power, the cause of untold deceit and damage to mankind.

My underpinning on this spiritual journey is the path beyond Advaita, Zen, and Sufism. This is the path of Nothingness, total surrender, falling in love with myself, and forever being in this Satsang of One.

Nothingness

Manifestation emerged from Nothingness.
Manifestation is Nothingness.
Manifestation merges into Nothingness.

For Nothingness to prevail, everything has to drop off. The dropping off had begun even without my knowing it. Just as realization and awakening are gradual processes, until their Happening hits you one day, so also, dropping off happens along with them. Just as the emperor shed his clothes one by one in the presence of the tailor until he stood stark naked, so also, you start to shed what has been accumulated inside and outside, materially, mentally, and emotionally, until all belongings and attachments disappear and you are finally left naked, as your true Self. This is the Self that gets hidden right after the first breath taken on emerging from the mother's womb, and stays hidden until *Satori* happens.

Dropping Off: Gifts

When your child comes home from the school playground, bruised, wearing dirty clothes and shoes, their body caked with dirt and soil, and their hair disheveled, you remove each piece of their clothing, march them to the bathroom, and hose them down with soap and water until they are squeaky clean and their sweet, innocent self again. Or take the story of the emperor who sheds his clothing, one by one, until he is revealed in his naked self, no different than that of the commoner.

When we start on our spiritual journey, we acquire many practices, absorb much knowledge, and gain much experience while shedding old, long-established patterns and habits that were clogging our consciousness, unbeknownst to us. They start dropping off one by one. We start to feel increasingly lighter, with each shedding stripping off another layer covering our true self. For me, among the many materialistic patterns that shed themselves was the act of giving and receiving gifts.

Right from childhood, we become conditioned to receiving gifts on our birthday, on festive occasions, after a good performance, and sometimes, for no reason. Very soon, it becomes an expectation. As we grow up and reach adulthood and maturity, with family and societal responsibilities, the innocence of receiving gifts as a child gives way to major gifting activities: weddings, anniversaries, showers, housewarmings, and any number of occasions. As with all human activity in this day and age, businesses were quick to come up with increasingly more occasions for gifting: Mother's Day, Father's Day, and almost every family member day; Valentine's Day; and so on, to the point that some people may find themselves receiving or giving a gift on almost all the days in the year! It has now become a serious activity that absorbs a good chunk of our time, effort, and money. Expectations about receiving and giving have become ingrained. Stress levels regarding what to gift go through the roof, and embarrassments over gaffes become commonplace. A good chunk of our precious time is spent on the unnecessary and frivolous. We start to focus more on the tangible and the materialistic, and totally ignore the intangible strands of human relationships based on intuition and connection.

When I was in the USA, a few days after Mother's Day, Maa asked me why I had not called her on the occasion and sent her flowers or something, like some of my other siblings. I replied, "Maa, they remember you once a year. You are with me all year long. I do not need a greeting card company to tell me when I should call my mom." Emotional and alone that she was, she started crying.

I have a large extended family, and for the longest time, I was absolutely diligent in sending cards, flowers, and gifts to each person on their birthday. Weddings are as common in India as mosquitoes, and as much of a nuisance, and gifts are inevitable. Most invitations have a clichéd line at the bottom: "Your blessings are the best gift." Yet, if you go empty-handed, you will turn red with embarrassment as you approach the bridal couple and see the stage laden with gifts. You are never sure whether cash is more appropriate than something in kind. If cash, how much? If in kind, what? You might spend sleepless nights pondering over this. And then there are all those invitations for parties, get-togethers, and celebrations, where you are torn between whether you should or should not take a gift. You chat and discuss with your family and friends about the right protocol, and whether that ubiquitous bottle of wine would suffice, or if it should be something more substantial. Sometimes you may even tear your hair out, not knowing what to do. Thank God, I decided to shave my head!

Enough is enough!

I had had enough of this. One day, I sent an email to all my family members and close friends that henceforth, I would not be indulging in the act of either receiving or giving gifts of any kind to anyone on any occasion, and I would appreciate it if they respected this. There was complete silence; not a single response or reaction. Of course, most of these people had already written me off as a wacko for having given up a lucrative career in the USA and returning to India to become a *sanyasi*. This was yet another of my hare-brained ideas, they thought. Their silence was bliss for me. It spoke volumes. The message had gotten across, loud and clear.

I made no exceptions. Many occasions, such as weddings and parties, came and went, which I attended. There were births and other joyous occasions in the family as well. The only issue I pondered was which of my many Fabindia kurtas I should wear (another shedding on my spiritual journey, as we shall see later). There was a tremendous lightness of being. Nothing to receive and nothing to wonder about what to do with the useless item you just received. And nothing to give. It was yet another aspect of the Zen lifestyle I had adopted: shedding everything unwanted, unnecessary, and meaningless. There were some who did not understand my philosophy. It did not matter to me. I had the conviction of my heart. And since the heart chakra was wide open, there was no less love and affection than before. In fact, I believe it became more bountiful. It was no longer riddled with materialism; it was pure and simple, freed from all shackles. The only giving and receiving now were hugs, hand-holdings, healing circles, and an exchange of energy. Each of these gestures and actions left a deeper impact and a greater sense of being.

This was one of the first and the most difficult sheddings that happened along my journey. It has been quite a few years now. Other sheddings have been easier, mainly because they have not affected others as significantly as this one. These are not seasonal like the shedding of a bird's feathers or the falling of leaves in autumn. There is a new conditioning, as Ramesh would say, and new sanskaras are formed. I keep getting lighter and lighter, getting to the core of my being, as innocent and pristine as the day I came out of my mother's womb. There is no going back.

Dropping Off: Attire

When I was in the corporate world in the USA, the dress code was suit and tie every day. For formal get-togethers, client dinners, banquets, and other similar occasions, it was black tie, that is, tuxedo. I hated it. With the IT boom, things became a bit more relaxed with casual Fridays, when one could drop the suit and tie, and (short of jeans and T-shirt) wear anything. What a relief! At least for one of the five workdays, one could breathe. There was some hope for the Vishuddhi Chakra to open up.

When I quit the corporate world and returned to India, I was looking forward to a gradual migration to the blissful, comfortable world of kurta pajama. However, I was in for a shock. As we say in Hindi, *"Angrez chale gaye lekin angreziyat chhod gaye* (The English have gone but left behind their Englishness.)"* In the hot, humid climate of Bombay and most of India, I saw Indian men dressed to the hilt in the same attire I had yearned to drop off for years in the USA. At least the cool climate of the USA provided some justification and necessity for that attire. I did not see any hope for any of the chakras to open up here, let alone the Vishuddhi Chakra.

I had embarked on a journey where there are many unknowns along the way. One does not know what to expect but keeps going along with the flow that is both sublime and subtle. There are no dramatic changes that happen on the spiritual path. As I got deeper into Advaita and Zen, the common theme that emerged clearly was the inevitable need for the self to break free of all shackles and years of hardened conditioning, and to soar like a free bird. As the consciousness rose higher, the dropping off of the unnecessary, irrelevant, burdensome habits was bound to happen.

A practical option

We are born without a stitch on our body, and that is the only time in our life when we are our pristine, pure self, born out of consciousness and connected to consciousness. It is downhill all the way after that. In tribal communities all over the world, children remain without clothes well into adulthood, and in many of these communities, even throughout their entire life. Certain tribal communities have been corrupted by the mores of "civilized" people who have insisted that it is immoral to reveal certain parts of your body to others, no matter how uncomfortable or unhealthy it may be to cover up. One needs to question why many realized individuals walked the lands of India and elsewhere, almost threadbare. Ramana Maharshi, Mahavira, Buddha, and Jesus Christ, to name a few. They had nothing to hide.

While I was not quite ready to shed it all yet, the changes were happening. As the chakras start opening up and getting energized, they need to breathe. And they cannot breathe when one is covered in tight clothing day and night. The body, the skin, the hair, the bones, they all need sun and fresh air to keep their cells fully vibrant and charged. One needs to charge our devices regularly by plugging them into a power source, or they will stop working. Using this analogy, we can understand that our body needs to be charged too by plugging into Nature. The cells need to connect with the moon, the sun, the planets, and the stars, and imbibe all the energy that radiates from them. Try walking barefoot in the morning on dew-laden grass, hugging a tree bare-chested, getting soaked in a rain shower, or sitting in the moonlight without a stitch on your body, and see how you feel.

Tight and layered clothing inhibits this. Why is it that during yog, pranayama, meditation, and other healing exercises, we are asked to wear loose, comfortable clothing? Why is it that when we come back from a party all clothed and bejeweled, the first thing we do is "take it all off"? It is human nature. We want to breathe. So why should we not want to breathe 24/7? Why only for a few hours a day? And specifically, why not at night while sleeping, when our body is busy rejuvenating and recharging all its cells?

My suit and tie had long given way to simple trousers and open-necked shirts. Kurta and pajama had gradually made inroads into my wardrobe, and not just as nightwear, as is common in India. Conventional trousers with zippers and belts gave way to drawstring pants with loose bottoms. Collared shirts gave way to collarless shirts, tunics, and *kurtis* with short sleeves or long flowing sleeves with no cuffs.

For the cooler climates, I discovered the beauty of the shawl, resplendently available in a multitude of designs, fabrics, and colors in different parts of India. Very soon, I had an enviable collection.

Dress shoes were history. I had discovered the pleasures of sandals and chappals, perfect for India, where one needs to take them off frequently.

Soon, I discovered stores that sell garments made from sustainable and eco-friendly fibers, which were appropriate for Shiva and Shakti. It did not take very long for pants and shirts to become extinct from my wardrobe. The kurta pajama (in its many variations) became the attire of choice for me almost everywhere: at home, at parties, weddings, formal occasions, business meetings, workshops, satsangs, or while traveling. I did get denied access to certain clubs, and I was glad for it, since I had no desire to hobnob with the leftover *angrezis* (Englishmen) in India. I declined formal dress code invitations, and very soon, they became a trickle. Again, a silver lining in the clouds. I started breathing easier and deeper. Sleeping in the buff became normal, and with that came peaceful sleep.

Dressing for the body

It is not too difficult to establish a correlation between our clothing and our health and wellness.

First of all, since our body is a product of Mother Nature and made up of the five elements, any alien material, such as synthetic, nylon, rayon, or chemically treated fabrics, will have an adverse effect on us, no different than any toxic or inorganic substance entering our food chain and bloodstream. The impact is rarely immediate, except in the case of allergies of certain kinds, but it happens, nonetheless. Once I realized this, it was only cotton and linen for me. I discovered the natural, organic beauty of *khadi* and the way it allowed my body to breathe. Along the way, I discovered fabrics made from bamboo and hemp, and I started breathing even more deeply and easily, wearing them. Once I saw for myself how silk was woven, by boiling the live cocoons in hot water, silk dropped out of my wardrobe. Even in the coolest climate, I found wool to be unnecessary. Layered cotton clothing of various textures was sufficient.

Secondly, those of us who belong to a certain generation may remember or know that our parents and grandparents never wore any underwear, including bras for women. My father always wore a dhoti, and my mother always wore a *sari*, two of the most practical and comfortable pieces of attire in the world. Underwear and bras (corsets and the like from the Victorian era were the origins of this) were yet another gift given to the "uncivilized world" by the "civilized English," along with the chair, the commode, high heels, toilet paper, and many others, all of which have contributed to health issues worldwide. It did not take very long for the Muladhara, the Swadhisthana, the Manipura, and the Anahata chakras to be imprisoned. The long-term results were inevitable.

My wanderings around the world revealed an amazing correlation between various ailments (in particular breast cancer and cancer of the organs around the lower chakras) and the lifestyle of the twentieth century. For instance, the correlation between the use of the western commode and constipation and other intestinal diseases, and that between sitting on a chair and lower back and spinal problems.

All of these dropped off for me, layer by layer, one by one. I felt a sense of freedom, once again soaring like a free bird, ever higher and higher. The spiritual journey continued.

Dropping Off: Tamasic Food

I was born and brought up as a vegetarian. Even after living in the USA and other places abroad for over forty years, I have never compromised. It was not always easy, but obviously not impossible either, since I remained hale and hearty. I always thought it was enough to be a vegetarian to be healthy. I was wrong. As a vegetarian living a fast-paced life, I was eating all kinds of packaged, frozen, processed, and chemically treated foods at odd hours. Often, I would eat in the company of hardcore carnivores, from the same table and kitchen. It did not seem to matter, so long as it was vegetarian.

But it did matter. The realization was one of the earliest, and perhaps the farthest-reaching, of all my realizations. I discovered what Krishna meant by "tamasic," "*rajasic*," and "sattvic," which he repeatedly used while instructing Arjun in the Gita's eighteenth chapter. The gunas that they represent apply to all aspects of life, but for me, they became particularly relevant in the context of aahaar. Aahaar is not just food. The closest English word would be "nutrition," and when I talk about sattvic aahaar as part of the spiritual journey, there is no English equivalent, just as there is none for karma, dharma, yog, dhyana, and many other Sanskrit words.

Saatvik aahar has been a very important part of my spiritual journey, as described in chapter eight, "The Spirit." Once I realized how vital it was to my progress on the path to Nothingness, *Tamasic aahaar* in all its forms dropped off.

The change begins

First, I discontinued all packaged foods. Next in line was fast food. Then, my consumption of refrigerated foods became minimal—no leftovers. I have not used the microwave in years, and non-stick cookware and plastic were banished from my kitchen. I learned the importance of organic food, not just for its benefits, but also, more importantly, for its role in protecting Mother Earth. She provides all our nourishment but has been ravaged for years by all the chemicals and pesticides that have polluted the soil, water, and air in the process of industrial cultivation. She needs to be nurtured back to health. Organic food became an increasing part of my diet, both at home and while eating out. This was more difficult to achieve in India than abroad. Sadly, over the years, I have found it easier to eat healthy outside India than in India. There is a far greater awareness of wholesome food in many other countries. This sounds counterintuitive, but it is true.

Lessons from Nature

As I got deeper into the world of energy healing, it became clear that the human body was but a microcosm of the entire Universe. There was no reason for human beings to have made their own rules contrary to the Laws of Nature. With spiritual awakening comes an acute sense of observation, whereby I noticed that the entire animal and plant world is up and awake well before the crack of dawn. Come twilight, they have already found their abodes for the night. Have you ever seen an animal or bird eating after sunset? If you water a plant at night, you are ensuring its withering away in a few days. The sun and the moon rise and set at their predetermined times. The entire Universe works with such clockwork precision that it has become very easy for science to predict its behavior. But we "intelligent" human beings have created such havoc for ourselves due to our unnatural habits that it is quite easy to know where to pin the blame for our suffering. We eat at odd hours, well into the night. We eat the wrong things at the wrong times. We do not pay heed to the simple rule of "local, seasonal, organic."

Healing through naturopathy (Food habits and fasting)

I started regularizing and regulating my meals. Reading up on naturopathy helped me understand the medicinal benefits of almost every ingredient (herb, fruit, vegetable, and grain) that goes into my meals. I found a book by Vandana Shiva, *Bhoole Bisre Anaj* (Long-Forgotten Grains), and discovered the pleasures of *ragi, jowar, bajra,* and many other grains that are oozing with energy and nutrition. Wheat and rice became rare in my diet. All of the diet-related bloating and heaviness disappeared.

I used to suffer from respiratory congestion and related problems for a long time, until I met a naturopath in Boston. Since I was a heavy consumer of milk and milk products, he suggested I try giving them up for a few months and see what happens. Sure enough, after three months, I was breathing free again, and I have not looked at milk since.

I became a deep follower of naturopathy. Regular detoxification became an essential part of my lifestyle. This was primarily in the form of fasting supplemented by an annual colonic, and later, regular trips to an Ayurvedic center.

Generally, fasting is a deeply rooted practice that Indians follow. But this has come about only as an adjunct to religion. Fasting as a tool of cleansing and detoxification would never have become so popular had it not been cloaked in various mythological anecdotes, stories, superstitions, and rituals (*Mahashivratari, Ekadashi, Saawan, Karwa Chauth*, and many more). In my workshops, when I talk about the importance of fasting as a healing practice, people are generally reluctant to adopt it. But they will not hesitate to do so were it suggested to them that they should fast once a month to appease a certain deity to alleviate some personal problem. I am always happy that the purpose is served, regardless of the way the message is delivered and accepted.

In naturopathy, there are strict rules around proper fasting, but unfortunately, these are not followed when fasting is undertaken without full awareness. Many people "prepare" for their fast by stuffing themselves to the hilt the night before and "break" their fast by doing the same. This does not facilitate any detoxification or cleansing.

I have adopted a simple fasting routine. Once a month, I only drink water for twenty-four hours; once a month, I only consume liquids for twenty-four hours; and once a month, I only eat fruits all day. The meals are light the day before and the day after the fast, allowing for the digestive system to fully benefit from the rest it gets.

The rule of naturopathy, "Medicine is the food of the sick, and food is the medicine of the healthy," became my mantra. If ever I was down with some ailment or had one of those low-energy days (my monthly period), I did not run to the medicine closet or the doctor anymore. Instead, I pulled out my naturopathy, homeopathy, and ayurvedic books and found the right remedy. Like many people in India, I became an amateur homeopath. I even started prescribing remedies as part of my healing treatment in my workshops. This can come about only from a deep sense of conviction in what one believes in. But now, it is no longer just a belief. Gradually, it has become my nature, my swabhav; a fresh conditioning, as Ramesh would say.

Dynamic outcome

As with almost every change that I underwent on the spiritual path, there was a silver lining to the change in my eating habits too. Since I had not renounced the world (as most conventional people would believe, given my lifestyle), I was still connected to friends, family, and acquaintances. Once they heard about my "strange" eating habits (most importantly, no heavy meals after sunset), invitations became rarer. What more could I ask for? It freed up my evenings for satsangs and workshops, which were typically preceded by a light meal or a potluck. No energy was wasted in trying to drum up metabolism, without the help of the sun, to try and digest all that heavy food eaten well after sunset, and then waking up all bloated and tired. Instead, my group and I used the energy cultivated all day long from the sattvic aahaar we had imbibed. The difference was not subtle; it was dynamic. Sattvic aahaar was truly the fuel necessary for me to continue on this enlightening journey. I was blessed.

Dropping Off: Clutter

A spiritual journey can continue on many different paths, all leading to the ultimate discovery of the Self. Just as all religions point toward one or more gods who only differ in name, shape, and form, so also, there are many paths for spiritual evolution. For me, it has been the path of Zen, the purest form of the Buddha's teaching, just as Advaita is the purest form of Hindu teaching. And for the most part, the two paths are joined at the hip like Siamese twins, except in one significant respect.

And that has to do with physical clutter.

In all spiritual paths, there is a gradual dropping off of various conditionings we have been burdened with all our lives, until we discover the very core and essence of our existence and understand our connection with Consciousness. This happens to allow the energy (prana) within us to flow freely, thereby enabling us to see more clearly, sharpen our intuitive skills, open our third eye, and connect with the higher Self. Anything that obstructs this natural course of spiritual evolution gets dropped off, be it clothes, food, people, or habits. All of this I discussed in the earlier parts of this chapter and will discuss it further as we move along.

On the Zen path, it is equally important that all physical clutter that surrounds us gets dropped off too. The Hindu path does not emphasize this, at least not directly. Consequently, a typical Hindu home or temple does not exude the same sense of peace and calm as a Japanese home or temple. It may contain the most awakened energy of a master or guru, but it will not necessarily be clean, simple, and clutter-free. Feng Shui is an aspect of Zen philosophy, and it believes that energy is blocked by unnecessary and misplaced articles. This applies to everything in any space where we spend our time, be it our home, workplace, or recreation area.

Japanese minimalism

When you visit a Japanese Shinto temple or a Zen monastery, what strikes you immediately is the stark nature of the space, embellished with selectively placed articles and furniture. It immediately radiates a sense of peace and serenity. The Osho Ashram is a perfect example of this. Meditation would happen naturally and effortlessly in such a shrine. If you are a lover of Japanese architecture as I am, or if you have visited Japanese homes or seen pictures of them, you will notice an extension of this same serenity within the four walls. No matter how small or big the space, it seems refreshingly light, and one immediately feels so relaxed. Everything is neat and tidy; every item is in its place. Only natural materials are used for construction. Walls are made of mud, grass, and wood. Floors are made from wood or bamboo, on which are placed tatami mats made from grass and jute. Shoji screens, made from rice paper and pinewood, serve as flexible walls. Futons made from organic linen and cotton are used for sleeping. Bathrooms are adorned with stoneware and wood. There is hardly any man-made or synthetic material in sight. The living space is in complete harmony with Nature.

I adopted many of these elements while designing my own living space, and the energy vibrancy is palpable.

Learning to let go

So what happens to all the stuff that we so diligently hold on to all our lives? If we look around our homes, we will find our drawers, shelves, and wardrobes bursting with documents, letters, photos, albums, artifacts, memorabilia, unopened gifts, useless gizmos, obsolete gadgets, clothes and accessories, toiletries and cosmetics, shoes and bags . . . the sky is the limit. In the USA, storage rental is one of the biggest businesses, catering to the American mania to "shop till you drop." We have a natural human tendency to hoard our memories, never knowing when they might come in handy. Thinking that, like our minds, we too have the infinite ability to hoard, we just expand our storage space, instead of discarding the old to bring in the new.

It is either a penchant for collecting something or an inability to discard and let go. When I cleared Maa's home upon her passing away, the attic was full of utensils meant for large families and cooking feasts and had not been used for decades. My brother had piles of read and unread newspapers and magazines. When Ayo and I cleaned out his study upon his passing away, there were stacks of printed emails. One of my sisters holds on to all correspondence, and another accumulates stuff discarded by others in the family. Yet another sister has saved clippings from various published media, and the fourth one hoards food items as if she is expecting a famine soon. We refuse to let go of the past lest it might slip away and never return. But we forget that it has already slipped away. What we need in the present moment is all that we need to have. And that becomes the bare minimum. Minimalism comes in, clutter moves out.

In India, there is a tendency to hold on to empty containers, old cartons, empty bottles, and sundry stuff. They all gather dust and cobwebs. In Zen, an empty bottle is not "no mind"; it is blocked energy. Out they go. Not surprisingly, even the digital world is not immune to the problems that arise from accumulating all kinds of data on our hard drives, both intentionally and inadvertently. Our computers are prone to crashing more often, they slow down considerably, and booting up seems to take forever. There are various programs and maintenance routines available to regularly clean the hard drives and get rid of the unwanted.

Living for the present

I look at my lifestyle in the present moment, and that tells me what exactly I need to live now. Everything else is superfluous and redundant. The past is gone, and the future will take care of itself. It resonates perfectly with my philosophy of living in the present moment. I am constantly going through my drawers, shelves, and wardrobes, either discarding or giving away items I have not used for extended periods of time and am unlikely to. All kinds of paper stuff, such as documents, bills, and reports, go through the shredder every month. Every time I buy a new garment, an old one gets discarded. My kitchen and pantry hold the bare minimum supplies, enough for the next week or two. I buy everything fresh and seasonal. No risk of spoilage or rotting, and better nutrition with fresh food. I have a refrigerator, but it is almost always empty, especially the freezer section. Nothing is frozen or preserved.

As within, so without

In Ayurveda and naturopathy, regular cleansing through panchakarma, fasting, and other detoxification methods is prescribed. This helps to restore physical vitality. So also in the physical world around us. It is all related. When we see a clean, uncluttered, tidy space around us, we immediately move into a comfort zone that allows us to breathe more freely and see more clearly. We feel refreshed, reenergized, and lighter. It's a huge burden off our shoulders. Moreover, when we start discarding unnecessary physical clutter around us, it becomes a potent symbol for also discarding unnecessary relationships, habits, thoughts, and ideas.

Dropping Off: People

One of the most important aspects of any serious spiritual ascent is the value of satsang. Satsang simply means being in the company of the sattvic or the purest, highest Self. As the chakras get activated, the energy starts flowing vigorously up and down the *Sushumna Nadi,* which starts to vibrate at a much higher frequency. This higher frequency now starts to seek out similar higher frequencies with which it can resonate, like a well-tuned orchestra, where every instrument and player is in complete harmony with each other. It transports each player to a different plane where they forget their individual self and become one with the entire orchestra. When Russian ballet dancer Nijinsky was asked how he could dance so sublimely, he famously said, "When Nijinsky dances, there is no Nijinsky."

As habits and conditionings drop off, what remains behind is the true self that increasingly starts to turn inward. Noise becomes abhorrent, silence becomes a solace. Words start to lose their significance. The body and the spirit start to speak through the emanating energy from the open chakras and nadis. This language of awareness and consciousness can only be deciphered and understood by others who are on the same plane. But since one has now discovered the Self and hopefully got the answer to the question "Who Am I?" there is no loneliness. It is a blissful existence with the full awareness of "I Am That." The company of others becomes irrelevant. I was well along on my Satsang of One.

Meaningful connections

As the social interaction, the attire, the food habits, and other aspects of my individuality changed or dropped off, there was no longer any inclination to be with someone who indulged in small talk and mindless chatter, or did not have anything meaningful to contribute to my spiritual development. This was misconstrued as arrogance and aloofness by many. It did not bother me. I found it easier to interact and communicate with a child or a teenager than with an adult. As Osho said, "It is very difficult, if not impossible, to get through to someone who has his mind full than one who is mindful."

I got involved with students in schools and colleges, mentoring them, providing guidance, and pointing them in the right direction in consonance with their swabhav. I challenged them to think about whether they wanted to be just educated or also wished to learn how to live their lives. It became a very fulfilling use of my time. Some institutes would insist on having a teacher or professor present during my interactions with the students, but I refused. They would be a drag. Students would become inhibited and would not open up. The satsang we created at each session was special.

When I returned from the USA, many childhood friends and other acquaintances were keen to reestablish a connection. But we had nothing in common. Only one friendship survived, that with Rajesh. We hardly ever met or talked, but the connection was strong. When we did meet, it was the easiest for us to pick up from where we left off. It helped that his wife, Meenal, was on the same wavelength, so we connected effortlessly.

New connections have been established, mainly from my workshops and sojourns around the world. I get drawn to individuals who have either discovered their true identity or are firmly on the path toward that. There is much in common to share and discuss. In true satsangs, hugging comes naturally and spontaneously. The chakras are generally open, so energy moves freely, creating a comfort zone for everyone. As soon as someone walks into this space with blocked energy, the antennas go up, looking for some vibrations on the same frequency. Finding none, we walk away.

Family satsangs

I belong to a very large extended family, and we have frequent get-togethers. We are generally a very close-knit family with a lot of love, affection, and caring among us, which transcends all generations. This is primarily thanks to my parents, who imbued this feeling in all of us as we were growing up. Like all large families, there are exceptions, and there is a fair amount of disagreement among us. We yell and scream and shout and get angry and upset. But when we meet, we have satsang. We reminisce and talk about our parents; we cook and eat until we fall asleep. This is not the spiritual satsang of chanting and discourse, but it is satsang for me nonetheless because it overflows with joy and happiness, and something that I look forward to. There is no spiritual nourishment in these family satsangs, yet it is something meaningful to some extent. However, blood relationship cannot be the basis for a meaningful connection, in fact it is rarely so. The connection has to be based upon something deeper. As the younger generation has veered away from the core value of respect for the elders and has developed a short attention span, thanks to the attachment to their devices, I find myself increasingly detached from this large extended family. I increasingly find myself in my Satsang of One in these gatherings.

The language of silence

My satsangs take many forms. We have dance, music, chanting, and other creative activities. We have cooking, potlucks, and eating together. We practice yog and pranayama together. We learn archery and Tai Chi. We perform Reiki circles and other healing activities. The male and female energies come together like a cosmic dance in our Tantra satsangs. We go for long walks in the forests, hike, climb mountains, and sit by the fireside. We sit in silence. Words become irrelevant during satsangs. Silence connects everyone. We sway and breathe like hollow bamboos creating their own music, all connected to that one Consciousness.

My favorite satsang is the satsang of solitude, when I am all alone with myself and I can hear Krishna playing his flute in my ears. This is Satchidananda, Satsang of One.

Dropping Off: Fear

The spiritual journey never ends so long as we keep breathing. It starts from the time the child takes the first breath inside the mother's womb and continues until the last breath. The only difference between individuals is whether they take each breath in awareness of this journey or are oblivious to it. That itself depends on one's destiny, what is meant to be, and is determined and known at birth itself. As with all his children, my father had gotten my horoscope prepared soon after I was born. It was one of those handwritten booklets in Sanskrit prepared by the family pandit. I still have it. Everything that was stated there about my life has come true so far. Subsequent readings by various astrologers have only confirmed this. I have no reason to doubt that the rest of the journey will follow the destiny carved out for me, clearly articulated the day I was born.

This series of "dropping offs" takes us higher and higher through each chakra. As we let go of accumulated layers of conditioning, the true self begins to emerge, and we start living according to our swabhav. The superficial, material, and emotional aspects of our life go through a transformation and bring us finally to the Ajna and Sahasara chakras. But there is one last dropping off remaining: our fears and insecurities.

Modern man is riddled with three main insecurities:
Fear of lack of money (material resources).
Fear of interpersonal relationships (dealing with the "other").
Fear of ill health and death (the unknown).

These three insecurities plague each of us right from the time we develop our ego and individuality. Money becomes the instrument of barter for almost every activity from the time we get our first pocket money. And if we are not privileged enough to get pocket money, we start finding ways and means to acquire this instrument, including begging, borrowing, and stealing. Life, as we know it, cannot be lived without this instrument. And once we have become beholden to its necessity, the sky is the limit. Satiation is almost impossible. Very soon, we are engulfed in the fear of never having enough, either for our necessities or for non-essentials.

On the spiritual path, this fear disappears once we turn the concept of material wealth into the concept of abundance and gratitude. We are a microcosm of Nature, and at any given point, we have just what we need. This is Universal Law. So, instead of pleading and praying for more all the time, we can be grateful for all the abundance we already have.

Once the teaching of being a witness, nondoership, and nonduality sinks in, the fear of interpersonal relationships disappears. You become comfortable in your own skin, of who you are; you fall in love with yourself, and the "other" does not matter anymore.

Health and death are inherent parts of the plan prescribed for each of us by the Universe. There is absolutely nothing we can do about it. Birth and death are two bookends, and we live our lives moment to moment, between them.

|| Satori! ||

|| East Is East, and West Is West
And Never the Twain
Shall Meet ||

—Rudyard Kipling

12.
|| The East and the West ||
|| Polarity ||

I discovered my Indian roots in the USA.
I became an Indian in the West.

When I talk of the East, I mean India.
When I talk of the West, I mean the USA.

For the most part, India represents the East, and the USA represents the West. The East and the West morph into the Near East and Eastern Europe. For those travelers who are observant, it is not so difficult to experience the subtle and not so subtle shades of differences as you travel West from India through the Middle East, Arab countries, Central Asia, Türkiye, and on to the Eastern European and Balkan countries, until you hit the full-blown West in Central Europe. From there on, it is all downhill until you reach the nadir in the USA, which exists primarily upon unbridled consumption and destruction of Nature. Here, you find that spiritual awareness is totally bankrupt.

As you travel east from India, you experience a more homogenous culture and lifestyle based upon a deeply ingrained spiritual value system. Buddhism and Hinduism made deep inroads throughout Asia, as did the Shinto tradition in Japan. Even developed countries with a Western influence, such as Singapore, South Korea, and Japan, are spiritual at their core.

And then, there is the rich, vibrant, and largely misunderstood Arab and Islamic world that straddles the East and the West, and has its footprints in every continent except, strangely, Central and South America.

Growing Up Indian

Before I migrated to the USA in January 1982, I was oblivious of the richness and significance of being an Indian. I grew up in a typical, traditional Indian family that followed a Hindu way of life. My parents were not overly religious, yet they followed all the festivals and performed all the necessary pujas and rituals throughout the year. Fortunately, they did not believe in visiting temples to pay obeisance to idols. Maa did have an altar at home and followed a daily ritual around it. Babuji could not be bothered with it. However, come Diwali, Dussehra, Holi, and other religious days, Babuji would be at the forefront to do what was needed as per tradition. I was expected to participate too. The rebel in me would surface because my conscience would gnaw at me for participating in something I did not understand. And my parents made no effort to explain anything to me. It was the typical blind faith that prevails in India. I revolted and refused to participate, and Maa and Babuji were not too happy about it.

Eventually, and ironically, it was the West that turned me back to India and its ethos, and for this, among other things, I am ever grateful to it.

Introduction to the West

In the 1970s, I saw the Bollywood movie *Purab Aur Paschim*, by Manoj Kumar. It left a deep impression on me. I was barely in my teens and oblivious to what destiny held for me. Whatever I knew about the West was primarily through my voracious reading of books (including English literature); my regular haunts, the British Council and American libraries near Churchgate where I lived; and watching movies. There was no internet.

All of this, as well as my English medium education, kindled an intense desire in me to migrate to the West. Two of my siblings, a sister and a brother, were already there, and family members would visit them regularly. The exposure to the USA was getting stronger. A close school friend of mine, Vinod, had already gone there for higher education, but surprisingly, he returned disenchanted. All the same, it did not discourage me.

Migrating to the West was also a form of escapism from the conservative and restrictive family and social environment I found myself in, not to mention the limited opportunities for financial upliftment and for giving vent to my raging hormones. I was still ignorant of the Universe's plan for me and definitely not aware of this East–West conundrum that would face me a few years later.

When I migrated to the USA, I landed in the cold, dry, wintry, and snowy landscape of New York City from the warmth of Bombay. Dilip Bhaiya, Lalita Bhabhi, and three-year-old Anmol were at JFK airport to receive me, along with Sita and Raj, Nirmala Jiji's best friends. With five hundred dollars in my pocket to tide me over until I got my job, I camped at Sita's place for a while, mailing out resumes, scanning the newspaper ads, and scouting the city for that elusive first break. When I could not take the cold rejections anymore, I moved to Dilip Bhaiya's place in King of Prussia, PA. Same routine with no luck. But at least I had Anmol to play with, and soon, we bonded.

Subsequently, I was back at Sita's place in New York. Even before I got the much-coveted green card, she had prodded and encouraged me, and even written to Senator Moynihan inquiring about my green card status. She was Nirmala Jiji's bosom friend from school, and by default, close to everyone in the family, with an extra-soft corner for me. Even in my early adulthood, I felt something uncomfortable about her and her motives. It was to become clear to me soon enough.

Sita and Raj had migrated to the USA much earlier. She was a schoolteacher, and Raj was now a stay-at-home husband on disability, due to an accident at the airport where he worked for Sabena Airlines. They had no children, like Nirmala Jiji. They were both chain-smokers and alcoholics, and ate chicken. It was a toxic atmosphere, made worse by the realization that she expected me to live with them even after I got a job, for obvious reasons.

Ironically, it was Sita who managed to get me an interview, which would land me that elusive job at Price Waterhouse, the crème de la crème of the then Big Eight. It was a dream come true. With my first paycheck yet to come and the five hundred dollars all but gone, I asked Pramila Jiji for a loan and rushed to get my first one-bedroom rental apartment in a not-so-desirable neighborhood. I had to get away from Sita. Hell hath no fury like a woman scorned, and this was to be my first experience of Kali in all her fury. By contrast, Raj was a very loving and pleasant person, a complete antidote to his wife. Against her wishes, he helped me with my move to the extent he could, and I was grateful for that. That was the last I saw of them.

Finally, "Home" in the West

I had finally set up home on my own in the West. I have lived for forty-four years in the USA, London, and Luxembourg, and visited every country in North America and Europe, as well as Australia, New Zealand, and what was left of "white" South Africa. It did not take me long to realize that the West and "white" are synonymous, and anyone who is non-white stands out like a sore thumb. The degree of segregation, tolerance, and embracement varied from country to country and also from people to people. Though Ramona and I are planning our exit from this world of arrogance, greed, superficiality, and shallowness, I am grateful for the sustenance the West has provided, the sensibilities it has inculcated in me, and for reorienting me back to my Indian roots.

The West used its physical might to destroy, plunder, and loot many countries across Asia, Africa, and South America during the colonial period, and caused unfathomable damage to the economic, social, and cultural fabric of these countries, the repercussions of which are felt even today. It is only fair and just that the Universe is making amends with reverse colonialism, not of the violent kind perpetrated by the West, but the pacifist form, which nurtures education, healthcare, culture, technology, research, and various soft skills lacking in the West. The West, as we know it today, would collapse like a house of cards under the weight of its own emptiness if all the non-whites were to migrate back to their own countries.

The Imperfect East and the Perfect West

The East is the cradle and keeper of civilization, but it is not perfect. The West is the cradle of unbridled consumption, arrogance, entitlement, and violence, and it is perfect.

This is the paradox that attracts the younger generation to the West.

The perfection of the West is based upon shallowness and a sterile style of living. The imperfection of the East is based upon its deep-rooted religious and spiritual traditions and practices, in a less-than-desirable living environment. They can never meet, except at the very superficial level of materialism facilitated by the internet. There is a cross-migration happening of the younger generation from the East running away from their roots to indulge in Westernized living, as portrayed by the media. The disillusioned from the West are moving to the East for spiritual salvation. The move toward the West is more prevalent, just as maya's influence is, over there.

The West has corrupted the East. "Yog" has become "Yoga" and nothing more than an aerobic exercise. The richness and variety of Indian cuisine have been ignorantly reduced to tandoori chicken, naan, and curry, a dish that is, in reality, non-Indian and a figment of the British imagination. The time-tested, centuries-old potency of Ayurvedic, Unani, Chinese, and Tibetan medicine systems has been denigrated and restricted by the West in order to promote its own toxic pharmaceutical drugs and dysfunctional medical system. The typical American high school student knows more about Prozac and other drugs (recreational and non creational) than the history of America. By the time a typical American is sixty of age, he or she is popping an average of ten pills a day. The American medical industry is among the largest employers in many states. In the East, the medicine cabinet is stuffed with herbs and home made remedies used for generations.

The West originated the practice of tipping as a display of their apparent abundance and superiority, even if they were financially strapped and living hand to mouth. The service industry in the USA quickly got trapped in this toxic practice which became an expectation rather than a reward it was meant to be. Like everything else, they quickly spread it to other parts of the world much to the amusement of the locals.

The West invented hybrid forms of cultivation and spread the seeds all over the globe, damaging local ecosystems, soil, and water sources. I carry out a simple test of eating a slice of fresh tomato in each country I visit, which helps me determine whether the soil and water there are contaminated. As I move West, the taste gets worse until I reach the USA, where the tomato is inedible.

The West has damaged the natural cycles of this beautiful planet of ours and ravaged it with nonstop wars. It invented the nuclear bomb and tested it on innocent Japanese. It then released GMO technology all over the world and is now unleashing another monster in the form of AI. The ignorant, gullible, and pliant East is maintaining a servile attitude, as it does with anything "white." One does not need divya drishti to see where all this is headed. But then, this is also a Happening.

The West can no longer claim the higher moral ground it once had in the early to mid twentieth century when it came to the rescue of Europe. Since World War II, it, along with its stooge, has launched more wars than any other country and killed innocent civilians, including children, than ever. The defense and arms industry has a stranglehold on the US economy. Bu contrast, India has not launched a single war ever. It has always been attacked upon and invaded throughout history and has always tried to defend its rich tapestry of secularism, culture and tradition.

The East has allowed the West to do what they have done. The East is gentle and is no match for the aggressive, vocal, and arrogant West, which made the East dependent on it due to its economic and financial might. The spirituality of the East is its strength and cannot be measured in yardsticks created by the West to determine development, and will not be tamed or controlled by AI. The East was a land of untold riches, peace, and tolerance before the West looted and tried to destroy it. It will survive the havoc caused by the West because it has always lived within its means and not on other people's money.

When I left for the USA, my father gave me just one advice; "never borrow from anyone". That is the way everyone lives in the East, within their means. Yet, when I landed in the USA, I noticed everyone struggling to live hand to mouth and borrowing to the max. It was a microcosm of what was happening at the macro level. With a financial and accounting background, it was not rocket science to realize that the perceived US property was based upon *borrowing from the rest of the world and printing money* for its insatiable spending. The USA is as bankrupt financially as its citizens. Most businesses are leveraged to the hilt. Lawyers specializing in Chapter 11 (bankruptcy law) are laughing all the way to the bank.

As a yogi and a seeker, my only solace is to be the witness and watch this Happening as well. It is as much ordained as any other Happening.

Indians in the West

The Indian diaspora in the West, especially the USA, is truly unique. The first generation that migrated in the 1960s and 1970s is stuck in a time warp. They have neither blended into the American way of life nor have they kept up with the Indian spirit. The fresh boatloads of Indian IT nerds who descend on the shores of the West now bring their own cultural baggage with them and confine themselves to their ghettos. The second generation that has been educated in the USA is a confused lot. They have American friends but Indian parents, American boyfriends and girlfriends, but want an Indian style wedding. They are addicted to Bollywood but attend rock concerts. It is a lethal mix. These NRIs behave conspicuously when they visit India, brushing their teeth with bottled water and cleaning their butts with toilet paper for one-upmanship over their Indian cousins.

But the issue is deeper. There is the individual psyche that governs each individual, and there is the broader psyche that governs each of the two hemispheres. At the individual level, there is tolerance, understanding, and bonding, but the glue is materialism, not spirituality. At the broader level, East and West can never see eye to eye. The spiritual, religious, and social conditioning of centuries has created a deep chasm between the two. To add to it are the wounds and scars that have yet to heal from the colonialism, violence, and repression perpetrated by the West for centuries, and continuing today in the form of racism and a self-imposed superiority complex.

In all my years spent in the West, I have not come across a single person of the Indian diaspora who has seriously taken to spiritual seeking. The confusion between religion and spirituality is more marked in the West than in the East. In the East, people by and large are fervently religious, with little or no understanding of spirituality. In the West, when I ask someone whether they are spiritual, I get the answer, "Yes, I go to the temple (or church) regularly." The problem in the East is not the presence of religion; it is the ignorance of religion. The problem in the West is not the absence of spirituality but the ignorance of spirituality.

Teachers and masters like Swami Vivekananda, Paramhansa Yogananda, Maharishi Mahesh Yogi, Swami Rama, J. Krishnamurti, Swami Sivananda, Swami Muktananda, and many others moved West and set up base there to introduce spirituality. In the vastness of the spiritually barren West, they have barely made inroads. On the other hand, Swami Prabhupada introduced the West to the *bhakti*-driven religious fervor of Krishna Consciousness and had a bigger impact. But like all religious movements, it soon lost its grounding and credibility, and became an embarrassment of sorts. Sri Chinmoy found the middle path and made quiet inroads through education and social work. The current crop of godmen from India make the mandatory annual visits to the West and do nothing to lift the spiritual consciousness of people mired in unbridled materialism, since they themselves are caught in the same web. The Dalai Lama has been partly successful in raising awareness of Buddhism, but the dogmatic kind, not the Zen awareness of the Buddha.

In my years of living and traveling in the West, I have found that the Himalayan Institute in Honesdale, PA, the Sivananda ashrams spread throughout North America and the Maharishi Vedic City in Iowa are the only repositories there for traditional Vedic, Advaitic, and Tantric knowledge. Fortunately, there are pockets of influence, like Baba Harihar Ramji, who are keeping the flame lit.

As I have traveled from Asia to the Middle East, Africa, Europe, North America, and South America, the differences in spiritual awareness are difficult to miss. My Wanderings have been a learning experience like none other, and I hope to continue with them until my last breath. As Robert Frost said, "I have . . . miles to go before I sleep."

The East Today

The Indian ethos is my ethos, but it is no longer the land that oozes spirituality from every stone and every leaf. On the one hand, it is fast descending into the abyss of fundamentalism and intolerance that is sweeping across the globe; on the other, Western shallowness has encroached into the psyche of the younger generation. The richness and depth of Indian wisdom in all walks of life are fast disappearing in these times of instant gratification. Personal, family, and community values have eroded in trying to keep up with Western standards. And this is all happening in the name of development and progress, which are just bywords for unbridled capitalism and consumption running amok.

But India is my country, and I was sad to have had to give up my citizenship when I acquired another. India is multifaceted inside its borders, but not so outside. It is not willing to accept the best of the rest of the world and would rather struggle along on its limp feet. When I came to India in 1993 to set up operations for Morgan Stanley, the country was ridiculed for its anemic "Hindu" rate of growth, but it has now leapfrogged its way to the top. As a seeker who has found the answers right here, I know that this is still the place to be for spiritual salvation, in spite of some of the worst living conditions in the world, in the midst of unimaginable filth and unhygienic conditions, open sewers, overflowing toilets, nonexistent or broken infrastructure, ramshackle housing, overcrowding, absence of basic civic sense, and some of the worst displays of public etiquette anywhere in the world, including the most obsessive, intrusive and rude mobile phone habits I have seen anywhere. India lives on its streets, sleeping, eating, washing, urinating, defecating, along with protesting, celebrating, fighting, and killing, surrounded by some of the ugliest and bleakest structures, all in your face. Most Indians remain nonchalant and uncaring about this depressive state of existence, and therein lies their unflinching attachment to blind faith and religion. Most people are seeking economic nirvana instead of spiritual nirvana. Religion and every activity connected with it is one of the fastest-growing businesses in India alongside economic growth.

India is globally equated to Hinduism, even though one-fifth of its population is Muslim and represents the third-largest Muslim population in the world. I have found it interesting that in many countries, I am identified as a Hindu and not as an Indian. For them, India is Hindustan, and all Indians are Hindus. No amount of pleading on my part convinces them when I tell them I am not a Hindu. It is beyond their limited sphere of living in ignorance. It is no different than being labeled a Hindu at the gates of a temple in India based upon how I look and talk and behave.

Being a Hindu is a way of life, and that is what it was always meant to be, according to the scriptures and ancient wisdom which refers to the

Sanatan dharma (eternal way of life) with no mention of "Hinduism". It was never meant to be an ism or a dogma or a religion like other organized religions. Ganga, Gayatri, Gita and Gai (cow) are the four pillars and symbols of sanatan dharma, It does not reside in temples but in Nature all around. Among all the major religions, Hinduism is the only religion that does not have a leading figure like Yeshua, Mohammad, Buddha, Mahavir, Guru Nanak, and Zarathushtra, and therein lies the strength and resilience of the Sanatan way of life.

Are You a Hindu?

Just in case you have ever wondered whether you are a Hindu, or taken for granted that you are a Hindu, or questioned the definition of a Hindu, you just have to visit one of the many temples in South India or the Pashupatinath Temple in Kathmandu, Nepal, to get an instant answer. I have never considered myself to be a Hindu, but I was told in no uncertain terms at the Lingaraj Temple in Bhubaneswar that I was one. It seemed like I was getting a badge of honor. Many who doubt being a Hindu would have been proud to have this declaration thrust upon them at the entrance of one of the most revered Hindu temples in India. I was a bit aghast that religion was being imposed upon me when, in fact, I had no religion!

In secular and liberal India, some temples allow entrance only to Hindus, and this is a known fact mentioned in all travel guides. In 2008, I was on a trip to Odisha with a motley group that consisted of Indians, NRIs, and foreigners. We were on our way to Konark for a full moon meditation at the Sun Temple. Full moon at the Sun Temple sounds like a contradiction, but what a blissful, empowering contradiction (but that is a separate story already related elsewhere)! We had to pass Bhubaneswar and Puri to reach Konark, and since the Lingaraj Temple in Bhubaneswar and the Jagannath Temple in Puri were listed in all our guidebooks as the top "sightseeing places," we decided to stop by. Having read that only Hindus are allowed entrance, some of the foreigners and NRIs were hesitant to even go near the temples. I had something else in mind, and convinced them to come along to at least admire the architectural beauty from the outside (they are actually dirty and ugly!), and if we were fortunate (or unfortunate, depending on one's perspective), the gods would smile and make us all Hindus for a day!

We reached the Lingaraj Temple, dutifully removed our shoes outside, and joined the long queue to enter. I led the group, followed by these individuals: Sam (an NRI and non-practicing Muslim, who looks totally Indian); Vijay (an ex-NRI, now in Delhi, a self-professed Hindu) with his American wife, Dolly (a Protestant converted to Hinduism, wearing a sari); Himanshu and his wife, Julie (non-practicing Parsis living in Europe but speaking Parsi-accented Hindi); Sonam (a practicing Sikh from Europe, who can throw choice four-letter words at you in Hindi, looked fairer and more "foreigner" in her jeans than Dolly); Michael, aka Mohandas (from Lithuania, who studies Sanskrit in Benares and teaches it in Europe, in kurta pajama, long hair, speaks chaste Hindi, but looks very much a foreigner, like Tom Alter an English actor speaking chaste Urdu); and Elia (a Jew from Israel who looks totally Indian with pierced nose, etc.).

Six others were "true" non-Hindu foreigners, who would never have made it past the entrance even if the gods were smiling, and therefore chose not to join the line.

I approached the three security officials (not sure whether they were cops) and was allowed to enter. Sam followed, without being questioned. Vijay was holding his wife's hands, and one of the guys stopped Dolly and started talking to her in Hindi. Vijay intervened, saying she was his wife and they were both Hindus. The guy said, "You may go, but is your wife born a Hindu or Christian?" Vijay replied that she had converted to Hinduism to marry him. She was refused entry, and they stood aside. The three guys could not figure out what to make of Himanshu and Julie. They were also holding hands and looked as Indian as all Parsis do, and were conversing in Hindi with the guys. Names were asked, Himanshu sounded Indian, and was allowed to go, but not his wife, Julie. Sonam's body language was such that the three guys dared not challenge her! She entered. Mohandas did not make it because he was speaking with them in such chaste Hindi that they doubted any Hindu could speak such perfect Hindi! Elia walked in.

I was watching all this and asked the officials why Dolly, Julie, and Mohandas had not been allowed.

They responded, "Only Hindus are allowed.

I replied that Dolly was a Hindu and that Mohandas was studying and teaching Sanskrit, and, perhaps, he could speak with the priests.

Their ostensible reason was that "converted and other such Hindus are not allowed."

I persisted: "But you have allowed so many non-Hindus, so why not two more. I am not a Hindu, so why did you allow me?"

Looking pointedly at the rudraksha mala on my neck and the red thread around my wrist, they told me, "You look like a Hindu, so you are allowed to go in." In fact, they insisted I go in!

I then pointed to Sam, Himanshu, Sonam, and Elia, and argued, "But you have allowed a Muslim, a Parsi, a Sikh, and a Jew to enter!"

Taken aback, they bemusedly said, "You are kidding. They are all Hindus. Non-Hindus don't look like this!"

I pointed to Sam and informed them, "His real name is Salim, and he is a Muslim." Then, unable to resist, I sarcastically added, "Should I ask him to drop his pants so that you can confirm it?"

The three gatekeepers to the Hindu gods had no clue what I was talking about! By this time, we were surrounded by bystanders, and it became quite a scene. Needless to say, none of us (true Hindus, Hindu lookalikes, pseudo-Hindus, or non-Hindus) entered the temple. A local journalist in the crowd who had witnessed the incident spoke with us, took some pictures, and apparently, this "event" was published in one of the local newspapers. I do not doubt that it was a nonevent for almost anyone who may have read that piece, just as it was for the hundreds who were entering the temple.

We repeated the same "event" at the Jagannath Temple in Puri, with almost identical results, except that Himanshu was also stopped from entering.

I had had a similar experience at the Pashupatinath Temple in Kathmandu, where I was in a group of two hundred Indians and NRIs led by Swami Chidanand Saraswati of Parmarth Niketan. We were on our way to Kailash Mansarovar. There were about ten "foreigners," including Sadhvi Bhagwati, who has been initiated by Swami Chidananda as his main disciple. She is an American Jew who wears saffron saris, recites the Gita, and gives discourses on Vedanta. All ten, including her, were not allowed inside the temple, even though she was with Swamiji, who went inside with the group. Some of us protested and stayed behind. Later, we asked Swamiji about this, and he had no clear explanation to offer.

I have been to 130 countries, visited numerous temples, mosques, gurudwaras, churches, synagogues, and other places of worship for various faiths and denominations. Not once have I encountered a place that is closed to people of other faiths, except sometimes during prayer time. India has yet one more unique distinction: denying access to God to the very people who represent God.

Despite having to remove footwear outside the main temple, these custodians and caretakers of Hindu gods cannot keep the temple grounds and the temple itself clean and tidy. Among all the places of worship of different faiths I have been to all over the world, the Hindu temples are the filthiest.

A few years ago, I was in Vrindavan, walking around near the ghats, which were all very filthy. A priest approached me asking whether I would like to have a puja performed. I replied, "Why don't you clean up these ghats and the streets first, that will be my puja." He was aghast! I walked on.

Chardham: Heaven or Hell?

In Zen, we say, "Not a leaf moves without reason."

Everything that happens all around us and in our lives is part of a grand plan. Nothing is random. Every cell of every creature, every grain of every stone, is connected to each other, has a role to play, and a story to tell.

For many who are on the spiritual path, all this may sound clichéd. But therein lies the truism. And the evidence appears before us consistently.

The Chardham Yatra in Uttarakhand is perhaps the most revered pilgrimage for Hindus. It involves visiting four far-flung sites in the Himalayas by road. One of them, Badrinath, is one of the four maths established by Adi Shankaracharya over a thousand years ago. The sites are inaccessible most of the year due to extreme weather conditions, and the rest of the time, the poorly maintained roads make the trip very treacherous. There are regular landslides and mishaps, causing fatalities along the route each year. In its infinite wisdom, the Government introduced a helicopter service. Soon, the helicopters started crashing, killing the passengers. This has not daunted the pilgrims or the Government (not surprising), and the story is repeated year after year. There are two ways of looking at this Happening:

The resolute Indian belief system

Millions of Indians are part of a belief system where God (does not matter which one) exists or resides in certain spots scattered around India. This belief has been perpetuated through a liberal dose of mythology mixed with a potent dose of vested interests from religious zealots and corrupt politicians. Year after year, there is a mad rush for the Amarnath, Vaishnodevi, Chardham, and Kailash Mansarovar yatras, all in remote mountainous locations with little or no infrastructure. There are numerous others, but these are the stars that clamor for attention, partly because they are accessible only for short periods of time and also because they offer pilgrims the thrill of navigating through treacherous mountain areas in North India.

Each of these yatras has had its share of tragedy and controversy over the years, including natural disasters that have befallen them. But none come close to what was seen in Chardham in 2013. Thousands perished in the landslides and flooding. These were people who were part of this belief system, who had gone on the yatra to experience God, be with God, or at least feel closer to God. Should God not have been happy that His devout followers had come to pay obeisance, braving such hardships? Should He not have been pleased and showered His blessings on these fortunate few who got to come for His darshan? So instead, why did He rain fury upon them? What happened to the deeply entrenched Indian belief system that attracts thousands of Indians from all over India to this part of the Himalayas, seeking salvation or penance for their sins or praying for something or the other? This is the land of *"Atithi devo bhava* (The guest is God)."* God Himself is not supposed to behave in this destructive manner. So what happened?

Are you sure God resides in these abodes?

The Law of Karma

India is one of those intriguing places where people will have animated and heated discussions, as if they are undisputed experts on the topic under discussion. And karma is one of the favorite points of debate. Most of the participants have no clue what the Law of Karma is all about. Ask them, and they will conveniently retort, "Oh, read the Gita; it is about karma." Since this is something that resonates well with most people here, let us look at the Chardham disaster from this angle.

If you believe in the most simplistic version of the Law of Karma, which suggests that your fruits are the results of your actions, then this tragedy is really easy to understand. One only has to shift one's gaze from the micro level to the macro level. The Law of Karma is not dependent on a belief in God. It transcends the gods themselves, who are also subject to this law. After all, even Krishna had to pay a price for the various lies and deceit he indulged in during the Mahabharat war. Indian mythology (part of the Indian belief system above) is replete with stories where various gods use this law in one-upmanship to establish their own superiority. The sage Narad Muni is often the catalyst for this. So, if man plays havoc with Nature, man will bear the fruits of that action. And it has, in Uttarakhand and elsewhere.

Mankind has plundered and destroyed the beautiful Himalayan mountains and all the meandering rivers that descend from them to become the mighty and holy Ganga. We swear by the holiness and divinity of this great river, yet turn a blind eye when its various siblings originating in the Chardham area are held captive through the unbridled building of dams, thereby impacting the ecology.

Thousands of pilgrims and other residents in the area flush tons of plastic and other garbage into these pristine rivers and the forests surrounding them. Roads that are poorly designed and maintained are cut into the mountainside, with scant respect for topology and geology. The already fragile infrastructure that can barely sustain the residents of the area is expected to handle the multitudes that throng there every year.

The fumes from the thousands of vehicles that clog the roads each summer are enough to choke the hardened and jaded urban dweller, not to mention Mother Nature, despite Her accommodating nature.

Dwellings and structures of all kinds, most of them precarious and of very poor quality, dot the landscape in every habitable area. Many of them are built right alongside the rivers. Riverbeds are eroded, and riverbanks are intruded into without proper reinforcement. Even a very famous ashram in the holy town of Rishikesh has not hesitated to reclaim a part of the Ganga as its own, so that it may accommodate ever-growing crowds for its famous Ganga Aarti. This structure too was swept away by the mighty force of the Ganga!

The Law of Karma never fails. As you sow, so shall you reap. Mother Nature is unrelenting. She will not allow mankind to tame Her. Every once in a while, She makes it clear who is supreme. But it is the unfortunate fate of mankind in India that it continues to remain in this self-imposed stupor of blind faith and ignorance.

I went on the Chardham Yatra more than thirty years ago when I was a student. Even at that time, it was miserable. I reached Kedarnath but refused to go to the temple. I came back to Joshimath and refused to go to Badrinath. Gangotri and Yamnotri were out of the question; there was litter and human waste all around. I could not find a single decent, clean toilet anywhere. When I could not hold my pressure any longer, I asked a priest nearby for help. He asked me to go into the open fields with a tumbler of water. The field was infested with flies. Somehow, I relieved myself and swore I would never come back.

Kailash Mansarovar

Mount Kailash in Tibet is believed to be the abode of Shiva here on Earth, and a visit there is considered the gold pennant for Hindu pilgrims. In July 2006, I had the opportunity to visit Kailash Mansarovar with a group led by Swami Chidanand Saraswati.

In March 2000, I attended the first International Yoga Festival organized in Rishikesh, and I was impressed with the organizational skills on display at the festival. It has since turned into a jamboree of sorts with over a thousand attendees from all over the world, claiming to be yogis and yoginis. But in 2000, it was a small group of about a hundred, which enjoyed personal interaction with the sages and teachers, including Swamiji himself. This is when I first met Himalayan Master Ved Bhartiji, a disciple of Swami Rama and a realized soul himself. Being in his presence was as mesmerizing as being with Osho. His depth of wisdom and his mastery of Sanskrit were awe-inspiring and pushed me further along on my journey. A few years later, I visited his ashram and spent a few days there, after he had already attained samadhi. My connection with the Himalayan Institute had been established.

At the same festival, it was my good fortune to also come in contact with Swami Bharat Bhushanji from Saharanpur. He was our Yog Guru (and one of the very few yog teachers who pronounced yog correctly) for two weeks, during which he made Patanjali's Ashtanga Yog come alive, combined with *mantra japa*. He was the first and last true yog teacher I met on my journey. At that stage in my journey, I was well established in *Hatha Yog* but lacked the discipline necessary to take it forward. Bharta Bhushanji provided that encouragement.

The Kailash Mansarovar Yatra was a disaster for me. It was poorly organized with inadequate facilities, and a sense of arrogance and a "make do" attitude pervaded the group. There were three groups of people: people living in India, Indians living abroad, and non-Indians. On these kinds of hardy trips involving difficult terrain, uncertain weather, and poor facilities, non-Indians tend to fare better, as they did in this case. However, quite a few others fell ill along the way with little or no medical help. I barely made it to Mansarovar, but the refreshing, cool breeze from the lake rejuvenated me. However, I was in no shape to do the circumambulation of Mount Kailash. I had to be content to stay back and watch Adi Kailash from my tent, waiting for the helicopter to arrive to rescue me and a few others. Chandrika was my savior in the form of a Shakti who had accompanied me from Pune.

The aborted trip to Mount Kailash reminded me of the trip to Kedarnath in 1975, where I fell sick as well and was miserable during the entire trek. Many years later, I could not have darshan at Bhimashankar (one of the fourteen Jyotirlingas) for strange reasons. The message was clear. I did not have to go looking for Shiva in all these places. He was reigning supreme in my Ajna, waiting for Kundalini to rise. And it did.

As an atheist, I did not go on these trips to seek God, and sure enough, I did not find him lurking behind some tree or hiding in some temple. Much later, as I continued along on my spiritual journey, I found Him sitting inside me all along!

Religion vs Spirituality

I am frequently asked to explain the difference between religion and spirituality. Depending on which part of the world I am in, my answer is simple.

In India: "If you go to Ayodhya to find Rama, that is religion. If you go inside yourself to find Rama, that is spirituality."

In the West: "If you go to the Vatican to find Jesus, that is religion. If you go inside yourself to find Jesus, that is spirituality."

Year after year, there are numerous instances of natural disasters, stampedes, and bus accidents killing hundreds and thousands of pilgrims of every faith all over the world. No faith is immune from this Happening, both in the East and the West. Yet it does not deter the others who follow in the same footsteps. It is easy to rent a car or book a train or flight and head to where you think you will find God, even though in the process you may actually end up in his lap! But it is much more difficult to stay where you are and find him right inside you because that requires years of practice, penance, perseverance and patience.

If we can strip the dogma from religious thought and bring any religious teaching down to the bare bones spiritual level, the following will make sense. It is not about the comparison of religions but the essence of the human spirit. Just as Hinduism has nothing to do with Rama or Krishna or any of the other godheads, Buddhism has nothing to do with the Buddha's teachings, Islam has nothing to do with Prophet Mohammed's revelations, and Christianity has nothing to do with Jesus and his teachings. All of these religions got "organized" thanks to the greed and power of certain individuals who took it upon themselves to "interpret" the teachings of the Teachers themselves.

Mudras in Orthodox Churches

I looked up at the icon again and again, not believing my eyes. I was in the St. Sava Church in Belgrade, Serbia. It is the largest Orthodox Church in the world. I went around and looked at some more icons, and the hand gestures stared at me again, almost wanting to tell me something. They were unmistakably similar to the mudras in Hindu and Buddhist traditions. My curiosity was now piqued, and I started clicking some pictures.

A couple of years before this, I had traveled extensively to Eastern Europe and Russia, which, along with Greece, are the centers of the Orthodox Church. I visited numerous Orthodox churches in these countries, each more resplendent than the other. One of the most beautiful ones I visited was in Vilnius. But I had never noticed the hand gestures on the icons until now.

It is important to understand that iconography is unique to the Orthodox Church and does not exist in the Catholic or Protestant Church. The latter has an altar, which does not exist in the Orthodox Church. The faithful and visitors are required to stand during the services in the Orthodox Church as there are no pews. These differences between the two (Orthodox vs Catholic and Protestant) are missed by most non-Christians while visiting the churches. But a closer and patient look will reveal some surprises, as it did for me.

From Belgrade onwards, as I traveled to the other Balkan countries (Bulgaria in particular) and Russia, I started noticing these hand gestures in almost all the icons in the Churches. These countries are predominantly Orthodox but have a few Catholic churches too. So, to make sure that my observation was valid, I also visited the latter and did not find any icons there, and therefore, no hand gestures.

In the Orthodox churches, I noticed that among all the hand gestures, two were most common: one, the tips of the thumb and the ring finger joined together, and two, the tips of the little finger and ring finger joined to the tip of the thumb. Both were formed with the right hand. The first one is the *Prithvi Mudra*, and the second is the *Prana Mudra*, two of the 108 mudras from Yog and Tantra practices. The third most common hand gesture I noticed was the tip of the index finger touching the tip of the thumb, the *Vitarka Mudra*, better known as Jnana Mudra.

How did these mudras come about in these Christian icons thousands of years after they had already become part of the spiritual and religious practice in India?

As part of this Happening, three other Happenings occurred within a span of a few days during the same trip to help me find the answer to this question.

First Happening: I stumbled upon *The Urantia Book* at the Mystic Fair in Zagreb, Croatia.

Second Happening: I finally read the book *Jesus Lived in India* in its entirety by Holger Kersten.

Third Happening: I met a defrocked priest of the Serbian Orthodox Church in Belgrade.

Let me start with the third Happening.

Jesus in India

While conducting a cooking workshop at Radost, a vegetarian restaurant in Belgrade, I started chatting with Maria, one of the chefs, who is a Krishna devotee. When I shared my observations about the hand gestures with her, her eyes lit up, and she enthusiastically informed me about an Orthodox priest who had done extensive research on the connection between Jesus and India, and, in particular, what exactly happened during the "missing years" of his early life and those after his "Resurrection." During his investigation, this priest had traveled to India and Tibet numerous times. Subsequently, he was about to publish his findings. But before he could do that, the Church got wind of it and defrocked him. Instead of a messiah, he had become a pariah!

Maria knew the priest and agreed to introduce me to him. I met him the next day over a cup of tea. He was a very unassuming person, radiating a certain aura that was very comforting. As I shared my observations with him, he smiled and said that what I had noticed was not random. It reflected the "Buddhist teachings and philosophy that Jesus had imbibed while visiting India and Tibet during the missing years of his life." I listened to him in disbelief as he shared anecdotes, tidbits, evidence, and other information he had gathered during his trips as part of his research. I sat there transfixed as he showed me pictures and references in various Indian and Tibetan scriptures alluding to the presence of one Yuz Assaf, as well as Issa Masih, visiting India and subsequently living there. His trail culminated just outside Srinagar in a dargah that is marked as the tomb of Yuz Assaf. Yuz Assaf was Jesus!

The priest's last statement as we parted was even more thought-provoking: "Jesus was the last of the reincarnations of Vishnu, after Krishna and the Buddha.

The priest's revelations jolted my memory, and I realized that I had actually visited this place in Kashmir in 2006. I had come across the book *Jesus Lived in India* that pinpointed the exact location, and I had gone there to find it for myself.

This brings me to the second Happening.

Whenever I am on a long trip like this one (over two months), I usually throw in a book for reading, assuming I will have some free time, which, of course, I never do. The book lies buried deep inside my suitcase. This time, for some strange reason, I was carrying *Jesus Lived in India,* and I had forgotten about it. After my meeting with the priest, I immediately dug out the book from my bag and devoured it with rapt attention.

Holger Kersten, the author of this book, is a German theologian and religious scholar. He has meticulously outlined in detail the missing gaps in Jesus's life and, in particular, shed light on the mystery of the

Resurrection and what happened thereafter. His trail from Bethlehem, Jerusalem, and Palestine took him across the entire Middle East and Near East, Afghanistan, Pakistan, India, and Tibet. It culminated in Anzimar, just outside Srinagar, at Yuz Assaf's tomb, the same one referred to by the priest.

While the priest's research notes were all in Serbian and, therefore, not readable by me, Kersten's book is in English. While some parts may appear to be conjecture and may not stand up in a court of law because of a lack of circumstantial evidence, the scientific and theological proof provided by him appears quite convincing to a non-Christian. Of course, to the Vatican Church, it was blasphemy, and the book and the author were quickly denounced.

Global Influence of India's Wisdom

Irrespective of whether one accepts and believes in the theories postulated by the two individuals above, one fact remains irrefutable: Civilization, as we understand it, had dawned in India before anywhere else in the world. Indian philosophy and thinking in the form of the Vedas and Puranas had developed and been documented thousands of years before Jesus was born. Krishna and Gautama Buddha had both reincarnated as Vishnu avatars and left a trail of their teachings and followers well before Jesus. It is quite possible that these teachings and belief systems made their way to various parts of the world. However, up until the last couple of centuries, Indian history was largely depicted through the oral tradition, with very little in writing. This is unlike Western history, which is largely written and, therefore, also easier to move around, manipulate and amend according to one's convenience.

The Western world, right through the ages, has never given credence to the depth of Indian wisdom and its impact on almost every aspect of life in the world. Authors like Kersten, Emerson, Tolstoy, Russell and Hesse in modern times, and travelers like Marco Polo have done that. It is also an indication of Eastern passivity versus Western aggressiveness.

And this brings me to the first Happening.

The Urantia Book is a two-thousand-page tome that was first noticed in the 1950s. It has no stated author and was compiled based on supposed revelations to some individuals who chose to be anonymous. It quickly became controversial due to its contents and the fact that no individual(s) took responsibility for them. In a nutshell, the book purports to reveal wisdom about the Universe, its functioning, God, and, in particular, Jesus and his life and teachings.

Skimming it (it is impossible to read the entire text due to the dense and science fiction style of writing), one gets the impression, that the author(s) took off from where the New Testament ended, and took it upon themselves to "reveal" the true nature of the Universe from the Western Christian perspective, to counter the widely accepted wisdom of the Vedas and Upanishads. Whether or not they succeed is not relevant.

The reason this book becomes relevant in the context of Jesus and India is twofold. One, it does talk about Jesus seemingly appearing in person to various individuals for a long period after the Resurrection. Second, it reluctantly acknowledges the fact that India was the beehive of all spiritual wisdom during the period of Jesus's early years, especially the Buddhist teachings and their extensive impact. It also mentions that the belief in reincarnation and the ability of wise men to predict the arrival of the next Buddha were strongly accepted beliefs in the East. But thereafter, instead of joining the dots and linking the birth of Jesus to this reincarnation, as recognized by the three wise men from the East who came following the Bethlehem star, they abruptly drop it like a hot potato on the premise that Indian spirituality and wisdom "did not fulfill its potential"! It is not important to go into the reasons for this. Suffice to say, Indian wisdom was very much acknowledged and known in the West, even to a reluctant latter-day Christian.

There are numerous areas of similarity and convergence between Christian theology and Hindu and Buddhist philosophy. This is evident more in the Orthodox Church and less so in the Vatican Church. Nikolaj Belimirovic is another Serbian Orthodox priest who has alluded to this connection. Just as Zen is the purest form of Buddhism, Sufi is the purest form of Islam, and Advaita is the purest form of Hinduism, the Orthodox beliefs emerge as a truer version of Jesus's teachings and life, though not in their entirety.

One can find a few similarities between Christianity and the Hindu and Buddhist traditions: The introduction to St. John's Gospel, "In the beginning was the Word . . ." reminds one of Aum, the primordial Word, the sound of Creation itself. Likewise, a parallel can be drawn between the Holy Trinity (The Father, The Son, and The Holy Spirit) and the Trimurti (Brahma, Vishnu, and Mahesh) or (Buddha, Dharma, Sangha). The use of holy water during baptism is similar to cleansing oneself through ritual bathing in the holy rivers of India. Chanting, for example, the Gregorian chants, is the Western equivalent of mantra chanting in the East. In the Christian tradition, one uses rosary beads while chanting or praying, while in the Hindu and Buddhist traditions, a similar form of prayer beads, the *japa mala*, is used. Fasting is common to both the West and the East. Just as the prophecy of the birth of Jesus was feared by King Herod, the foretelling of the birth of Krishna was feared by the tyrant king Kansa. And finally, Jesus was a healer, and so was the Buddha.

This is how the hand gestures start to make sense. If Jesus was indeed a Bodhisattva, his spending time in India and Tibet during his formative years starts to fall into place. Upon his return, his teachings earned him the wrath of the Jews, since they were totally opposed to the latter's concept of God. He was hounded, betrayed, and ultimately crucified. But as foretold by him, he rose from the tomb on the third day, not just in spirit as mentioned in the Gospels, but in body, since he never died on the cross. His appearances after the Resurrection are not just visions, but of flesh and blood. Only, no one is aware of this except the few who were with him throughout this time, and who accompanied him as he crossed Mount Olive to head to the East, to India, his spiritual home, where he had come from. Osho, a master of modern times, himself acknowledges this, no less.

Amen!

Journey of a Vegetarian

Along with Hinduism, India is associated with vegetarianism. I consider myself fortunate to have been born in a vegetarian family, but I discovered true vegetarianism in the West, just as I discovered my Indian roots while living there.

Are you a vegetarian?

Yes? Let me ask you again.

Are you really a vegetarian?

If your answer is still yes, read on and see if you still maintain that you are a vegetarian.

Well, why are you a vegetarian? Is it because you were born and brought up a vegetarian and have continued to be so? Or is it because you want to live healthy? Or because you believe that killing animal life for human consumption is wrong? Or perhaps a combination of one or more of the above reasons?

Many of those who claim to be vegetarians fall in the first category (especially in India). Since they were born to vegetarian parents and brought up in a vegetarian household, they take vegetarianism for granted and never question what makes one a vegetarian or what it really means. They mostly either remain unaware or choose to ignore that in their day-to-day life, they may be intruding into the animal world inadvertently.

The health benefits of a vegetarian diet are well researched, well documented, and well known. This includes the known biological fact that the human body is designed only for a plant-based diet and not for the consumption of dead animals. However, the moral aspect of being a vegetarian, that is, the justification for killing animals for consumption, is subjective and debatable, and a matter of one's personal choice.

True spiritual learning and growth can only be experiential and not anecdotal. What follows is a discussion based on my own experience around the world.

Am I a vegetarian?

Yes. I was born to vegetarian parents and brought up in a vegetarian household. For the most part, my circle of immediate family and friends comprised vegetarians, and a vegetarian diet was the only one I knew and accepted. As in most Indian vegetarian families, our meals centered primarily around dal, sabji, roti, and rice in various forms and combinations. I never gave this aspect of daily life any thought.

It was only after I went to the USA that everything changed. The vegetarian diet that I had taken for granted in India went for a toss. I was exposed to a very different culture, with food habits alien to my insulated Indian mind. I was now forced to verify every item I bought at the grocery store or ordered in a restaurant. Fresh produce (fruits and vegetables), grains, cereals, lentils, and dairy products were obviously not a problem. This was in the early eighties, well before "hybrid," "GMO," and "organic" became buzzwords. I started coming across ingredients and names that I had never heard of before, such as polenta, soya, tofu, and gluten. I would avoid any strange or unknown names, not wanting to risk ending up eating meat in some form. The silver lining was that I started cooking and called my mother regularly to ask how to make my favorite items: sabudana khichadi, upma, poha, and various vegetables and dals. I started experimenting on my own. If I had to eat out, I would seek Indian restaurants.

This was about the time when vegetarianism was starting to become more prevalent in the USA and Europe. As with almost everything else in the USA, a plethora of writings, commentaries, and other information on the benefits of being a vegetarian was circulating, which focused on the health benefits and the moral aspect. I started taking a hard look at my own background and asked myself why I was a vegetarian. This was also the time when people in the USA and India inquired how I managed to survive as a vegetarian. In India, it was generally understood that anyone migrating to the USA would inevitably start consuming meat. For Americans, vegetarianism was a fad, totally misunderstood, and riddled with ignorance and arrogance about their own "superior" diet.

This was the turning point for me. From being a "born into a vegetarian family" vegetarian, I became a conscious vegetarian, fully aware of why I was one. Most importantly, I no longer needed to be defensive about being one. Yet, it was an uphill task for me, especially because I was rising up the corporate ladder, interacting with the business world, and traveling extensively. Business lunches and dinners, meals with colleagues, invitations to homes and parties, room service, and flight meals all became obstacles to be overcome. But my resolve introduced me to various support groups, such as vegetarian societies, and I became more involved as an activist. Most importantly, I started understanding the importance of knowing exactly what it was that I was consuming. I made it a habit (to date) of not buying any packaged item without reading the label and knowing the ingredients.

Meanwhile, many vegetarian Indians coming to the USA were shedding their vegetarian diet, partly as a necessity (so they claim), and also as a status symbol, and to appear to merge into the mainstream, without having to come across like a square.

As I quit the corporate world and immersed myself fully into spirituality, I became more sensitive to what was on my plate. Why is it that all the teachers and masters, retreats and ashrams, and all places of spiritual growth and learning all over the world (not just in India) are vegetarian? As the energy channels open up and energy starts moving through the chakras, one inevitably becomes sensitized to one's environment, especially food and nutrition. At the physical level, the body starts rejecting any animal-based food. Intuitively, one starts sensing something is wrong even before one has taken the first morsel. I learned and realized for myself the reason for this: the simple truth that when an animal is about to be slaughtered, it immediately becomes cognizant of it and becomes tense and stressed. This negative energy remains in the flesh and bones even after it has been slaughtered. Any healer or energy therapist can recognize this, whether it is the negative energy of individuals, food containing killed animals, hybrid produce, or food laden with preservatives, chemicals, and fertilizers.

I have a fondness for authentic Neapolitan pizza, and Neapolitan pizza without the buffalo mozzarella or fior di latte (cow's milk mozzarella) is like *pani puri* (fried hollow shells with tangy water) without the pani (water). I soon discovered that almost all cheese contains rennin, which is derived from a cow's stomach. I was depressed and disappointed on learning this. I do not have a particular liking for cheese except mozzarella, especially mozzarella made from buffalo's milk, fresh and creamy. I was not going to accept defeat, so I researched this and found that any cheese can be made with a plant-based rennin and that such cheese was available at many places. I also discovered that certain pizza places do use vegetarian cheese. It was not the end of the world after all!

My attention now shifted to items that we generally do not associate with being vegetarian or otherwise: personal care items (toothpaste, soaps, shampoos, perfumes, lotions, etc.), health supplements (vitamins, antioxidants, etc.), and medicines. One can argue that some of these are not consumed by the body, so what is the problem? Well, first of all, all these items are absorbed into the body directly or indirectly. Secondly, if being a vegetarian is a belief and a way of life (this is where the question "Why am I a vegetarian?" again arises), then should it not extend to everything that touches one's daily life? Should one not question everything that one utilizes and see if it involves a slaughtered animal? Where does one draw the line? What about clothes and footwear? What about the use of leather? What about furniture and other household items? I looked at every item that I was buying, consuming, or using, and made a conscious decision whether I would continue to use it, stop using it, or substitute it with a known vegetarian alternative. This was based on a fair amount of my own research, supplemented with loads of information available on the web and discussions in groups and forums.

The most disconcerting part of this conscious exercise was the discovery that almost every item we use at home or outside contained the remnants of killed animals. Conversely, the most comforting part was the discovery that there was a vegetarian or close-to-vegetarian substitute available for most items. If one were sensitive and cared enough about being a vegetarian, one would seek them out. If not, life would go on as before.

The thing that bothered me the most was the use of animal products in various supplements that I was taking: vitamins, antioxidants, and immunity boosters, some in capsule form. I learned that capsules are made from gelatin, which is also derived from various parts of a cow and other animals. However, it was not long before I found brands that used capsules made from plant-based gelatin. Even non-capsule-based formulations are now widely available in vegetarian versions. The problem is with allopathic medicines, and so far, the all-powerful pharmaceutical industry has not been influenced enough to research and introduce vegetarian versions of its various drugs. Until then, I am happy to continue with ayurvedic and homeopathic treatment. The key, of course, is to stay healthy so as to avoid a situation where one may be forced to take allopathic medicines.

Vegetarian mishaps

The first interesting experience I had was just after arriving in the USA. One of the easiest and cheapest things to eat out would be a slice of pizza. The first time I went to a street corner pizza place in New York, I saw "pepperoni slice" on the items listed. My mouth started watering at the idea of a hot, spicy pepper on my slice. I was about to take my first bite, when I saw a poster on the wall advertising pepperoni with a picture of a lump of meat. I almost threw up! This experience was typical of those undergone by Indians new to the USA.

Soup of any kind is one of the most common items in vegetarian fare. In my early years in the USA, I discovered French onion soup. The description typically listed the ingredients as onions, croutons, and cheese. In particular, I used to frequent a hotel in Boston during my business trips there. I would end up ordering French onion soup from the room service menu. One day, I came across the recipe for this soup in a magazine. I was shocked to read that beef stock was an ingredient in this soup. The next time I visited the hotel, I spoke with the chef, and sure enough, beef stock was used in the French onion soup on their menu. It had never crossed my mind to think of the stock that is used in soups. It was a big learning experience, and ever since, I always ask about the stock in the soup, unless I am certain of it.

I was a long stay guest at a top hotel in the suburbs of Bombay, where everyone knew I was a hardcore vegetarian. They had just opened a new pan-Asian restaurant, and I was invited to dine there. As is common in many restaurants in India, the menu clearly indicated which items were vegetarian. I scanned the menu, and seeing one of my favorite items, Som Tam (a raw papaya salad), I ordered it. As soon as it was served, I knew something was wrong. I took one small morsel, and sure enough, it smelled as well as tasted of fish. I called my friend, the restaurant manager, and explained that this item, listed as vegetarian, contained fish. He said that was not possible, and called the new Thai chef who had made the salad. She came to the table all smiling, expecting to receive accolades for her cooking. I asked her whether the salad contained shrimp paste, and she excitedly affirmed that it did contain shrimp paste, especially imported from Thailand! The restaurant manager apologized profusely.

Some years earlier, I had a similar experience with Pad Thai (stir-fried rice noodle dish) at another Thai restaurant. Ever since I realized that shrimp paste or fish oil is an essential ingredient of Thai food, I have avoided that cuisine unless I am eating in a vegetarian Thai restaurant.

There have been a few other mishaps along the way. I have been served a beef burger instead of a vegetarian burger at a restaurant in the UK, and a chicken sandwich instead of a vegetarian sandwich at a coffee shop in Pune, and also at a major hotel in Rabat, Morocco.

In some cases, when the error is pointed out to the staff, they coolly remove the dead animal from the dish and bring it right back! It has happened on flights as well.

Veggie all the way (around the world)

I have been to 130 countries so far, and in no country did I starve or feel famished because of being a vegetarian. And I rarely have to rely just on fruits, salad, or bread. I always like to try out the local cuisine, or at least something with an international flavor. Eating in an Indian restaurant (and almost every country I have been to has one) is always a last resort when there is absolutely no other option. As soon as I reach a hotel, I have someone write the following on a piece of paper in the local language: "No meat, no fish, no seafood, no chicken, no eggs." If there is a local word for vegetarian, I have that written down as well. I carry this with me all the time and show it to the waiter and confirm that he has got the message. It is not enough to just say "vegetarian" since there are as many interpretations of the term as there are countries. I have come across many "vegetarian" restaurants that include eggs, chicken, or seafood in their menu. It is also not enough to say, "I eat only vegetables," because then I am served nothing but a plate full of raw vegetables! Life has definitely become easier since the advent of the internet.

Some years ago, I discovered www.happycow.net, a website listing vegetarian restaurants in over a hundred countries. I never leave home for my destination without checking this listing. Through happycow.net, I have experienced some of the best vegetarian meals around the world, covering almost every type of cuisine. It carries reviews of restaurants and lists grocery and health food stores that sell prepared vegetarian meals. Furthermore, it is updated regularly by real diners.

Traveling is a great learning experience from every point of view, and especially as a vegetarian, one gets to see so many different perspectives on this lifestyle. From the delicious, fresh, and wholesome cuisine of the Middle East (falafel, baba ghanoush, hummus, tabbouleh, and baklava) and the olive-oil-drenched and sun-ripened cuisine of Italy (pastas, pizza, antipasti, minestrone, and breads) to the couscous of Morocco; the paella (similar to biryani) of Spain; the empanadas (think samosas) and other delicacies of Central and South America; the fresh, steamed tamales of Mexico; the dumplings, rolls, noodles and soups of numerous vegetarian Chinese restaurants all over the world; the rijsttafel (think thali) of Indonesia; the roti canai (think paratha) of Malaysia; the momos of Tibet; the Ethiopian injera with an array of vegetables and lentils (think thali served on a large dosa); the list is endless. Some of the best falafels I have had are on the streets of New York and in Rotterdam. My first experience of rijsttafel was in Amsterdam, as was my first couscous on the Left Bank in Paris. The best pizza I have ever had was at a nondescript joint somewhere on the border of Luxembourg and Germany with Martina and her friends!

Some of the most sublime dining experiences and meals I have had are outside India. When I was living in Boston, I heard about DiCocoa's in the middle of rural Maine, about three hours away from Boston. This café is open just once a week, every Saturday evening, for a tasting dinner. The first time Anjali and I went, I did not know what to expect from this vegetarian restaurant in the middle of nowhere. There was no menu, no prices. One has to call in advance to let Cathy know you are coming.

Once you reach there, you are completely in her hands. It is a one-woman show. No help of any kind, either in the kitchen or outside. Right from the first course, it turned out to be a feast for the senses—the taste, the aroma, the presentation. Each morsel was sublime. She would emerge with each course and explain in detail what it was and where she learned to prepare it. There were flavors from all over the world. This went on for about two hours while I was comfortably reclined on various cushions thrown all around. It was as if we were her house guests. When it was time to pay, there was no bill. She asked me to drop whatever I wished to pay into a big box. She has no way of knowing who paid what. It has been one of the most memorable dining experiences ever.

I remember Sublime in Fort Lauderdale, one of the best vegetarian gourmet restaurants in the world. We showed up without a reservation and was told it may be a long wait. The ambience was so inviting and the people were so nice that I would have waited even if I were to be the last person to be seated. I am glad I waited. It was one of my first experiences of fine dining in the vegetarian world.

Hangawi, a Korean restaurant in Manhattan, is the closest to the temple cuisine of Japan and Korea that I have come across outside these countries. Temple cuisine is part of the Buddhist tradition prevalent in Japan and Korea. It is typically found in Buddhist temples and entails traditional sitting on the floor with a low wooden table placed in front, and being served by male and female students or residents of that temple. Numerous small bowls consisting of various items are placed on the table, and each item is explained. The entire experience is very similar to the traditional style of eating in many Indian households even today.

I also remember Gandhi in Budapest. I went to the restaurant expecting it to be an Indian one. It turned out to be anything but! It is nested in an underground cavern of sorts, dimly lit with candles, communal tables, and a limited menu. There was no sign of India anywhere. Later, when I asked about the significance of the name Gandhi, I was told it was because of the non-violent nature of the food that was served!

There is this wonderful restaurant, Malabar, in Santa Cruz, California, run by a Sri Lankan. All his staff, inside and outside the kitchen, are women from various parts of the world. While the restaurant is open every day, on Saturday evenings, he has a tasting dinner; no menu, no price. One never knows what will emerge next from the kitchen, adding to the excitement of the dining experience. At the end, one pays whatever one wishes. The first time I dined there with a group of ten, I offered to pay $150. He refused, saying it was way too much! How can the food at such a place not be sublime?

And then there is David Bann in Edinburgh, Greens in San Francisco, and many more eateries, far too numerous to mention here.

For those from India who crave Indian fare but do not care for the ubiquitous chana masala and matar paneer found in the majority of Indian restaurants all over the world, there is Govinda and various restaurants run by disciples of ISKCON and Sri Chinmoy (under different names in different countries). These places offer no-frill, wholesome, inexpensive, vegetarian meals, Indian and otherwise.

I also learned a hard lesson while flying. Many airlines offer special meals when booked in advance. Some of these meals are religion-based, such as a kosher meal, a Hindu meal, a Muslim meal, and the like. I remember ordering a Hindu meal on a flight and finding chicken on my plate. Later on, I made inquiries and found that in the Western mind, a Hindu is an Indian, and since chicken is a popular part of Indian cuisine, it is usually offered in a Hindu meal! From then on, I realized I needed to specify "vegetarian " and why I did not consider myself a Hindu.

Vegan vs vegetarian

A vegan avoids all animal products, including dairy and honey, whereas a vegetarian consumes these two. A vegan believes that consuming dairy and honey supports the animal rearing industry, which is responsible for harmful practices toward animals. I do not subscribe to this view. This is where I believe the ability to make an informed decision is important, rather than blindly following a path.

It is true that in the West and other parts of the world, milk is procured from cattle that are primarily reared for slaughter and are subjected to harmful and painful practices. The process of cultivating honey at commercial bee farms is similar. However, not all milk and honey is derived in this manner. There are many dairies that rear cattle only for the milk, and the cattle die a natural death. This is definitely the case in India. Similarly, since honey is the natural byproduct of beehives, there are many sources of honey, both in India and abroad, that follow the natural process of producing honey. The key is to look for dairy products and honey from these sources.

By blindly avoiding all dairy and honey, I believe the vegans are missing out on several health benefits that can be obtained from these products. According to naturopathy and many other systems, milk itself is not considered fit for human consumption, but its byproducts, such as butter, ghee, and yogurt, are extremely healthy and, in fact, essential for a vegetarian. A mother's milk is the only milk appropriate for a child, and this should be continued for as long as possible. Any other milk cannot be a substitute for mother's milk. Experientially, it has been shown that consumption of milk (especially cold milk) is one of the major causes of various respiratory and digestive problems. Undigested milk produces phlegm. This has been my own experience.

In the USA, I developed various respiratory problems, such as congestion, sinusitis, wheezing, breathlessness, constant colds, and sore throats. Some of these were attributable to the harsh, cold, and dry climate of New York. But in spite of temporary relief from various remedies, including homeopathy, they recurred frequently. In Boston, my naturopath asked whether I consumed milk. A glass of milk a day was a habit with me since childhood. This was supplemented with ice creams, milk shakes, cold coffee, and sundry other forms of milk all the time. He suggested I try eliminating milk from my diet and see if it helped. I gave up all consumption of milk, except in tea and coffee. Sure enough, within three months, I started to feel the difference. I have continued with this habit, except when I need to have a bit of warm milk as part of an ayurvedic remedy.

However, when milk is converted into yogurt, its characteristics change completely. The live bacteria in yogurt work wonders for one's digestive system. Similarly, butter churned out of yogurt, and ghee clarified from butter, are very essential sources of good fat for a vegetarian. The vegans, I believe, are missing out on this important element of a vegetarian diet.

All vegetarians are not equal

There are many vegetarians, especially in India, who avoid onions and garlic or all root vegetables. This is mainly for religious reasons. Those who avoid all root vegetables believe that by uprooting them, they are harming the soil and various forms of insect life that survive in and around the soil. Even as a hardcore vegetarian, I find it difficult to subscribe to this viewpoint. Uprooting vegetables when they are ripe is no different from plucking fruits and vegetables from the branches of plants and trees, or plucking certain fruits and vegetables like melons and pumpkins that grow along the ground.

Similarly, onions and garlic are avoided by certain vegetarians because they believe these have tamasic qualities that impurify the mind. These individuals are primarily devout followers of Krishna. In all my readings about Krishna, I have yet to find any mention of this practice directly attributable to Him that validates this belief. This is yet another blind belief based upon someone's interpretation that forms the core of religious practice. Onions and garlic have tremendous health benefits. They are particularly beneficial in warding off inflammations, infections, and heart diseases, and are considered superfoods. I cannot imagine my diet without them.

Silk is another item that is avoided by all vegans and some vegetarians. I generally avoid silk unless I am sure it has been procured from silkworms that have not been killed for their cocoons.

Like everything else, one needs to discriminate between blind faith and rational belief. With awareness, one can do this and reap the benefits of a full and proper vegetarian diet.

Vegetarianism in India and elsewhere

The vegetarian experience in India and the one abroad are not necessarily the same. The difference lies in the callousness, indifference, and ignorance you encounter in India, and the caring and understanding you are welcomed with in most places around the world.

For a supposedly vegetarian country like India, happycow.net lists only 176 vegetarian restaurants out of a total of over 13,000 worldwide, and the majority of them are South Indian. The website does not include restaurants that serve vegetarian dishes alongside animal-based dishes, and I subscribe to this policy as much as possible. The negative energy emanating from having slaughtered animals in a common kitchen is enough to contaminate the vegetarian food. All food imbibes the vibrations of the person who has gathered it, prepared it for cooking, cooked it, and served it. Therefore, it also follows that a person who is working with dead animals in any way will transmit that stale and negative energy to the vegetarian food as well. This is easy to experience if one is sensitive enough and vibrating at a higher frequency by having the same dish in a mixed vegetarian restaurant, and later, in a vegetarian restaurant. I extend this belief by not sharing a table with someone who is not a vegetarian.

By and large, this hybrid restaurant culture is not prevalent outside India. First of all, there are far more vegetarian restaurants serving varied cuisines in most parts of the world than there are in India. Secondly, even in a mixed restaurant, the chef and the kitchen staff are very sensitive to their vegetarian clientele, and either have separate sections or separate utensils or take special precautions. This is partly due to the risk of legal action in certain developed countries that have laws protecting consumers from being served items that may be contrary to their belief system or their health requirements.

A few years ago, McDonald's and Pizza Hut were sued by a group of Indians in the USA for including beef seasoning in their french fries and animal-based flavors in their pizza sauce, respectively. These food items are commonly consumed by Indians while traveling abroad, under the assumption that they are vegetarian. Both companies had to settle the lawsuits and amend their recipes.

When I was served a sandwich with chicken in a restaurant at the Hilton Hotel in Rabat, I sued the hotel company in the USA; they immediately apologized and settled with me. This is in stark contrast to my experience with Café Coffee Day in Pune. When I tried to take action against them for serving me a chicken sandwich, I got nowhere and became an object of ridicule for trying to do something so stupid. The typical reaction was, "Why didn't you just ask for another sandwich?"

Lard is a common medium of cooking all over the world, including India. It has been banned in many cities and countries, including New York. Of course, it has been banned not because it is an animal product but because it is a monounsaturated fat, and all monounsaturated mediums of cooking have been banned. I wait for the day it will be banned in India.

Similarly, MSG, a staple additive in Chinese and other Asian cooking (while not a direct concern for vegetarians, since it is not derived from an animal product, it is extremely harmful to human health), is increasingly avoided in the West but used liberally in India. I have seen people who avoid onions and garlic but lap up Chinese cuisine laden with this chemical.

I am not a fan of the pretentious fine dining cuisine culture anywhere in the world, be it the Michelin kind or otherwise. How many of these white-glove, fine dining restaurants cater to vegetarians, except as an afterthought? Some of the most sublime, sattvic, and spiritually alive meals I have had have been either on the streets or hole-in-the-wall dining spots. On the one hand, it is generally true that it is easier to find vegetarian meals in the East than it is in the West, on the other, in New York alone (the haven for vegetarian dining), I have dined in vegetarian restaurants serving practically every type of global cuisine: Mexican,

Korean, Chinese, Ethiopian, Vietnamese, Guatemalan, Peruvian, Sri Lankan, Tibetan, Afghani, and Middle Eastern. I have attended dinners organized by the Natural Gourmet Institute in New York (specializing in vegetarian cooking) with special tasting menus, and many other culinary institutes in the USA and Switzerland.

It is far easier to find vegetarian items on the shelves of supermarkets outside India. They are clearly labeled and, in the UK, this practice has been the law for a long time. In the USA and most European countries, while not a law, it is very prevalent. If one is not sure, one will always get an informed answer upon inquiry. In India, that is not the case. Knowing fully well that a can of Heinz baked beans comes in both vegetarian and animal versions, I picked the animal version from the shelf of a famous supermarket in Pune and asked one of the assistants whether it was vegetarian. He stared at me and said, "Yes, of course. They are baked beans!" If he had bothered to read the ingredients on the label, he would have noticed chicken stock in it.

A vegetarian outside India has, generally speaking, made a conscious decision to become a vegetarian. It is rare that they are born into a vegetarian family. It is rare to find a completely vegetarian family that is not Indian. Even the Indian diaspora has increasingly taken to consuming meat as their way of blending into Western culture. Therefore, they are far more committed to the belief and cause of vegetarianism and apply it to daily life far more diligently than a vegetarian in India.

If one were to compile statistics, one would find that more people in India are starting to eat meat than those turning vegetarian. It is the opposite in the Western world. Being a vegetarian is a way of life for those who are conscious vegetarians. They apply it to all aspects of their life. In India, being a vegetarian mainly implies cooking and eating a vegetarian meal. Sometimes, this is further reduced to cooking and eating a vegetarian meal only at home. Or worse still, some vegetarians themselves do not eat meat but have no problem cooking and serving meat at home.

In various workshops and talks, when I inform people that pizza and jello, two of the most favorite items consumed in India, contain pieces of dead cows, I get nothing but a blank stare. How is it that if a piece of dead cow is served on a plate along with dal and sabji, one would immediately raise a hue and cry, but if the same piece is camouflaged in a slice of pizza or a cup of jello, one does not even bat an eye?

A conscious vegetarian would never step into a McDonald's, even though many now offer vegetarian items on their menu. He is aware that McDonald's is responsible for slaughtering millions of cows a year to serve their customers all over the world. In *Dhamma*, it is said that an action that even indirectly causes harm to anyone is unwholesome. By stepping into McDonalds to have a vegetarian burger, a vegetarian is supporting a business that is causing untold harm to the environment.

I have come a long way in my journey as a vegetarian, from being a born vegetarian to an embarrassed vegetarian, a defensive vegetarian, and a conscious and fully aware vegetarian. Today, when I go to a restaurant, I usually have to ask whether they serve any vegetarian items. I wait for the day when a carnivore goes to a restaurant and has to ask, "Do you serve meat?"

Until then, let me ask you once again.

Are you a vegetarian?

Empty Talk

I was invited to speak at the World Aqua Conference in New Delhi. The main topic was the sustainability of water, but all five elements were covered. In my talk, I pointed out the paradox of holding this conference in a city where air-conditioned comfort was as common as sipping water from plastic bottles, but no one cared a hoot. They were too busy looking for something to eat. With collective arrogance, we had gathered to discuss the Five Elements. But just as Brahma, the Creator, the Supreme Being, is self-knowing, knowledge of the Five Elements is experiential, and that alone can reveal the beauty, the magic, the interconnectedness, the Whole.

I suggested that the next conference be held in a village, under a banyan tree, next to a river or well, sitting on the ground in Sukhasana, enjoying the fresh, warm air. The organizer said, "No one will attend."

India is the land of talk, talk, and more talk. And slogans, slogans, and more slogans. Everything is in the face or over the top. Subtlety and nuanced sensibilities do not exist here. Take something, multiply it a thousand times, and you will find it in India. I am told that India has the largest number of entries to its credit in the Guinness Book of Records.

Authenticity and selfless service do not need any validation or recognition.

India is that bulwark that separates the East from the West. The East begins with Japan and gradually morphs into India. The paradox of India lies in its shining as a spiritual beacon amid a cesspool of filth, open toilets, stray dogs and broken roads. In a land of such magnitude, extremes, and misplaced priorities, how does one find spirituality and wisdom? One breath at a time, one step at a time, one Happening at a time. That has been my journey of One, mainly while being away from my own country.

But All Is Not Lost

Ramona and I came together to create PraMonA, an offspring of the East and the West. We have ventured on a journey that has become a Satsang of Two. It is spiritual strength that brought us together, not just for ourselves but to offer hope and show the path to others. This is what the Shiva Shakti connection is all about. If Ramona and I can come together despite upheavals in our individual lives, there is no reason why the East and the West cannot do so with mutual respect. However, spirituality is the only path on which this meeting can happen. Otherwise, they will both go to the dogs, literally and metaphorically, as is happening currently.

People in the USA spend more on dogs and are concerned more with their care than their own or their family. The business of pets is a multi billion dollar business in the West with puppy factories feeding the mania. Cats in homes cause more allergy related problems for their owners, but to no avail. Sheryl, my Reiki teacher was surrounded by cats and suffered constantly with respiratory issues. So did Bonnie, my astrologer, who suffered from asthma and finally succumbed to it. Both were in denial, as are millions other. People in the West simply refuse to see the connection between their health and the unhygienic conditions created in their living space with animals around. Dog poop is left on the streets or carried home in grocery bags. Human beings are not allowed to urinate in public, but dogs are. People walk them into supermarkets and restaurants with a sense of entitlement that dare not be challenged in spite of laws to the contrary. Unfortunately, people in India are fast following suit, whether it is with stray or pet dogs.

Tattva (the Truth or Reality) is everywhere, in every cell. The Gayatri Mantra talks about *bhu, bhuvah, swah* (earth, air, Heaven). Quantum mechanics talks about the randomness of Nature. But human beings only talk about consumption with no reference to sustenance.

A man who throws garbage, a man who jumps the red light, and a man who rapes. All three are offenders to varying degrees. But what is common to them? All three are an imbalance of the elements and the chakras and live in ignorance and darkness.

All knowledge about the entire manifestation revealed to the Indian sages has been enshrined in the Tantras, the Vedas, the Brahma Sutras, the Upanishads, the Bhagavad Gita, and other Indian scriptures. All that is to be known is already known. It is just a matter of opening one's eyes and living in awareness. But, from the land of awareness, we are moving to the world of zombies, Gen Z and beyond.

Free up your chakras and let them breathe so that they may experience the Five Elements. The human brain is the only organ in the human body that is not governed by any chakra.

Let the East not race toward beating the West at its stupidity and shallowness. Let it cherish and revel in its traditional knowledge that far exceeds all knowledge that the West can ever come up with, no matter how many Nobel prizes it may win. Let us open up our scriptures in all their wisdom and glory, and cull the pearls of wisdom that lurk in every shloka, mantra, and stuti. Let us again revive Sanskrit, the mother of all languages.

We do not need science to prove the existence of Nature. We need our five senses to experience Nature. AI will always be artificial, no matter how intelligent it is claimed to be. AI has the ability to take over religion, but it will never touch the human spirit. Fads, trends, phases, and eras will come and go, but the spirit remains the same, forever. This is why the Hindu philosophy is called *sanatan* (eternal).

The human body is a microcosm of the entire Cosmos! When Arjun asked Krishna to show him a glimpse of the *Brahmanda,* Krishna just opened his mouth, and the entire cosmos was right there for Arjun to see.

The multitude of gods and goddesses who exist in Indian culture, reflecting different attributes and virtues, were originally all concepts created by the early sages to impart spiritual wisdom in a more acceptable form. It is no different than telling a fairy tale to a kid with princes, fairies, demons, giants to convey a lesson. These spiritual concepts in the form of gods and goddesses soon started getting personified with names, faces, and attire, an army of gods and goddesses sitting in Heavenly abodes, watching over mankind and every move that it was making. Unknowingly, the sages had unleashed a monster that took the form of religion and idol worship. The concepts themselves were quickly forgotten. From being a concept of abundance, Lakshmi became the goddess of wealth, and instead of being grateful for the abundance they already had, people started asking Her for more.

Spirituality, the genesis of religion, veered off from this blind faith. As I said at the beginning of this chapter, Babuji worshipped Lakshmi as the

Goddess of Wealth every Diwali, and I refused to go along with that. Many years later, I discovered the same Lakshmi as one of the 108 Shaktis with the power of abundance that She radiates upon everyone. And I surrender myself to Her every time I read or recite *Saundarya Lahiri* or *Sri Sukta*. There is no Hanuman flying around in the skies with his tail wagging, yet I recite Hanuman Chalisa regularly as it embodies the spirit of fearlessness. I do not need to go to any temple to find any of these concepts. They are right inside me.

Be the change that you wish to see in the world.
Leave the rest to Nature.
Leave Nature alone.
Stop playing God.

I was seven. I was standing on the balcony looking at the sky filled with the stars and the moon. I wondered, *Where have they come from? Who am I?*

That was the beginning of my Satsang of One.

	Aum Namah Shivaya	
	Aum Namah Vasudevaya	
	Aum Namah Hanumantaya	

|| Know the Truth, Rest in Peace
Truth Is Known by Its Own Simplicity
If They Heed Not Thy Call, Walk Alone ||

Glossary

Words appearing in italics can be cross-referenced within the glossary.

A

Aahaar	Nutrition
Aarti	A Hindu ritual of worship, in which light from a flame is ritually waved to venerate deities
Abhaya Mudra	A *mudra* expressing fearlessness
Abhimanyu	Arjun's son, in the *Mahabharat*
Adi Shakti	The First or Eternal Mother Goddess
Adi Shankaracharya	An Indian Vedic scholar, monk, and teacher of *Advaita* Vedanta
Advaita	Philosophy of nonduality
Agamic	Pertaining to the Agamas, a body of post-Vedic scriptures
Agiary	A fire temple, a place of worship for the Parsis. Its hierarchy is lower than that of an *atash behram*
Ajna Chakra	The sixth chakra, or the third eye
Akashic Records	A cosmic database containing every soul's past, present, and future

Anahata Chakra	The fourth chakra, or the heart chakra
Ardhangini	The other half of oneself, or wife
Ardhapadmasana	Half Lotus Pose for meditation
Arjun	One of the five *Pandavas* in the *Mahabharat*
Asana	A yogic posture; a seat
Ashram pranali	Ashram tradition
Ashtavakra Gita	A Vedanta text in the form of a dialogue between Sage Ashtavakra and King Janaka
Atash Behram	A fire temple, a place of worship for the Parsis. Its hierarchy is higher than that of an *agiary*
Aum	The primal sound, also known as "Om"
Avadhuta Gita	An *Advaita* Vedanta text written by Sage Dattatreya
Avatar	The incarnation in physical form of a Hindu god on earth

B

Bajra	Pearl millet
Bal Krishna	*Krishna* as a child
Beej mantra	Seed *mantra* or primordial *mantra*
Bhabhi	Elder brother's wife
Bhagavad Gita	A part of the *Mahabharat,* wherein *Krishna* imparts spiritual instruction to *Arjun*
Bhaisahab	Elder brother
Bhakti	Devotion
Bhogi	One who enjoys
Bodhisattva	One who compassionately refrains from entering *nirvana* in order to save others

Brahma	The Creator, one of the Hindu *Trinity* of gods; Saraswati's consort
Brahma Leela	The divine play of *Brahma*
Brahma Muhurta	The spiritually auspicious time before dawn
Brahmachari	A celibate
Brahmanda	Universe

C

Chakra	An energy center in the subtle body
Chakra cleansing	The practice of clearing the seven *chakras* in the human body to ensure a free flow of the life force
Chakravyuh	A maze or labyrinth
Chanakya Niti	A collection of Sanskrit aphorisms on the art and science of politics and governance, ascribed to Chanakya, an Indian teacher, philosopher, and economist
Chhappan bhog	A traditional offering of 56 different food items presented to Hindu deities
Chhatri	An elevated, dome-shaped pavilion resembling a chhatri (umbrella), made as a memorial
Chi	Life force in Chinese
Churan	A marinated mixture of powdered herbs used as a digestive

D

Dal	An Indian dish made with lentils
Dargah	A shrine or tomb of a revered *Sufi* saint
Darshan	To be in the presence of a holy person or deity; to present oneself to a devotee or seeker

Deeksha	Spiritual initiation from a guru
Devar	The younger brother of a person's husband
Devi	The divine feminine
Devanagari	The alphabet system used for Sanskrit, Hindi, and some other Indian languages
Dhamma	Buddhist term for *dharma*
Dhammapada	A collection of sayings attributed to the Buddha
Dharma	Righteous living
Dhritarashtra	The blind king of Hastinapura and the father of the *Kauravas*
Dhyana	Meditation
Dhyana Mudra	Meditation *mudra*
Divya drishti	Divine sight, or supernatural vision
Divya shruti	Divine hearing
Durga Saptashati	A 700-verse text praising Goddess Durga

E

Ekadashi	Eleventh day in the Hindu lunar month

G

Ganeshji	The elephant-headed Hindu deity known as 'the remover of obstacles'
Gauri Shankar	A rare, naturally joined pair of beads symbolizing the union of *Shiva* and *Parvati*
Gayatri Mantra	A powerful Vedic *mantra*
Ghats	A series of steps leading down to a body of water

Ghazal	An Indian lyric poem, typically on the theme of love, which is set to music
Gobar	Cow dung, used as fuel, manure, and a traditional, eco-friendly plastering material on walls in rural India
Gopi	Female cowherd
Grihastha Ashram	The second (householder stage) of the four traditional Hindu stages of life
Guna	One of the three fundamental qualities of Nature (gunas), according to Indian philosophy
Gurdwara	A Sikh place of worship
Guru–shishya	Teacher–student (relationship)

H

Haiku	A Japanese couplet or poem
Hanuman Chalisa	An ode to *Hanumanji* consisting of 40 verses
Hanumanji	The Hindu deity revered as a divine vanara (monkey) and a devoted companion of Lord *Rama*
Hara	The energetic area around the abdomen, including the *Manipura Chakra*
Hatha Yog	An ancient Indian system of physical postures and breath control
Hatha Yogi	One who practices *Hatha Yog*
Havan	Vedic fire ceremony
Haveli	An Indian mansion decorated with exquisite artwork, built by rich merchants

Homa	Similar to a *yagna* but shorter in duration and less elaborate

I

Ibadat	A comprehensive term covering all acts of righteousness, surrender, and adoration of God in Islam

J

Jijaji	Elder sister's husband
Jiji	Elder sister
Jnana Mudra	Wisdom *mudra*
Jnana Yogi	One who practices Jnana Yog, or the path of knowledge
Jowar	Sorghum
Jyotirlinga	A pillar of divine light representing Lord *Shiva*; there are 12 sacred Jyotirlinga shrines in India
Jyotish/jyotish	Vedic astrology; its practitioner

K

Kaal Sarp Yog Puja	An astrological ritual performed to alleviate the malefic effects caused by the placement of all seven planets between *Rahu* and *Ketu*
Kaam vasana	Intense sensual desire
Kakasana	The Crow Pose, a yog *asana*
Kaliyuga	The Dark Age, as per Indian scriptures
Kama Sutra	An ancient Indian Sanskrit text on virtuous living and the art of love
Karma	Actions or their results
Karmic	Pertaining to *karma*

Kartik Ekadashi	The eleventh day of the Kartik month in the Indian lunar calendar
Kartik Shukla Paksha	The waning half of the Vedic lunar month of Kartik
Karwa Chauth	A fast kept by married Hindu women
Kashmir Shaivism	A spiritual tradition which believes that everything is an expression of pure Consciousness, known as *Shiva*
Kauravas	The 100 sons of King *Dhritarashtra,* the antagonists to their cousins, the *Pandavas,* in the *Mahabharat*
Kavach	A shield; a talisman
Ketu	The descending (south) lunar node in Vedic astrology
Khadi	An Indian homespun cotton cloth
Ki	Life force in Japanese
Koan	A paradoxical riddle in Zen teaching
Krishna	A *Vishnu avatar,* the protagonist of the *Mahabharat*
Kundalini	The divine feminine energy coiled up like a serpent at the base of the root *chakra*
Kundli	A Vedic horoscope
Kurta pajama	A type of simple Indian attire
Kurti	A short *kurta*

L

Lagan nu bhonu	Typical fare served at a Parsi wedding
Lakshmi Narayan	Narayan is *Vishnu,* and Lakshmi is his consort

Lalita Sahasranama	An ode to Goddess Lalita with a thousand attributes
Laxman	*Rama's* brother
Leela	Cosmic play
Lingam	The sacred male organ that is the source of all Creation

M

Mahabharat	A Hindu epic written by Ved Vyas about the war between good and evil
Mahajaap	Marathon chanting
Mahamrityunjaya Mantra	A Vedic *mantra* to appease *Shiva*
Mahashivratari	A Hindu festival to celebrate the mating of *Shiva* and *Parvati*
Mala	String of beads, often used as an aid in chanting
Mamiji	Maternal uncle's wife
Manipura Chakra	The third *chakra*, or the navel *chakra*
Mansika	Reciting a *mantra* internally
Mantra	A sacred sound, word, or phrase
Mantra japa	Chanting of *mantras*
Masaji	Mother's sister's husband
Math	A spiritual center
Maya	The illusion or appearance of the phenomenal world
Mohalla	Neighborhood
Moksha	Liberation from the cycle of birth and death

Mudra	A symbolic gesture using fingers and thumbs to channelize the vital force
Mukhi	Refers to the number of "facets (mukha)" on the *rudraksha* bead
Muladhara Chakra	The first *chakra*, or the root *chakra*
Muni	An ascetic who observes silence or introspects
Munim	A traditional Indian accountant

N

Naada Brahma	The primordial sound, *Aum*
Nada	Sound
Nadi	An energy channel in the subtle body
Nadi Shastra	Ancient Indian astrology based on palm leaf readings
Namavali	A "garland of names" of a god or goddess, which is chanted in their praise
Navarasa	The nine fundamental emotional states in Indian classical art forms
Neem	An evergreen tree with medicinal properties
Nirvana	The final release from desire and suffering

P

Padmasana	The Lotus Pose for meditation
Panchakarma	An Ayurvedic five (panch)-step detoxification and rejuvenation process designed to cleanse the body of toxins
Panchamrut	A nectar offering made from five (panch) ingredients

Pandavas	The five heroic brothers, the protagonists of the *Mahabharat*
Pandit	A Hindu priest, scholar, or teacher
Panya	Glorious
Parvati	*Shiva's* consort, also known as *Shakti*
Pedhi	An old-style office with thick mattresses and cushions to sit on
"Pra" "deep"	One who sheds light
Prakriti	Mother Nature; one's inherent nature or constitution
Pranayama	A system of yogic breathing exercises
Pranic Healing	A no-touch energy healing technique that uses the life force to accelerate healing
Prasad	An offering of food made to a god
Pratyahara	Withdrawal of the five senses
Puja	The act of worship or a ritual ceremony related to it
Puranic	Pertaining to the Puranas, a set of scriptures that propound Vedic Teachings
Purdah	Veil
Putra shokh	Intense grief caused by the death of one's son

R

Raas Leela	A divine, playful dance between *Krishna* and *Radha* and the *gopis*
Radha	*Krishna's* consort
Ragi	Finger millet

Rahu	The ascending (north) lunar node in Vedic astrology
Rajasic	Pertaining to Rajas, one of the *gunas*
Rama	A Hindu god, the seventh *avatar* of *Vishnu*, and the protagonist of the *Ramayana*
Ramayana	An ancient Indian Sanskrit epic authored by Sage Valmiki, detailing the life, adventures, and moral journey of *Rama*
Rangoli	A traditional, colorful design drawn on the ground to attract auspiciousness
Reiki	A Japanese healing modality
Rishi	An Indian sage
Roti	Indian flatbread
Rudraksha mala	A string of rudraksha beads (which are the dried seeds of the rudraksha tree found in India and Nepal) symbolizing Lord *Shiva*'s tears and offering spiritual protection to the wearer

S

Saawan	Monsoon
Sabji	Vegetable
Sabudana khichadi	An Indian dish whose main ingredient is sabudana (sago), made from the starchy extract of tapioca roots
Sadhak	A spiritual practitioner or seeker
Sadhana	Spiritual practice
Sadhu	An Indian monk
Sahasrara Chakra	The seventh *chakra,* or the crown *chakra*

Samadhi	The last of the eightfold steps of Patanjali's yog
Sambhog	Sacred intercourse
Sangam	Union
Sanjay	*Dhritarashtra's* personal advisor and charioteer; also one of *Krishna's* 108 names
Sanjivani	A legendary life-restoring herb used to revive *Laxman* in the *Ramayana*
Sankalpa	A spiritual vow of intention
Sanyasa	Renunciation of worldly life
Sanyasa Ashram	The fourth and final stage of the traditional Hindu stages of life, signifying complete renunciation of worldly life (family, possessions, ego) to pursue ultimate spiritual liberation
Sanyasi	A renunciant, or one who has taken *sanyasa*
Saptarishis	The seven sages sent by *Brahma*
Sari	A garment worn by Indian women consisting of a length of fabric elaborately draped around the body
Satchidananda	The ultimate reality of Existence (Sat), Consciousness (Chid), Bliss (Ananda)
Sati	A historical Hindu practice where a widow immolates herself on her deceased husband's funeral pyre, or soon after his death
Satori	Sudden enlightenment
Satsang	A spiritual gathering
Sattvic	Pertaining to Sattva, one of the *gunas*

Sattvic aahaar	Pure nourishment, which nurtures the Sattva *guna*
Saundarya Lahiri	A poem penned by *Adi Sankaracharya* in praise of the Mother Goddess
Seth	A rich businessman; a title for a person of high social status
Shaivya	Connection with *Shiva* or *Shiva* energy
Shakti	The Mother Goddess, the Divine feminine energy; also (in the context of this book) a woman who has had a significant impact on the author's life, as well as women in general
Shakti Peeth	"Seat of *Shakti*," one of the 51 places of worship dedicated to Goddess *Shakti*
Shaktipat	Transfer of spiritual energy from a guru to a disciple
Shayari	A form of Indian poetry in Urdu
Shiatsu	A form of acupressure of Japanese origin
Shila	Foundation
Shiva	The Destroyer, one of the Hindu *Trinity* of gods; *Shakti's* consort, the Divine male energy
Shivaling	An idol depicting the *lingam* and the *yoni*
Shivoham	A Sanskrit *mantra* meaning "I am *Shiva*"
Shloka	A Sanskrit couplet, a common form of writing used in Hindu scriptures
Shraddha	An annual Vedic ceremony to commemorate the deceased
Shrapit dosha	An affliction indicated in the chart as per Vedic Jyotish

Siddha mala	A *mala* containing 14 rudraksha beads, ranging from 1–14 facets, conveying spiritual achievement, or siddhi
Siddha peeth	A sacred, spiritually charged site associated with a perfected master (Siddha)
Sixty-four Yoginis	Sixty-four forms of the Divine Goddess
So Hum	A Sanskrit *mantra* meaning "I am That"
Somras	The divine nectar that *Shiva* and *Shakti* imbibe from each other
Sri Laksmi Tantra	One of the many *Tantra* scriptures focused on the Divine Goddess
Sri Sukta	Devotional hymn to Sri Lakshmi
Sri Vidya	A *Tantra* philosophy devoted to the Goddess
Sri Yantra	A highly potent *Tantra* mandala
Stuti	An ode to a deity
Sufi	The followers of Sufism, a mystical Islamic tradition that emphasizes the direct personal experience of God
Sufiyana	The *Sufi* way of life, including poetry and music
Sukhasana	The Easy or Happy Pose for meditation
Sukshma	Subtle body
Sushumna Nadi	The central energy channel (*nadi*) in the subtle body that runs along the spinal cord from the base (*Muladhara Chakra*) to the crown of the head (*Sahasrara Chakra*)
Sutra	Buddhist scripture

Sutradhar	In Indian theatre, the character who introduces the play, sets the scene, and provides commentary; also a metaphor for someone playing the same role in real life
Swabhav	One's inherent nature
Swadhisthana Chakra	The second *chakra*, or the sacral *chakra*

T

Taiji	The **wife of a** *tauji*
Tamas	One of the three *gunas*
Tamasic	Pertaining to *tamas*
Tamasic aahaar	Impure food, which increases *tamas*
Tandava	The Cosmic Dance performed by *Shiva* in a trance-like state
Tantra	The oldest of all Indian spiritual philosophies about the divine male and female energies
Tantric	Pertaining to *Tantra*
Tapasya	Intense spiritual discipline or austerity
Tarot	A set of 78 illustrated cards used for spiritual guidance
Tauji	One's father's elder brother
Thakkar	A caretaker
Thali	An Indian meal consisting of various dishes served in a large metal plate called a "thali"
Tithi	A date as per the Hindu lunar calendar
Trinity	The Hindu *Trinity* of *Brahma*, *Vishnu*, and *Shiva*

Triveni Sangam	The holy confluence of the Ganga, Yamuna, and Saraswati rivers in Prayagraj
Tulsi	The holy basil plant
Turiya	"The Fourth," referring to that which is beyond the three states of waking, dreaming, and deep sleep

U

Upamshu	Whispering a *mantra* softly, with the lips moving, but audible only to the practitioner

V

Vaastu	An ancient Indian science of architecture, design, and placement
Vaid	An Ayurvedic physician
Vaikhari	Saying a *mantra* aloud
Vanvaas	Literally, "living in the forest"; figuratively, a period of forced seclusion from society
Vashishta Gufa	The cave where Sage Vashishta meditated
Vasudhaiva Kutumbakam	The whole world is one family
Veena	An Indian string instrument
Vipassana	A way of self-transformation through self-observation
Vishnu	The Sustainer, one of the Hindu *Trinity* of gods; Mahalakshmi's consort
Vishuddhi	The fifth *chakra*, or the throat *chakra*
Vritti	Fluctuation of the mind

Y

Yagna	A form of Hindu ritual worship performed in front of a fire, where Vedic *mantras* are chanted
Yatra	Pilgrimage
Yog Sutras	A text on yog written by Sage Patanjali
Yogini	A female yogi
Yoni	The sacred female organ that is the source of all creation

Z

Zazen	A type of Japanese meditation, typically of the Zen Buddhist tradition

Connect with the Author

Your thoughts and feedback, upon reading the book,
would be very meaningful to me.

Website: www.tantien.org

YouTube Channel: PraMonA

Email: TanTienPraMonA@yahoo.com